EYEWITNESS WAR

EYEWITNESS WAR

The Publishing Corporation U.K. Ltd

First published in the UK in 1995 by
The Publishing Corporation UK Ltd of Colson House,
Knight Street, South Woodham Ferrers,
Essex CM3 5ZL. Tel & fax: (01245) 320462

Produced by Marshall Cavendish Books, London
(a division of Marshall Cavendish Partworks Ltd)

EYEWITNESS WAR
ISBN 1-897780-32-X
A record is retained by The British Library

Cover illustrations: Front: Survivors of the raid on Dieppe, August 1942 (John Frost Newspapers). Back: Ghurkas advance in Tunisia, March 1943 (Marshall Cavendish Ltd)

Editorial personnel: Sarah Halliwell, Tim Cooke (text); Paul Cooper, Wayne Humphries, Ricky Newport (design).
Printed in the UK by The Guernsey Press Co Ltd

Some of this material has previously appeared in the Marshall Cavendish partwork
EYEWITNESS WAR

Contents

Introduction

Looking back some 50 years on, the true meaning of World War II has become blurred under layers of interpretation. For political historians, it marked the inevitable outcome of the rightwing politics that fed on people's discontent during the 1920s and 1930s – the Nazis in Germany, the fascists in Italy, and the militaristic regime in Japan – and the eventual triumph of democracy over dictatorship. For scientists it marked a period of rapid and often beneficial progress which saw the birth of radar, for example, and advances in the treatment of disease and injury. For military enthusiasts, the use of bombing and the demand for resources signalled the introduction of a new way of fighting, a total war in which everyone had a part. For social historians, the domestic upheavals caused by the absence of men and the new working roles of women marked a watershed after which society would never be the same. And for the millions who lived through it, at home or on the front line, the war was a profoundly personal event which would influence the rest of their lives. If the truth of the war lives on anywhere, then it is in their memories that we should look for it.

As the years pass, so those who endured the war grow fewer. Those who do survive were young people then, who should have been falling in love, starting families and building careers. Instead they found themselves in a world of violence, separation and chaos. But this new world was also a place of comradeship, of victory and of triumph. Their memories run the full range of emotions, from happiness to grief, from resignation to rage. Extraordinary incidents and acts of remarkable courage are remembered in a modest, matter-of-fact way that illustrates better than any textbook what it was like to live through nearly six years of global war.

Eyewitness War gathers the memories of people from all nations: civilians and troops, defenders and attackers. From the desperate days of May 1940 when it seemed that Hitler's shadow would fall across the whole of Europe to the dropping of the atom bombs that ended the conflict, the story of every major campaign is told in the words of those who lived through them. Their voices create a memoir of all aspects of the war, from the sands of North Africa to the jungles of the tropics, from the tactics of top generals to the quest of ordinary soldiers to find comfort amid the chaos of battle.

The war began badly for the Allies. In 1939 and 1940, Hitler's troops overran much of Europe and drove the British back to their island home, where only the bravery of RAF pilots and the resilience of the population saved them from invasion. In North Africa, too, the Germans and their Italian allies won initial victories in their drive towards the Suez Canal and the oil fields of the Middle East. But there, again, their advance was checked at El Alamein by Montgomery's Eighth Army, who with their American allies drove Rommel's *Afrikakorps* from the continent. Meantime, in the east, both Britain and the US suffered defeat as the Japanese rampaged through south-east Asia and the Pacific. But victory would come, as troops on both sides fought among some of the war's harshest conditions on previously unknown Pacific islands whose names would never be forgotten: Guadalcanal, Tarawa, Iwo Jima, Okinawa.

In Europe, meanwhile, Hitler had sent his troops east into the Soviet Union in a quest to overthrow communism. But like Napoleon a century before, his army would face an unbeatable enemy – the Russian winter. In Berlin, the *Führer* retreated to his bunker as his Reich crumbled. To the south, his ally Mussolini had been overthrown as Allied troops fought their way through Italy and into southern France. To the north, the Allies launched their long-anticipated invasion on 6 June 1944. Despite fierce resistance on the beaches and in the Normandy countryside, they fought their way to Paris before turning to the Rhine, the final barrier before Germany. Overcoming Hitler's last gasp resistance in the Ardennes, the Allies at last bridged the mighty river. Yet the final assault on the heart of the Reich would come from the east, where the Red Army had driven their enemy back into the streets of Berlin. In April 1945, after Hitler had committed suicide, the Germans surrendered.

In the east, the war raged on as the Americans fought their way closer to Japan. But a new weapon had been developed which would make an invasion unnecessary. On 6 August 1945, an atom bomb detonated over Hiroshima; three days later, another devastated Nagasaki. Against such weapons the Japanese were lost, and on 2 September 1945, they surrendered. World War II was over.

DUNKIRK

Triumph in Defeat

In early 1940, Hitler's troops overran northern Europe, pushing the British Expeditionary Force back to the French port of Dunkirk. In response to government appeals, a flotilla of craft crossed the Channel to aid the evacuation, which took more than 300,000 men off the beaches. They left behind massive casualties but their resilience was celebrated as the 'Dunkirk spirit'

Robert Holding, with the 4th battalion, Royal Sussex Regiment, had survived a series of seemingly inescapable batterings by the advancing Wehrmacht. His company nearly wiped out, he is among the stragglers who arrive in war-torn Dunkirk, hoping for a passage back to England.

"From all sides now I could hear the roar of enemy artillery, and in many places the chatter of machine-gun fire was almost continuous. Over the town hung a pall of black smoke, above which enemy bombers, flying in close formation, wheeled, dropped their loads and departed, unchallenged and quite unhindered. On the road, our pace was now reduced to a crawl. The reason for this soon became apparent in the form of a road-block manned by military police. As each man reached the barrier, he was asked the name of his unit, and then directed to the area allocated to his division.

The sun had now set, but the town was lit by a fiery red glow from the burning dock area, and from landward by flickering gun flashes and the deadly white glow of flares. On through this eerie ghost town we continued our weary way, stopping at intervals to be checked and redirected by police, until I finally found myself once more outside the town, still heading eastward toward the unmistakable sound of bursting shells. After a while we were directed off the road down a sandy track where quite suddenly I was confronted by an extraordinary sight.

There before me, lit to an almost daylight brilliance by a large passenger ship that blazed from end to end just a few hundred yards out to sea, was a long sandy beach that stretched as far as the eye could see. To the landward of the beach, acres of grass-tufted sand dunes seemed to move like an ocean as their shadows shifted in the flickering light of the burning ship. But it was the men that rivetted my attention. They lay in their hundreds, huddled along the edge of the dunes or in long columns stretching down to the sea. Most were sleeping the sleep of sheer exhaustion – many were sleeping their final sleep. I wandered around for a while, trying to find someone that I knew. Unsuccessful, I made my way to the dunes to find a place to sleep.

I awoke with a start in the chill light of dawn. Cold and bemused, I lay trying to collect my wits. All along the beaches orderly queues were forming, seemingly by common consent, for no-one appeared to be organising them. The sea was completely empty of shipping of any kind. I looked in vain for any sign of the ship that had been burning so fiercely the night before – nothing remained of it. It might never have existed. Nearer the shore, small pieces of wreckage and a number of bodies floated, moving gently on the flat surface of the unbelievably calm sea.

I was soon dozing off, only to be awakened by the sound of approaching aircraft. A flight of Stukas, followed by a second, then a third, passed overhead. One could almost feel those hundreds of men holding their breath. The aircraft passed on, heading for the columns of smoke that hung over the docks. The sound of their screaming sirens and thundering bombs came rolling along the beach toward us. One could not help but shudder at the sound – and be thankful that we were not the target.

We were not, however, to be left in peace for long. From somewhere inland, the sound of gunfire heralded the commencement of an artillery barrage. Soon the shells came screaming in, sending up great clouds of sand as they burst among the dunes – which fortunately absorbed a lot of the blast and shrapnel. We rode out the storm til it stopped as suddenly as it had started. The guns turned their attentions to other targets. The dead and wounded were collected and carried back to the dunes, where makeshift dressing stations had been organised.

Our attention was now rivetted upon a smudge on the horizon

which, in due course, was revealed as a destroyer, heading straight towards our beach. It came to within a few hundred yards of the shore, turned broadside on and began to lower its boats. Unhurriedly and calmly, the boats plied back and forth, carrying as many men as they could safely cram aboard, but never seeming to make any impression on the endless queue which edged forward.

The evacuation continued unhindered, save for the arrival of a group of Stukas which, on being greeted by a hail of fire from the destroyer, moved further down the beach, seeking a softer target. I was now chest-deep in the sea, and estimated that two more journeys would see me safely aboard. The boat returned, took on its load – I was now at the head of the queue, with the water lapping at my chin.

I watched intently as the boat drew alongside the destroyer. This time however, the soldiers did not climb up the scramble nets to the deck. Instead, there before my disbelieving eyes, the boat was attached to its davits and was hauled aboard. This procedure was followed by the other boats and soon the destroyer began to move. At an ever increasing speed it headed for the open sea. I cannot remember what my feelings were at that moment. I just stood there. Perhaps it was never intended that I should be taken off – perhaps at that moment I no longer cared.

So the night dragged on into a misty dawn. Once more the orderly queues began to form. I joined the one nearest to me in a repeat of yesterday's tableau. Slowly the mist cleared, revealing a sea empty of any kind of vessel. The enemy, spurred no doubt by the sight of so many of his quarry getting away, started the day with renewed urgency. From the land and air he was pounding the town and the beaches. Our column scattered with each attack, to reform immediately the danger had passed.

I was again knee-deep in water when, as yesterday, in an almost carbon copy, the shape of a destroyer hove into view, steamed toward us, turned broadside to the shore and began to lower its boats. Once more, the queue shuffled forward, deeper into the sea. As before, the wounded were brought down to be given priority of place in the boats, and again the unwounded, unhesitatingly and without complaint, gave up their places to accommodate them. This in spite of the fact that the sound of enemy machine-gun fire was now so ominously close that it seemed certain that this destroyer represented the very last opportunity to escape from these beaches.

The time dragged interminably. I was again chest-deep in the water. I counted the men in front of me. Next time, I would make it

– or would I? With bated breath I watched the boat ease up alongside the destroyer, where to my relief, the men began to scramble up the nets. Slowly, oh so slowly, it came nearer. I suddenly felt some life returning to my body. The numbness started to leave my brain.

I reached out my hand and touched the boat. At the same moment, a formation of Junkers 88s came roaring in. They swept overhead, on towards the town. A sailor leaned over, grabbed my belt and unceremoniously hauled me over the side."

Brigadier F P Barclay, DSO, MC, then a captain in the 2nd Royal Norfolks, recognised the debt owed by those who got away to the last defenders of Dunkirk.

"Well, the first thing I'd pay tribute to is the men and the morale that we had in the battalion, which was absolutely wonderful. It was the most thrilling feeling to experience the spirit of the chaps who were with you. On the other side, I think we were shockingly badly equipped. Some of the equipment we got we'd not trained with. It

Safely evacuated from Dunkirk, the lucky ones look forward to a week's leave

only joined us when we were mobilising. So far as training in the orthodox forms of warfare went, we were fine, but we hadn't done enough movement at night by transport.

We had tremendous courage in our men and the way they held out when the Dunkirk withdrawal was going on – they never got to Dunkirk themselves – they were stopping the Germans interfering with the withdrawal of thousands of other people. Which they did successfully and I mean, the battalion was practically wiped out doing it. But, such was the determination to put the biggest possible spanner in the Germans' advance, that it succeeded in letting the better part of the British Expeditionary Force get back to England."

Pilot Officer John 'Chalky' White, of No. 32 Squadron of the RAF, saw Dunkirk from above while giving air cover to the rescue boats.

"We arrived at Wittering for a break, and learned that we had to leave for Dunkirk. We patrolled it the best we could – the town was covered by a huge pall of smoke and it was very difficult indeed to see any low-flying enemy aircraft such as Stukas. We were ordered to patrol at 15,000 feet in Hurricanes with Spitfires at 30,000 feet.

I met two young officers who had been posted to our squadron at St Pancras. It was about 4.30 am when we finally reached Biggin Hill. We had to go straight out to the aircraft, and I remember telling them, 'For heaven's sake keep your eyes open all the time'. I was worried stiff as they were brand new to the squadron and there they were – expected to fly into the heat of the action within the hour.

Over Dunkirk we got mixed up with a whole lot of 109s. It was a question of flying around in tight turns and firing at any 109 you could, while making sure that no-one was on your tail. Those two poor youngsters were both shot down and killed on that first mission – that was the end of their war experience.

I know a lot of the troops on the ground said that there was no Air Force protection – I can assure you that whatever aircraft and men we had out there were trying to provide air cover.

Troops were coming back without equipment – bedraggled, grey, dusty and dirty – and I remember thinking 'My God, this is the pride of the British Army.'"

BATTLE OF BRITAIN

The Glory of the Few

Hitler had conquered western Europe and now set his sights on Britain, resolving to batter the island into submission from the air. In the summer of 1940, vicious dogfights raged in the English skies. But the bravery of a few hundred pilots of the RAF, combined with the resolve of civilians steeled by the threat of Nazi invasion, would result in defeat for the mighty Luftwaffe

Flight Lieutenant Peter Brothers of 32 Squadron, now Air Commodore, CBE DSO DFC, made flying his entire life, and was at the forefront of the action in the south east.

"The philosophy of taking on German bombers and fighters was based on the fact that the Hurricanes should attack the bomber formations and the Spitfires the fighter cover. Of course it never worked out like that. Either you weren't together with the Spitfires when the raid happened or, by the time the first flight went in to attack the bombers, the fighters were already coming down – so one of you had to play rear-guard action and take on the fighters. This usually fell to my lot, although I did get mixed up with bombers on occasions.

If you had the time and the height, you got into a favourable position up-sun – but again that didn't usually work out, because one was always scrambled on the late side. This was because, until the controllers were certain that it was a raid and not a spoof to draw you into the air, there was no point in launching you. If it was a spoof, by the time you were refuelling, the main raid would come – and this was what the controllers were trying to avoid.

As a result, it was rather late when we got the word 'Go'. That

The scramble – pilots rush to their planes for immediate take-off

usually meant that you were at a disadvantage heightwise, so you'd have to take the bombers head-on. That, we discovered, was one of the best ways. They didn't like that, as they didn't have forward-firing guns – or very few of them did.

You could break up a formation and, once you'd scattered it, you had a good opportunity of shooting down an individual aircraft without being involved in crossfire from the rest of the formation. Also, by the time the fighters got as far as London, they were at the limit of their range.

Life was much simpler afterward, when we were doing sweeps over France – you planned those. During the Battle of Britain, there was a lot of time for sitting around and waiting – and then there was the panic of the scramble.

The only time I felt positively sick was when I hit a chap straight in the cockpit. I thought 'I didn't mean that – I only meant to hit a wing off'. That was the game side of it – we all rather hoped the chap would jump out and be taken prisoner rather than be killed.

One got very tired. When we were operating, we were at readiness half an hour before first light at about 3.30 in the morning, and we'd finish about half an hour after last light – say 10.30 at night.

By the time you'd gone over to the mess and had a meal (and I often used to go back and take a crate of beer for the ground crew, and have a chat with them to thank them) and were in bed, it was around midnight. Then you were back down at the aircraft by 3.30."

On only his second bombing mission, Oberleutenant Hans Gollnisch of the Stab II/KG30 bomber unit was grounded by an RAF fighter as he approached his target.

"In early September 1940, my unit was transferred from Denmark to Chievre, Belgium, in order to concentrate bomber groups for bigger raids on England. It was my second mission of this kind when on 9 September we took off from Chievre to meet about 200 bombers at 5,000 metres over Cap Gris-Nez.

After a wide swing eastward, we headed for London, escorted by hundreds of German fighters. The targets were the docks and the shipping in the Thames, and could already be seen, when we were suddenly hit by a very short burst of fire from the machine guns of the RAF fighter that had evidently approached from below and behind, unseen.

Our plane was badly damaged and the situation was grim – the control column didn't work any more, as a bullet must have severed the elevator cables, and both engines were hit, the right losing gasoline, the left oil.

Then the observer, *Unteroffizier* Rolf, reported that the gunner, Diebler, was lying dead in a pool of blood, a bullet having pierced the artery of his neck. I gave the order to shed the cockpit roof in order to bail out, but then I found that I could just about control the aeroplane by the trimming wheel, which to some extent replaced the elevator. Thinking of our dead gunner, I decided to stay in the plane and make for the Channel. If our engines kept going long enough, we could get down on the water and maybe get back to France in the rubber dinghy which was carried on board. So I turned south for the shortest route and jettisoned our bombs. However, we now had no guns to defend ourselves against further attack, as these had gone with the roof, so I dived for cover in the clouds 3,000 metres below.

Unfortunately, in the clouds the engines stopped and didn't want to start again. By now we were too low to bail out, so had no choice but to make a very difficult landing with no use of the control column. I couldn't even let out the flaps, because the electrical system had failed!

I was very lucky to make a good landing as another problem was that of all the fields being covered in all sorts of poles and obstacles like old cars – as a defence against a possible landing by assault gliders in an invasion. However, I got us down in one piece and after we had lifted out the dead gunner, we set fire to our aeroplane and gave ourselves up to police and soldiers."

Lieutenant Ulrich Steinhilpher was based with the Third Squadron of Jaggeschwader 52, flying Bf-109s out of Coquelles, opposite Folkestone across the Channel. He was in the thick of the fighting in English air-space, and saw much to find fault with in the way the Luftwaffe was led.

"I consider I lasted quite well – right up to 27 October. In August we were mainly trying to hit the British fighters and their airfields, but they wouldn't come up and fight. That's where Dowding was so damned clever – he wouldn't release the fighters unless we came with bombers....

We weren't told there had been a change of tactics but when on 15 September, we escorted a mass of bombers in two waves to London, it was obvious that things had changed. Now we didn't attack the airfields any more, but just tried to keep the people of London in the shelters. Although the fighters did their best, there were huge losses to the bombers and by October the daylight use of bombers had been virtually stopped. Instead they concentrated on the use of fighter-bombers, Bf-109s which had a single underslung 250 kg bomb. The pylon which was fitted to the under-side of the 109 to carry the bomb was the same as that which should have been employed to carry long-range fuel tanks. Because of Hitler's insistence on the reprisal bombing of London, this valuable equipment was given to the fighter-bomber wings instead of the fighters. It was a decision which cost us dearly. On one mission some 235 109s were lost on the way back home, mainly because of lack of fuel, 19 of whose pilots drowned in the Channel.

So in October we started the so-called 'Waves'. The idea was that if bombs fell on London every 20 minutes or so then the whole population would stay in the shelters. One day we flew from Coquelles to London and back seven times.

My last flight was on 27 October. It was nine o'clock and very cold. My new aircraft was having its first overhaul so I opted to fly my old aircraft, 'Yellow 2', which had become a spare. It had been sitting around on the ground for two or three weeks, and in the cold nights condensation had begun to build up in the grease around the mechanism of the propeller.

When we were approaching London I could see the moisture in the grease was beginning to freeze. I should have returned to base but there was so much talk at the time of *Kanalkrankheit* (Channel sickness) – that people were returning to base with faults which 'cleared up' on landing, or not being able to fly because of 'sickness' – and I didn't want to be counted amongst them.

In the turn over London we got into trouble very high. Spitfires were diving through us and I couldn't act as usual with very high revolutions on the engine and a coarse pitch to gain speed. Instead there was a bang and I thought the supercharger had exploded, but the engine was operating well enough. So I started the usual gradual descent towards home and passed through some cloud. Taking my oxygen mask off I realised the cockpit smelt like a steam locomotive – the engine was boiling. In the brief dogfight [with the Spitfires] I had been hit in the radiator.

From then on I had to switch off the ignition and glide until the oil had cooled and then restart the engine to gain some height. On the third try I was very low because the oil temperature had not seemed to come down much and when I pushed the throttle forward I could feel the engine was going to seize – and it did. I was in radio contact with Coquelles and they said they would send the air-sea rescue, because I had said that if the engine stopped I would have to bail out.

I had real trouble getting out. Normally when the canopy release is pulled the whole unit comes off. This time only the lever came off in my hand and the canopy stayed in place. I had no option but to open the centre section which tilts and the slipstream tore this away but the back part stayed in place. When I tried to get out, my parachute got stuck. I took a chance and somersaulted backwards and my left leg was injured when the main chute deployed. I was so low when I got out that I saw the aircraft crash, right in the middle of a herd of cows.

A Home Guard man was the first person I met when I was testing my leg. A shot was fired and I saw a man with a shot-gun aiming at me. He didn't know it but I didn't have a weapon. New orders were that we could not carry side-arms any more because the bodies of aircrew had been recovered from the Channel with gun-shot wounds to the head. It seemed some pilots, half-drowned, had taken what our High Command had considered to be the 'easy' way out and shot themselves."

THE BLITZ

Surviving the Bombs

In the winter of 1940, Hitler ordered a massive bombing campaign to crush Britain's cities, in revenge for Allied raids on Berlin. The Luftwaffe bombarded towns and cities throughout the country for seventy-six nights, bringing death and destruction to the British population. Finding themselves for the first time on the frontline of the war, their resilience and courage was tested to the limit

Peter Wood was living in Tulse Hill in south London and working in the City. On 7 September, just before the Blitz, he was playing football near Crystal Palace when he heard some unseasonable thunder. He looked up to see the sky full of German bombers – but the game went on.

"Literally dozens of Germans, accompanied by smaller aircraft which I took to be fighters, were going over at about 500 feet. There didn't seem to be any gunfire from our defending forces at all. Fortunately for us, they overflew us, because they were obviously heading for the docks, for what was, as we know now, the first bombing of the docklands at that time. We shrugged our shoulders and carried on to finish our game of football.

After that the bombing of London increased in volume and the routine was to sleep in a reinforced cellar where my wife's family lived in Tulse Hill, and when the all-clear went in the morning, you just got up, washed and dressed and went to work.

After just over a month of this, I remember the all-clear going, and it was still dark. We came up out of the cellar and went out into the street and I had literally walked up a hill. A 500-lb bomb had peeled the road up about 50 yards from where I lived. This was, I suppose, the nearest thing to bombing that we got – except that about a month later I was walking my wife to her place of work, and we saw a hole in the gutter. We both peered down it, wondering what it was, then when we came back in the evening, that road was all blown up. It was an unexploded bomb, which had gone off during the day, and a bus had actually gone into the hole.

Like all of us living and working in London, we were members of the ARP and did our stint of fire-watching and generally helping the fire brigade and police as best we could. When we were in the shelters we played pontoon or poker most of the night and drank tea or cocoa. We didn't sleep very much because the anti-aircraft guns were going constantly. We could feel the bombs hitting the area. The extraordinary thing was, when the 500-pounder came so close to us, we didn't actually feel much from it. We must have been so close to the epicentre of the explosion that we didn't actually feel it.

Working in the City, sometimes you had a normal run through on the bus or tram – we had trams in those days – sometimes you would be diverted and you wouldn't get to the office for four or five hours. On some days, the damage was so bad that you just gave up and went back home.

Our area was not as badly affected at this time as later on, in 1944 when the V1 and V2 attacks were going on. That was much more devastating than even the [Blitz] bombing. The incendiary bombs were serious because they would start the fires going, then they would drop high explosives into the fires to stop you from putting the fires out.

Life went on as normally as possible. People got to the stage where, as soon as they had had tea or supper, they would take their bedding and go to the Anderson shelter – it became a way of life. The extraordinary thing was that people were not badly demoralised – the more they suffered, the more determined they seemed to be that they would beat this thing."

Ballard Berkeley, actor, served as a special constable in London's West End during the worst of the Blitz, and was responsible for keeping order in the midst of chaos.

"Sometimes we were called in because of the looting that was going on. It was one of the most awful things, I remember thinking – one heard of all the bravery and courage – and then there were also some very nasty things. Some of the looters at the Café de Paris bombing, for instance, didn't have time to do otherwise than cut people's fingers off to get their rings.

One night, the City was really having a bad time – you could hear the guns, see the lovely red sky down there, and we wondered if they were coming up our way or not. Then we heard a bomber overhead – the drone of the engine. You could always tell the difference between the German bombers and the British. There was the usual screech, and then came down a whole whoosh of incendiary bombs, right across the road. Eventually my beat seemed to be more or less clear, and I saw a tremendous blaze in the direction of Dean Street and Old Compton Street. I went down there and it was a bedding factory that was ablaze – it looked as if the north side of Old Compton Street and Wardour Street was going to be burned down. Because the fire service couldn't cope with all this, they had decided to evacuate the area.

It really was the most extraordinary thing – I'd just put a case of something across the road to save it, and was coming back to get more – then suddenly everything stopped and there was complete and utter silence. I heard no bomb coming down, no explosion, but whether the explosion had deafened my eardrums or not, I don't know – but everything was silent."

Bomber pilot Lieutenant Walther Freiherr (Baron) von Silber, of the III Staffel First Group Kampfgeschwader 53, Legion Kondor, was sent to bomb London. His crew did not return.

"The night of 10 May was very clear. We were flying at 4,800 feet, towards the target area around the Houses of Parliament. The Heinkel was hit by fire from the ground, and I immediately pressed the emergency button releasing the entire load of bombs. We then went into defensive manoeuvres. The Heinkel was hit for a second time and we were on fire. *Feldwebel* Fischer reported that two of the crew were dead and a third was wounded and unable to crawl through the narrow hatch doors, which were smothered in flames.

The fire on board was getting worse and worse, and it now looked impossible to rescue *Feldwebel* Fischer. So I gave him the order to bail out over the mainland. I still wanted to try and force-land in the Channel, and hoped to reach the French coast by dinghy. But the

An ARP recruitment poster appeals to civilians to help during the chaos of the Blitz

Heinkel 111 was now impossible to steer because of the raging fire on board, She began to fall away and then went into spin. I managed to clamber out. Whether the parachute was forced open while I was climbing out, or whether I unconsciously pulled the rip-cord, I cannot remember.

I was taken prisoner by members of the Home Guard. There was a big difference in their attitude to the enemy in comparison to the active troops. The worst experience I had was with an English interrogation officer, who seemed a rogue. During five and a half years of imprisonment, I got to know and respect many English officers, but I certainly regret this incident of English politics."

Kenneth Turner, in the Chief Clerk's Department, had to deal with the administrative problem of identifying and dealing with the hundreds of bodies returned to the mortuary after the 14 November raid on Coventry.

"Three or four days after the raid, the Medical Officer of Health who was responsible for the mortuary and the Chief Constable who was in charge of public morale had a serious difference of opinion. The Chief Constable was saying that unless people could go to the mortuary and identify their dead, there would be riots and trouble, and the Medical Officer of Health was saying that conditions at the mortuary were such that it was impossible for anyone to do this.

They came to consult the Town Clerk and he asked me to inspect the mortuary and give my opinion of it. He sent me off with a bottle of whisky in my pocket, and when I got there, I found I needed it. The mortuary staff were engaged in fitting bits and pieces together to make whole bodies, and in many cases there were no means of identification or anything of that sort. The whole place was literally a shambles.

I came out and a crowd of about two or three hundred had gathered. I said I'd been in and made an inspection, and that it was not possible for them to go in. That led to great shouts and so on, in particular from some service chaps in the front row, who had been allowed home on compassionate leave. I picked a sailor and an airman from the crowd and said 'You can come in' and took them inside. They were both violently sick in a couple of minutes. They came outside and said, 'It's right, what he says', and the crowd accepted it and dispersed.

After this, people couldn't arrange for private burials – it would have been impossible for four or five hundred individual graves to have been dug – and of course they couldn't choose which was their body out of all these. So it was decided and accepted that the whole lot be buried in a mass grave."

NORTH AFRICA

A Vast Theatre

Mussolini sought to take advantage of the war in Europe to expand Italy's empire in North Africa by confronting the British troops stationed in Egypt to protect the Suez Canal. But in 1940 and 1941, Richard O'Connor's Western Desert Force inflicted a series of defeats, capturing the port of Tobruk and winning a decisive victory at Beda Fomm

Sergeant Bernard Griffith left home and joined the army at the age of 17. After a few months with the Royal Horse Artillery in India, he found himself on the way to North Africa in 1939 where, serving as an Observer Post driver, he took part in the campaign which culminated in the battle of Beda Fomm.

"At first light you stood to and then moved out of the leaguer area at about 5.00 am to prepared gun positions at certain times and new positions on others. At that stage I was an Observation Post driver-operator, so was the last back into the leaguer every night and first out every morning – so I was generally about four miles in front of the gun position, mainly attached to the infantry. At that time, our total hours of rest, if there was any, was about three per night.

You didn't draw any money in the desert – there was nowhere to spend it. You got two bottles of beer and some cigarettes – when it arrived, the beer immediately used to explode because it was hot and it had been shaken about over hundreds of kilometres of desert. So when you went back, you had all your credits, as they were called. Pay was two bob a day then – that didn't accumulate to much. The form was, you arrived in Cairo. You got a local to introduce you to a gharry – a horse and truck – and he took you to a hotel – a sleazy place in the backstreets. The first thing you did was take off all your muck. You used to drop everything on the floor and give the bloke so many piastres to go out and buy you underwear, socks, KD shorts (khaki drill), slacks, shirts – and you lay in the bath for two hours.

The first stop of most of the 7th Armoured Division was the American bar in First Street, which we called the Beaulac. You used to have steak, egg and chips and a big bottle of Stella lager, which used to blow your head off if you had too much of it. Then we used to go round the cinemas and the shows they put on – varying types of show and, to be quite blunt, fornication – as you can imagine.

After a little setback after the first Italian push in October 1940, Jock Campbell formed us into 'Jock columns'. The ammunition used to be put inside the vehicle, the crew used to sit on top of the ammunition, and you'd go bounding across the desert at last light and do a right hook, generally, and come up behind an ammunition supply and dump the men and ammo. You'd drop into action just before first light, provided your navigation had been good, and fire like bloody hell on the enemy concentration – then get the hell out of it. It was a hit and run thing.

If you were caught behind enemy lines, the idea was to get away fast from the enemy concentration, find a little undulation and camouflage yourself up. For the whole day, you just sat there, getting cooked by the sun. There was no light, no smoking, no noise and you just sat there for the day – and at last light you made your way back to your own lines.

Christmas 1940 I shall never forget. I was in a cave. We had started our advance on the Italians and we reached a load of caves to the west of Sollum. You had so much food issued to each truck and the driver normally was the cook. We had one tin of bully, one tin of marmalade, a lump of cheese and a tin of herrings. Our sergeant put the lot in one can. That was Christmas dinner 1940.

There was a shortage of water, petrol – and terrible terrain. It was raining cats and dogs, and we were soaked to the skin. Vehicles kept breaking down, we didn't get any replenishments. We were going into battle with the ammunition we had, and we'd no idea if we were going to get resupplied or not. We were down to almost nothing and morale was low. However, when you dropped into action, you knew you were cutting off the Italian Army, and the world was your oyster.

At the end of it, it was pure elation. We found these Italian forts – full of food, chocablock. We just gorged ourselves silly for a few days. They all had water – literally hundreds of containers. We started tipping it around the place, washing our socks in water instead of petrol. They had bottles and bottles of Chianti, and we just tipped it back – we made hay while the sun shone."

General Sir Richard O'Connor GCB DSO MC, recalls his planning and execution of the campaigns leading up to Beda Fomm – Bardia and Tobruk. As major general, he commanded the Western Desert Force and later became lieutenant general.

"It was absolutely vital that secrecy should be maintained, and that meant, not only keeping the project from the enemy, but it was just as important to keep it from our own men. Only two senior staff officers were told to start with, and it was not until a week before that anything was written on the subject.

The troops were not told until they were already on the ground – only three days before the operation was to take place. Leave for Cairo was only stopped three days before, as the biggest source of danger was officers and other ranks going to Cairo and talking about what was going on – quite innocently, of things that the enemy could pick up... and everything that happened in Cairo went straight to Italy – so we took every possible step we could to make sure, first that the enemy didn't know and, no less important, that our own people didn't know.

We'd formed our plan – we decided that we would advance between the most southern enemy camps, then we would pass right through and get behind the camp and so actually attack them from their own side. In order to give this the best chance of success, I wanted to carry out a rehearsal – and obviously we couldn't call it a rehearsal for the operation because nobody knew about it.

During the day we had to enlist the help of the RAF in keeping the enemy out of the sky, because of the enormous amount of dust we produced in our advance to the forming-up places. The supply problem was vital and we were always on the edge of a shortage. Our five-day dumps very shortly ran out, and so we had to have our supplies moved in convoys.

It was very important, from my point of view, that I should have absolute control of what was to be sent up. It was a subject that I dealt with every day – and I was absolutely *au fait* myself with exactly the situation of where these various convoys were and when one could

British troops man a trench outside Bardia, December 1940

expect them. Our operation entirely depended on how this worked.

The forts we had to overcome were of a strength of about a division each – or sometimes more. For the original attack against the first one I was very insistent that we should attack them from the west – that is, from the way their rations would come. Secondly, I knew that by having our operations behind their front, we would be protecting ourselves against enemy air attack – they would damage their own people. So from every point of view, the right position to start from was attacking the enemy from a most unexpected quarter. That was the basis of the first one, and it was preceded by a heavy, short, bombardment which came as a complete surprise to the enemy and was immediately followed up by the infantry tanks, which blasted their way into the camp, closely followed by the infantry.

The Bardia and Tobruk operations required an entirely different technique. Their defences were of a different quality. They were strong, actual fortresses, with a very large anti-tank ditch surrounding them – and wire. There was no way of getting the tanks in except to bridge the ditch – and we couldn't bridge the ditch while the enemy was shooting at us. So we had to have a preliminary operation by the infantry, who would go in the night before the actual attack. They would, with the help of a very heavy artillery barrage, advance and make a bridgehead in the line at a place we selected, and immediately that was completed, the sappers would make a series of bridges over the anti-tank ditch.

Instead of attacking Benghazi direct, I decided to direct a force south west which would cut off all the enemy troops which were fighting in the Benghazi area. It was a gamble that the Armoured Division had to move over about 150 miles of unreconnoitred land – more of a gamble than might have appeared necessary, because I refused to have the area reconnoitred except from the air. I knew that if we began sending patrols out in that area, it would at once warn the enemy that it was our intention to attack from that direction. They would have fallen back earlier and we would not have caught them as we did."

Sergeant Francis McGoff, later Warrant Officer, was with the Royal Army Medical Corps during the desert campaign. His memories are of the extraordinary desert conditions.

"The men used to get desert sores – you used to wash all your clothes in petrol too – you didn't have water. We thought we'd found the answer to it when we captured a load of Italian anti-diphtheria vaccine – we tried using wet dressings of this on the sores – and they cleared up! But then a few days later they broke out again.

The desert sores started as a little blister. This would burst and a whacking great sore would appear. We used to brush them with stiff nail brushes and scrub them with carbolic soap until there was a nice blood flow, then we'd dry them off in the sun. Then we used to grind up MB693 tablets – and that used to clear them up – but not permanently. We had to stop that eventually, because there were vast temperature changes in the desert, so pneumonia was a very common complaint. There were blokes having to be evacuated to base with pneumonia, but if you treated pneumonia cases with MB693, the patients were better in five days – a marvellous treatment. But, they found too, that the chaps who had been treated topically with the stuff – when they were treated with it internally, the areas on their skin went black. There were a hell of a lot of deaths too – so we had to stop using the MB693 for skin treatment."

ATLANTIC WAR

Atlantic Sea Hunt

As an island, Britain was entirely dependent on convoys coming across the Atlantic for vital supplies. Throughout 1941, as German attacks on shipping brought imminent threat of starvation, a bitter contest was fought for control over the seas. The sinking of two ships, the German Bismarck and HMS Hood, marked the end of the battleship era

One of only three men to survive the sinking of HMS Hood, Able Seaman Robert Kilburn had a tale of horror which is just as terrifying today as it was then.

"Our radar had picked up two ships going south, so we turned to follow them. We expected them to be the *Bismarck* and *Prinz Eugen*, but until we actually sighted them, we weren't sure. We closed towards them and opened fire at 25,000 yards – 12 and a half miles. *The Bismarck* and *Prinz Eugen* answered immediately: the third, fourth and fifth shells hit us and the fifth blew us up.

I was on the upper deck, with only two other people. The others were in a shelter deck – a shell had killed all of them, about 200 men, but I didn't realise that at the time. There was a fire on board the upper deck and the ammunition was exploding. The three of us were waiting for the ammunition to stop exploding before putting the fire out. We were laid on the deck, and then there was this terrific explosion. It was most peculiar, the dead silence that followed it – I don't know if we were deaf.

One of the other men was dead and the other had his sides cut open and all his innards were tumbling out. I went over to the ship's sides to be sick.

I noticed that the ship was rolling over and the bows were coming out of the water, so I started taking off my tin hat, gas mask, anti-flash gear, overcoat, oilskin, so that I would have a chance to swim. With the ship rolling over, I just went into the water.

I was terrified. I had a small rubber life belt on, which was partially blown up. I started swimming away from the ship. I had a tight belt on, so I took my knife out and cut the belt off to breathe better. The ship rolled over and the yard-arms, which had been broken during the action, hit me across the legs and the wireless aerials tangled around my legs, pulling me down with the ship. I cut my seaboots off with the knife and shot up, like a cork out of a bottle. I must have been about ten feet down by then. The ship was about ten yards away from me – and she just sank. There I was in the water. There wasn't any down-current, which presupposes that the bottom had been blown out of the ship.

I swam around on my own at first. There was a large pool of oil about three miles along with a lot of flotsam and jetsam in it. I didn't want to go in the oil, but I could see small rafts – biscuit rafts – which were about a metre square. After about an hour, I was so cold that I had to get in the oil and swim to a raft. I was quite close to Ted Briggs – he was on a raft. He wasn't well, because he'd swallowed some oil fuel. I held on to his raft because I thought, 'If I'm going to die, I've got some company here'. We were in a state of shock and very, very cold. I had read stories about when you were really cold you just went to sleep and died, so I tried to go to sleep, because it seemed a really nice way to die.

We were rescued about four and a half hours after the explosion by a destroyer called *Electra*. They heaved us over the side like sacks of potatoes. They tried to give me a cigarette and I was so cold that they had to put it in my mouth, then remove it when I started coughing. We were so cold we couldn't move."

Commander Ronald Hay, a naval pilot when the sea war started, found himself struggling against the shortcomings of outdated aircraft – and the non-cooperation and rivalry between Britain's armed forces.

"The *Bismarck* didn't need the Home Fleet – admittedly, though, the *Victorious* took a hand in it. We could have done without the Coastal Command as well, because the *Bismarck* was lost for an agonising 36 hours or so. Eventually the *Bismarck* was discovered – in fact we got the first sighting report from our sorties long before we got any information from Coastal Command. As for the part the Home Fleet played in it, it was a disgrace in many ways. For some strange reason, either because their blood was up or they wanted to avenge themselves, they closed the race, opened fire at about 20,000 yards and closed it down to about 6,000 or 7,000 yards – and when you've got great big guns like that, hurling shells at high velocity, they were simply going across horizontally.

Of course, the whole point of distant gunnery was that you sent it right up there, got lots of gravity to make it plunging fire, going right down the funnel to blow up in the bowels of the ship – which would cause havoc. Of course, they closed the range down to 6,000 yards because there was no opposition from the *Bismarck*, then all they were doing was firing their shells straight through, horizontally, hitting this big armour with a thump, but nothing else happened.

Naturally, the superstructure was a total shambles, but the ship wouldn't sink. At the same time, we had 21 Swordfish, each with a 19 inch torpedo, hanging around waiting to sink the darn thing, but the *Dorsetshire* was told to sink it. They fired quite a few torpedoes, but nothing happened very much, and then, because there was a report of a submarine, they called off the rescue ship and left the rest of the men to die. Meanwhile, 21 Swordfish had to ditch their torpedoes safe into the sea. The whole thing was really pathetic.

I met the Gunnery Damage Control Officer of the *Bismarck* after the war, in Kiel. You can believe this if you want to – he told me that he blew charges and opened the seacocks down below himself, as he was one of the few survivors – I think there were only about 33 survivors, actually. This was apart from the carnage on the upper deck – so the ship was never sunk by the Navy. It was sunk by a German Damage Control Officer, presumably to stop the Navy from boarding the ship and getting secret logs and equipment."

Frau Elizabeth Heinz was a secretary in her early 20s in the German embassy in Montevideo. Her account, written at the time of the scuttling of the Graf Spee, took the form of a letter to a friend in Germany dated 21 December 1939.

"We suddenly heard on the radio that a battle was raging between

German and English cruisers at Funte del Este and Piriapolis. One news announcement followed close on another. First we were told that the English cruiser *Exeter* had been destroyed by the battleship *Graf Spee* – and we were astonished by this – we couldn't believe that a German battleship was here, off our coast. When I came home from the office and heard the news on the radio, the battle was already taking place in Uruguayan waters. At 9.00 pm we were told that shots had been exchanged, then the cruisers had disappeared in the fog. One cruiser was heading full steam for Montevideo and would reach Montevideo in 90 minutes. Apparently it was a German cruiser, but the nationality could not be confirmed – two other cruisers were following it. The radio announcer was practically tripping over himself as reports flooded in. Ten minutes later it was confirmed that it was a German cruiser, followed by two English. Ten minutes later: German embassy officials had gone to see the Uruguayan government – then a few minutes later – they were asking permission to dock in Montevideo. They were asking for a certain number of beds to be made available at the military hospital. The reports became more and more frantic.

It was announced that the German cruiser had dropped anchor in Montevideo harbour and was unloading its dead and wounded. How proud we Germans were of our 'boys in blue', of the beautiful ship – my tears are welling up again. The next day, Friday 15th, the 36 dead men were laid to rest.

In the meantime, a whole fleet had assembled off the La Plata estuary, waiting for the *Admiral Graf Spee* to leave the harbour: a huge mousetrap was set. The labourers worked day and night on the cruiser. On Saturday, from early morning until late into the night, everyone was asking: *saldra* or *nor saldra* – will she leave or won't she? It was all in vain, even the efforts of our German ambassador. Even the right granted to every country to have the time to patch up the ship again was denied to him. He was told she had to leave port by eight o'clock on Sunday evening. She couldn't even leave before this (the night of Saturday to Sunday was foggy and the weather was bad – this would have facilitated her escape), for according to the law, a given time must elapse following the departure of the last ship until any cruiser is allowed to leave. The English had been very cunning about this. A small English vessel left the harbour and by 6.15 on Sunday evening the time was up – which left the German cruiser with only 105 minutes in which to leave the port. The tension and excitement amongst the population rose to breaking point. The harbour was packed with people as the time grew closer and closer.

Will she leave – to a certain death with all those brave young men on board? There must be a way out – a loving God would not wish this to happen. Then around seven o'clock the anchor was raised and the ship began to move. The whole crowd froze. They couldn't believe their eyes, they didn't dare to breathe. The women fell to their knees and prayed for the blonde boys. We Germans were as white as a sheet. The ship slowly left the harbour one hour before the deadline. The crowd was dumbstruck and then gradually regained their senses and began waving and shouting. The ship left the dock, flying a massive German flag. We rushed home to listen to the radio. Then a few minutes before eight o'clock, we heard a dull blast. The sun had gone done now, it didn't need to shine anymore. Giant flames and explosions. Reports spread like wildfire, the captain and crew have been saved. Then others, the propaganda stations, reported, 1,000 young men in the bloom of youth have been sent to their deaths by one solitary man, who only needed to say one word. That man sits in Berlin – Hitler! Then we could see *Tacoma*, the German steamer, which had been in the harbour a long time, and the whispers went round: the crew had transferred on to the steamer during the night and now they had been taken by Argentinian tugs which were waiting nearby."

A British sailor keeps watch over an Atlantic convoy, May 1941

BALKANS AND CRETE

Captors & Captives

Drawn by rich natural resources and a strategic position in the eastern Mediterranean, Hitler launched an attack down through the Balkan pensinula towards Greece in 1939. The Allies withdrew to the island fortress of Crete, which in May 1941 became the target of a large-scale German airborne assault. Despite fierce fighting, the invaders won the island in less than two weeks

Corporal Jack Gardner of the 1st Battalion Argyll and Sutherland Highlanders was taken prisoner on Crete and held in Germany until the end of the war. He remembers the Crete campaign as a terrible waste of time, men and money.

"My battalion was called out of the desert – Egypt – in May 1941. We landed on Crete in small landing craft. During the landing a lot of the landing craft were wrecked by the turbulent seas. All we knew was that we were being sent to a place where we would see some action, but we didn't know the exact name or location. It was just a job to us regular army men.

We were marched inland overnight to take position and we were then sent out in platoons. I was left behind as rear guard, overlooking an area near a house. There were a lot of Stukas flying about. Then I saw the Germans going over in the Junkers. The troops below were more or less decimating the men that were jumping out. Some of them never came out of the aircraft because the aircraft had already been riddled with bullets, so they must have been dead or injured.

We soon realised that it was a very disjointed affair. There wasn't any cohesion in it because there wasn't any means of communication. Communication was literally non-existent – it was guess-work. Where should the front be, when there were parachutists being dropped off in different parts of the island? Most of us thought 'What the hell are we supposed to be doing?' It was totally chaotic. We were wandering about like lost souls in the night.

We had been on Crete for about four days before they tried to evacuate us. We were waiting in the hills to be evacuated. We could hear the British destroyers at night, ramming the Germans who were coming to Crete from Greece. We didn't have much food because you couldn't get supplies. We were buying food off the Greeks.

We were captured when we were waiting to be evacuated. Somebody walked down and the Germans stopped him and sent him back with a message that the Germans had surrounded us. The senior officer decided that there was no point fighting, so ordered us to destroy every weapon that we had.

We were marched up to Heraklion. It took two days – you just kept going. I wasn't apprehensive because the Germans had taken prisoners before. Fear didn't enter our minds because they are civilised people. It had happened, and that was that. I don't think that there was a man on that march who was frightened either. We had very little communication with the Germans during the march. They were told not to antagonise us because we were front-line soldiers, and the Germans had a lot of respect for front-line men. One of the Germans said to me that he didn't know why we were fighting each other.

We were held prisoner on Crete for four or five days in different places before we were taken to Greece. They kept us behind barbed-wire fences. You couldn't say the treatment was bad, because they didn't have much either. You got one meal a day, that was all, because they didn't have much food. When we were down at Suda, the Germans were using British stocks of food from the *York*. I was on a work party and a German asked me 'what's in this tin?' There wasn't a label, but I guessed 'peaches' and it was. He gave me a tin, and I opened it up. They tasted good – it was the first tin of peaches I had had in over a year."

Gerhard Schirmer, age 29, was a Captain in the 2nd Battalion of Paratroops Regiment 2, and was one of the thousands of German soldiers who dropped on to the island of Crete as part of Operation Mercury.

"General Student had a tactical plan. He wanted to build five Riegel (locking positions) – one at the airfield at Maleme, which would involve capturing the airfield at the same time which we needed as a base for reinforcements), one near Canea at Suda Bay, one at Retimo, and one each to the east and west of Heraklion. This last would involve capturing the airfield at Heraklion.

This plan was good, but reconnaissance had underestimated the strength of the English, Australians and New Zealanders. The English troops had camouflaged themselves splendidly and reconnaissance yielded very unsatisfactory results. Also, the English had unfortunately armed the Cretan population – who fought in their Cretan costumes, which was against every rule of war.

My battalion was to be assigned 48 to 50 Ju-52s. Well, the units which had been put in at Heraklion and Retimo assembled in the second wave at about midday. In the first wave in the early hours of 20 May, the units who had been deployed at Maleme and Canea were to jump. Because of the terrible problems with the dust on the airfields, the order of the units who were to jump was changed, and I was now the first.

I didn't get my eight aircraft as planned – only four. That meant I had to leave more than one complete company behind. This altered the whole plan of invasion. Before the start there was only a

Retreating from Greece, British soldiers rest in the shade while their officers dicuss plans

very short time to instruct the company leaders and decide who would be left behind.

While I was doing this, running through my mind constantly was the foreboding – how could I carry out this mission without almost one and a half companies out of my four? But, we were lucky – we were the first to jump in the area of Heraklion, and where we jumped there was hardly any defensive fire.

It wasn't long, however, before the first attacks came, principally from the New Zealand and Australian forces. The 3rd Battalion Paratroop Regiment 1 attacked the town of Heraklion, but the western edge of the town was magnificently defended by the English. There was an ancient ten-metres-high town wall, in which there were few gates, and it was impossible to get in. The Battalion had to withdraw. Next day Major Schulz and I took one company from my already tiny front and attacked Heraklion again. This time we succeeded in getting into the town along the coast. But the counter-fire was so heavy that we had to pull our forces back again – it was impossible to reach the airfield.

Very heavy fighting ensued. The English attacked – we counterattacked. It was a period of uninterrupted fighting. We'd planned to bring in a mountain regiment to Maleme from Greece and from the Peloponnese, using boats – little boats, fishing boats, in fact, since there were no other ships available. This little fleet did set off, about a hundred of them, but the English Eastern Mediterranean fleet got between them and the land, and the mass of these boats were sunk. Italian cruisers and destroyers were to provide protection for these boats, but once the English fleet arrived, they turned tail and headed back to Italy. So, no mountain regiment – which was meant to pick up paratroopers and bolster the attack. No, we had to carry on alone in Heraklion. That was an unbelievably difficult situation, especially as the losses were very high.

We had a stroke of luck. A rather weak battalion of paratroopers was dropped into my position on 25 May. This was a significant reinforcement. We had to carry on. We advanced with the two battalions in a row, one man behind the other, keeping the old front line only thinly occupied.

We marched off, headed south, right up to the edge of the mountains, and then bore left, heading east. We passed south of Knossos to reach the Lion Mountain, just south of the airfield of Heraklion. We wanted to take this. The English still held it, though somewhat feebly now. We took this mountain on 28 or 29 May, and then the next day we wanted to attack the airfield from this mountain, but once this attack was finished, there was no resistance at all – the English had all boarded ships, again near Heraklion, or others had gone off in lorries to the south of the island to Petra, and had boarded ships there. They were gone, and we had the airfield,

Short Sunderland flying boats – the only aircraft to help in the evacuation from Greece

but with absolutely our last ounce of strength.

When we had taken Lion Mountain, there was a little Arabian chapel up on the top, painted white. I got in there and lay down, gave over command of my battalion to a Company Leader. For the first time in days, four days, I think, I could get some sleep. I slept for quite a number of hours and eventually, when they woke me, they told me that the English fleet had been firing its 280 mm guns at the mountain and the hits from the shells were less than 50 metres from the little chapel. I heard absolutely nothing. That shows how battle-weary we all were.

It was a hard fight, but we knew whenever you fought against the English, it was a fair fight. We were able, and this happened in Crete also, to send over envoys and agree on a ceasefire of, say, an hour, so that both sides would retrieve their wounded, put them under cover and see that they were looked after. Anything like this was unthinkable in the fight against the Russians."

BARBAROSSA

Scorched Earth

Driven by his hatred of Communism, in June 1941 Hitler launched Operation Barbarossa, designed to vanquish the vast Soviet Union. Three armoured thrusts aimed at strategic targets and the capital, Moscow, threatened to bring a rapid victory as the defending Russians retreated, destroying everything in the Germans' path. Triumph seemed inevitable – but it would remain elusive

Lieutenant Ekkehard Maurer was with the German 32nd Infantry Division. Along with the rest of the German Army, he was convinced by the intelligence reports that the Russians were ill-equipped and unprepared. On 22 June, they advanced with confidence over the Russian borders, unaware of the winter perils.

"Well, being as young as we were at the time, I think we had a lot of confidence in ourselves, as any young men would have. The second point – we hadn't lost a battle, so we were used to being victorious. We saw a tremendous concentration of German armed forces, and also got intelligence reports which seemed to prove that the Russian Army was not of a very high standard. We had some contacts with the Russians in 1939, when they advanced in Poland, and we met halfway. Our impression at the time of the Russian military as a whole was not very favourable. They were poorly clad, they were not very well equipped – they were hardly motorised until then.

All of this led to some measure of confidence. On the other hand, I think we were quite conscious of the fact, even we young ones, that no army had ever conquered Russia permanently – that there was no final and lasting victory of an intruder into Russia. We didn't admit it to ourselves, but there was this awkward and uneasy feeling that we may win battles in Russia – but we may not win the war.

On the morning of 22 June 1941, my battalion commander and myself (I was his adjutant at the time) were in our foxholes, very close to the barbed wire. Just before the artillery barrage began, he whispered over to me something like, 'Don't ever forget 22 June 1941, at 3.15 in the morning', then he paused for a moment and said, 'Well, I don't think I have to tell you not to forget it anyway! At this very moment, the worst decline – the worst disaster – of German history in many centuries, is going to begin.'

It was a beautiful summer with no problems, but right after an attack across the River Dnieper on, I think, 1 October, we ran into very severe difficulties. It started snowing and becoming cold around 10 October and then we knew immediately that we were totally unprepared and unequipped for what was lying ahead of us. You might say it was a mistake to start this attack, and you could also say that, with regard to the human beings involved, it was a crime.

I felt terribly angry. We had no gloves, no winter shoes – we had no equipment whatsoever to fight or withstand the cold. We lost considerable amounts of heavy and light equipment, then, due to the cold, we lost a lot of people who got frostbite. We had not even the most primitive things to fight it. We were cutting strips off our overcoats to wrap around our hands instead of wearing gloves, for example.

As it became colder towards the end of November and early December, most of our artillery had become completely unusable. Guns didn't fire any more, even our wireless equipment didn't work properly any more because the batteries were frozen hard. So there was no way of communicating, even between the advancing lines and artillery batteries in the background.

We could hardly take care of our own wounded, not to mention dealing with the enemy. We were afraid to become wounded and become the prey of the enemy. We had seen enough of the enemy to know that in cases like that, prisoners were hardly ever taken, so a good many people, when it came to a decisive moment, opted not to stick his head out as far as he might have done otherwise."

Dmitrii Gavryushin, an infantry battalion commander, was amongst the many Russian troops cut off behind the advancing German front line, trapped by the sheer speed of their attack. His escape from captivity was to last an agonising three months on the run.

"Having fought for 14 days without a break, I was bruised, but stayed in action. I was later wounded in the arm and hand. On 24 July I was put in the Mogilev hospital. On 26 July, the town was captured by the fascists and the hospital was not evacuated because it was encircled.

Another two days later I, and some soldiers from my battalion, fled from the hospital. We changed our clothes in someone's home and set off in the direction of our troops.

We went in the guise of civilian prisoners who had been working at the airport and had been wounded in the bombing. After five days, the fascists detained us at the front. We were held for three days, and then sent to one of the Smolensk hospitals.

Having spent three days there, and having carried out an appropriate intelligence appreciation, we ran away from this hospital and, after 15 days, caught up with the front line near Shmakov, where they again detained us.

After five hungry days, they put us in a truck and sent us forwards. Catching up with a group of our prisoners of war, they put us out of the lorry, joined us to the column, and hurried us on. Hunger, and the pain of my wounds, stopped me keeping up with the fit ones, and I lagged behind, with the fascist escort all the time pushing me on with rifle-butt blows to my back. Having spent the night gathering our strength, we ran away in the morning. After several days, we reached the settlement of Stodolishche and bumped into our surgeon. We asked him to change our bandages. He uncovered our wounds and they were already gangrenous, with little worms crawling about."

Alex Vanags Baginskis was a young teenager when Germany invaded Latvia. He recalls the people's delight at being freed from the existing oppressive Communist regime, and their subsequent disillusionment.

"I was living in Riga, the capital of Latvia, with my mother when the Soviets invaded. We woke up one morning – 17 June 1940 – and the

A Soviet poster assures citizens that Hitler will not succeed where Napoleon failed

tanks were in the streets. I was thirteen years old and very intrigued. I looked at the tanks and the soldiers – they were scruffy, their uniforms didn't look nice and they were all armed. At the beginning, they said that nothing would change – but it did.

I remember very clearly reading in a Soviet paper in April 1941, a little, insignificant notice about German troops going through Finland. They were just passing through Finland to Norway. I was good at geography and I wondered to myself....

People were hoping that the Germans would come. They are our historical enemies. They arrived with the Bible and the sword in the 12/13th centuries and subdued our people, forcing Christianity on them. They ruled us until World War I, but even the Germans would be better than the Russians.

Early in 1941, the Soviets suddenly started increasing the number of troops in Latvia. Artillery moved through at night, the horses' hooves wrapped in rags. We couldn't hear them, but we could see them. In spring 1941 the Russians suddenly wanted to build 80 or 90 airfields – and you don't build bomber airfields for defence – they were planning something.

In June, whispers started going around that the Soviets would deport people. These people were described by the Soviets as 'socially dangerous elements'. One night, over 35,000 people, out of a population of about 1,600,000, were deported. Quite a number were shot as well. You can imagine the shock of going to visit my uncle the next morning to find the whole house empty.

A number of people, including my mother, took to the woods to stay with a family who lived near a farm. There were about 30 or 40 people living there with us in the woods.

About a week later , the war began. Suddenly, early one morning, the German aircraft arrived over Riga. We were up on the roof, binoculars in hand, watching the dive-bombers and the anti-aircraft firing. The Germans didn't bomb the town – they bombed gas tanks, oil tanks. Within two days, the Red Army was retreating. Single German aircraft would fly over in the evening dust and fire on the road. You could see the tracers. Once I saw a Soviet fighter take off, trying to catch a German plane. His aircraft was shot and exploded in the woods.

We returned to Riga a couple of days after the Germans arrived. A home guard and scout groups were organised. I was a scout. There was still some hard fighting to do – there was a lot of street fighting in Riga old town with the remaining Soviet troops or local communist militia.

There were burnt-out tanks with skeletons inside which had sunk into the pavements and we couldn't move them. They remained for a long, long time. There were lots of things for kids to do – aircraft and tanks to look at. I remember going to a Soviet airfield with fighters lined up there. The Germans didn't want the aircraft and there were boys there with screwdrivers, taking everything apart. You could find ammunition, machine guns, rifles – I had a whole arsenal!

At first everything was very patriotic – it was a feeling of relief. We all, even us kids, thought 'We're free now'. The Latvian flag was everywhere. The honeymoon lasted for two or three months, before the German Party people came and that was it. The national front was forbidden, national patriotic songs were forbidden, our anthem was forbidden. We were an occupied country again."

MOSCOW

Defeat in the Snow

As the winter of 1941 took its toll, the ill-prepared and weary German troops of Operation Barbarossa faltered. Although they came within 20 miles of Moscow, the city remained out of reach. The Soviets resolutely defended their homeland, with civilians joining in the struggle to drive back the aggressors. The tide had begun to turn

Unterscharführer Strong with the SS (equivalent to the rank of lieutenant) was part of the attack on Moscow which took place on 2 December 1941.

"We could only advance step by step toward our final destination – Moscow. Fierce cold all around us – and all this with poor accommodation and insufficient food for the fighting troops. The supply problems were getting worse all the time. These were the main causes of our crisis – without these problems, we would have been much nearer our destination. Nevertheless, the troops forced through, advance after advance, with superhuman effort, and fought themselves through all kinds of adversity with incredible patience.

Many of the soldiers had managed to steal Russian overcoats and fur hats and were hardly recognisable as Germans anymore. All our winter clothing had been infested with lice and was impossible to wear. To keep the engines running, we had to light fires underneath the sumps. Some of the fuel had thickened and we had no glysanthine to prevent the drinking water from freezing.

The already dwindling fighting strength of the units was depleted further as more and more men were picked off by the cold. The troops could not take much more. The innumerable losses would completely destroy the fighting strength of the company.

Half-frozen German troops were fighting on in the merciless cold, which sometimes sank to 45 degrees below freezing, in their normal uniforms, their normal leather boots, no gloves, no overshoes, no scarves, facing a merciless winter.

With the Russian prisoners, things couldn't have been more different. They wore the best winter clothing you could imagine. Their winter uniforms were thickly lined with padding. They had felt boots, fur gloves and fur hats. To stop themselves freezing, German soldiers took precious winter clothing from the dead Russians.

Over the precincts of Moscow hung giant flash rockets like the stars of Venus, and tight packs of searchlight beams hurtled around the sky, went out again, then appeared, ghost-like, clawing the air again at other places, criss-crossing in giant packs of beams. Between them, the flashing pearl garlands of heavy Russian flak. The light trails from shells sent long threads of dark red and orange into the night sky.

Moscow roared, the loud thunder piercing the December night. Heavy German bomber squadrons attacked Moscow through the night from the air, bringing death and confusion to the centre of the enemy's power base. Along the contours of the distant hills, you could see the flash from the exploding rows of bombs, until half an hour later, the night became silent.

Moscow had opened the prisons and had released the armed prisoners. In the factories, workers' brigades had been assembled. Women and children were put in to dig trenches. Fresh Siberian troops were on their way. The streets of Moscow were filled with the Red Army, marching to the front."

Lance Corporal Maria Ivanovna Morozova had been working on a collective farm in the Proletarsky district of Moscow when war broke out. Not yet 18, she graduated from an accountancy course and took a rifle-training course as the Germans drew nearer to Moscow. By this time, national fervour was at fever pitch.

"Soon the Young Communist League Central Committee made an appeal to the young people to volunteer to defend their homeland, as the enemy was already approaching Moscow. Not only I but all the girls wanted to go to the front. My father was already there. We thought that we alone were like that... but when we came to the military registration and enlistment office we found there quite a few young girls. We were subjected to a rigorous selection.

The first thing that was needed was, of course, hardy health. I was afraid lest I would be left out because I had often been ill in childhood and was rather weak. Besides, girls were also refused if they were leaving their mothers alone. I had two sisters and brothers, much younger than myself, but it still counted.

As we were in Moscow, we decided then to proceed to the Young Communist League Central Committee and debated for a while who was the bravest and would do the reporting. We thought that we would be alone there but it proved next to impossible to make our way through the corridor, let alone reach the secretary. Young people from all over the Soviet Union had come to the place, many of them from the occupied areas, seething to avenge the death of their nearest and dearest.

We finally made it to the secretary in the evening and were asked: 'Well, how are you going to fight at the front if you don't know how to shoot?' We answered that we had already been taught that. 'And you know how to make a bandage, don't you?' And you know, during that very course at the military registration and enlistment office a district surgeon taught us how to bandage wounds. We had another advantage in that there were 40 of us capable of shooting and giving first aid. We were told, 'Go home and wait. You'll be given a positive answer.' And a couple of days later we had call-up papers.

We still did not know where we would be assigned, but it did not matter much what we were going to be – our only wish was to get on to the front. It turned out we had been assigned to a women's sniper school. We began to study, learning garrison duty regulations, disciplinary regulations, camouflage, terrain and chemical warfare defence. We learned to mount and demount the sniper's rifle with closed eyes, to determine wind velocity, to evaluate the movement of the target and the distance to it, to dig in and to crawl. We could do it all. Upon graduation I got top grades in shooting practice and drill. I remember that the most difficult thing was to get up at the sound of alarm and to get ready in five minutes. We would take boots a size or so bigger so as not to lose much time when putting them on. We had five minutes to dress, to put on our boots and to fall in.

We eventually came to the front to join the 62nd Rifle Division outside Orsha. The commander, Colonel Borodkin, grew angry: 'They have thrust some girls upon me.' But then he invited us to have lunch with him. We would have been his daughters as far as age was concerned. The next day he made us show how we could shoot and camouflage ourselves on the terrain. We were quite good at shooting and even did better than the men snipers who had been recalled from the front line for a two-day course. Then came the turn of terrain camouflage. The Colonel came and walked about inspecting the glade, then stepped upon a hillock but still saw nothing. Suddenly the hillock under him begged, 'Oh Comrade Colonel, I can't stand it any longer, you're so heavy.' What a big laugh everybody had. He just could not believe that it was possible to camouflage oneself so well. 'Now', he said, 'I wish I had not referred to you as "some girls".' We went 'hunting' (in the snipers' idiom) for the first time together with fellow sniper Masha Kozlova, camouflaged ourselves and lay in wait, me observing the terrain and Masha holding the rifle. Suddenly Masha said: 'Shoot, shoot! See, there's a German...'. 'I'm observing. You shoot!' 'He'll be gone while we are arguing here,' she said.

'I have to make a fire map first,' I persisted, 'to designate the check points, locating the shed and the birch-tree...' 'Are you going to mount paper red tape, like they do at school? I've come here to shoot and not fiddle with papers!'

While we were arguing like that the German officer indeed gave orders to his soldiers. A cart appeared and the soldiers were busy passing some load along the file. The officer stood there for a while then said something and disappeared. Meanwhile we went on arguing. I noticed that he had already showed up two times, and if we did not do anything about it the next time he appeared we would miss him altogether. So when he appeared the third time, I decided to shoot. Then it occurred to me that he was after all a human being, even though he was an enemy. My hands began to tremble and a chill went down my spine. I was seized with inexplicable fear... I could not bring myself to take a shot at a human after plywood targets. Nevertheless, I braced myself up and pulled the trigger. He swung his arms and fell. I don't know if I killed him but I began to shiver knowing I'd killed a human being...."

From a Schultzstellung (protection position), Hauptsturmführer Dr Med. Windisch of the Small Divisional Command Staff SS Division 'Reich', watched the furious battle unfold around the city of Moscow.

"It was afternoon and we were standing beside the Magistrale, protected by the woods, observing the enemy, who were circling around in tanks on the other side. A battery of 8.8 flak had been put in position and was firing on the Russian tanks. Our grenadiers from the Regiment 'Deutschland' had broken through into the enemy's network of positions north of the Magistrale and were pushing on further, in a bitter struggle with huge losses.

Meanwhile, the 'firework display' began. I had never seen anything quite like it. We were standing on the hill, with three generals beside us, watching anxiously the movements of our own troops and those of the enemy.

Suddenly I heard the unmistakable noise of the Russian rocket shells, the so-called 'Stalin's organs'. They were definitely meant for us, for everybody disappeared suddenly into cover holes. Since I hadn't dug one myself, I couldn't disappear without leaving a trace. So I quickly threw myself behind a tree and watched the terrifying beautiful display of rocket shells crashing down. I will never forget the sinister black, red and violet flare from the shells.

The air all around was full of the explosions of shells crashing down. Suddenly behind us all hell broke loose. I hadn't a clue what was going on there, and ran to my friend Mix, the Ic (third General Staff Officer) of the Division, who lay under cover, not far from me. He laughed and said, 'That's our multiple rocket launchers!'

You should have heard this terrible ear-shattering scream. It mixed in with the bangs of the Russian shells hitting, there was a whistling and roaring from the firing and hits of the artillery, from machine guns, mortars and multiple rocket launchers. The effect of the latter on the enemy must have been devastating. The battles lasted all through the night. The effects of our launchers had been a decisive influence on the battle."

PEARL HARBOR

Tora! Tora! Tora!

The United States had resisted becoming fully involved in the conflict. But in the early hours of 7 December 1941, the Japanese Navy launched a shock air attack on the base of the Hawaiian US Pacific Fleet and a stunned America woke up to find she had been plunged into war. The struggle was no longer merely a European conflict, but a worldwide battle to the death

Mitsuo Fuchida, the brilliant commander of the Hawaii assault, led the Akagi Flying Corps into the fray. He recalls his part in the first wave which struck the US base.

"The enemy ack-ack was fierce. The nearer we got, the more it concentrated on the high-level bombers. The bombs sent filthy black smoke pouring up into the sky. Then a hail of bullets closed in on me. I looked down to see where it was coming from, and could see firing coming from the main fleet in Pearl Harbor, but also here and there there were flashes from the guns on shore, sparkling and glittering. 'The shore ack-ack's joined in,' I thought. At that instant, the aircraft juddered, as if something had slammed against it. Lieutenant Mitsuo Matsuzaki, at the controls, yelled through the speaking-tube, 'Commander, have we been hit?' I didn't know, so turned around to look. The answer came from Mizuki in the seat behind, 'I think we've been hit aft by cannon fire – there's a big hole in the fuselage and one of the control cables has been cut. I'll try to mend it, but I don't think I can reach it.'

'Can you still fly her?' I asked Matsuzaki. 'Yes, we're OK', he said. Closing in on our objective, it was tricky adjusting the course for the bombing run. It was time to drop now. I concentrated all my attention on the pathfinder's bomb. The instant it left his aircraft, I tugged at the release and dropped ours at the same time. Thinking we were out of range, I felt a sense of relief, then the shock of an explosion passed into me through the seat. The firing came closer. In one intense moment, I thought, 'Let the bombs go, quickly, now'. I glanced down, to one side. We were already into Pearl Harbor, and over Ford Island. Bits of broken cloud floated beneath us.

The pathfinder banked sharply to starboard, signalling, repeat, repeat. We were skimming over the streets of Honolulu, turning again into the bombing run. A patch of cloud had made us miss our aim at the very moment of release.

As the first squadron followed us again into a bombing run, there was a huge explosion close to our objective. A deep red flame burst up into the sky, followed by soaring dark smoke. Then white smoke, to a height of what looked like 3,000 feet. That must be the magazine! A shock like an earthquake went right through our formation and my aircraft shuddered with the force of it. It was the *Arizona* going up."

Lieutenant Commander Robert Lee Simpson was Radio Officer on board USS Argonne when America was suddenly pitched headlong into war.

"I was in my cabin on the main deck, having previously been awakened by our mess boy. I had just put on my white uniform coat when I suddenly heard several terrific explosions which rocked the ship.

I grabbed my cap and dashed down the passageway for the main radio room transmitting station aft. Some men only had time to put on their shorts and shoes in their mad rush to battle stations. The uniform for the day was white shorts and undershirts, which caused many sailors to suffer severe flesh burns.

Six torpedo planes had already made their runs on the *California* directly opposite us. Great clouds of smoke poured from her hull as the torpedoes tore into the ship, tearing open huge holes in the side. The *California* sank slowly as they abandoned ship.

Oklahoma, only a few yards astern of *California*, was hit by six more torpedo planes. The port side armour belt of heavy steel was torn off by the exploding torpedoes, exposing a gaping hole about 200 feet long. The watertight compartments had not been closed. The water rushed in and she immediately capsized and went down with all hands within ten minutes. Her crew were caught like rats in a trap.

Cutting torches were used at first, but had to be abandoned because the trapped men were being cremated by the flames. Air drills were then used to gain entry into the double bottom compartments.

The navy department announced later that indications were found inside the ship that three men had lived for 16 days. They had consumed all their emergency rations and had marked a calendar with an X for each day from 7 December to 23 December."

Lieutenant Colonel H H Blackwell wrote to his wife from the United States Army base at Fort Shafter, Honolulu, Hawaii, after the lightning raid by the Japanese on Pearl Harbor. His letter was returned to him by the military censors.

"I was rudely awakened just before eight o'clock by the terrific noise of bombs and cannon... At first I thought it was dynamite blasting in a tunnel – but when I heard the whistling sound preceding the explosion of some of the closer ones, I jumped out of bed and ran out to investigate.

When I got outside I was perfectly dumbfounded. Black columns of smoke were rising from Pearl Harbor Navy yard about three miles distant and the sky was filled with puffs of black smoke from AA shells. It looked like war, but I just could not believe that Japan could make an air attack from such a distance without our navy having some warning.

The attack caught both the army and navy completely by surprise. Being Sunday morning, most everyone was still in bed. Our AA guns were not in firing positions, but were parked at Shafter or other posts. We were on alert against sabotage, and in a condition of readiness which allowed three hours to go into action in case of attack. We had frequent drills on going out into battle positions and everyone had been trained thoroughly on just what to do (thoroughly should be qualified, however, since 80 per cent of our troops have had less than eight months' service, and the organisation of the Brigade was not completed).

We had found that this took about three hours. However, as soon as we found out that this was the real thing, we cut the preparation time in half. Speed limits were ignored. Some units began firing within 45 minutes from the time they were alerted. All units began firing before the attack was ended, and we shot down four or five planes. The AA fire I first saw was from the Navy.... "

Minoru Genda, on the staff of No. 1 Air Fleet in Japan, was charged with the detailed planning of the Pearl Harbor raid – and solving the problems too.

We were not convinced [about the use of torpedoes] but that was the time when all the senior officers were together – not one of them said it was impossible. Mind you, no-one said he was certain we could bring it off.

There were unsolved problems with high-level bombing. It's unusual for carrier-borne aircraft to carry out high-level bombing against an enemy fleet on the high seas. Torpedo bombing is so much more effective. However, high-level bombing has its strong points. It simplifies a concentrated attack using a large number of planes – but its success rate is low.

However, something startling occurred. The aircraft-carrier *Akagi* was doing bombing exercises against a target moving away freely, from a height of around 9,000 feet. A formation of nine aircraft scored four hits. That's a success rate of 45 per cent. And they did it three times running. If that could be maintained, it was far more effective than dive-bombing. So, I thought, if we can't use torpedo bombing, we can attack Pearl Harbor with high-level bombers. I was that confident."

Ensign H D Davison was on board the USS Arizona on 7 December, expecting a routine Sunday, when the first Japanese dive-bombers struck.

"It was just before colours, in fact, I had already sent the messenger down to make the eight o'clock reports to the Captain. Then I heard a dive-bomber attack from overhead. I looked through my spyglass and saw the red dots on the wings. That made me wonder, but I still couldn't believe it until I saw some bombs falling. The first one hit up by the air station. I sounded the air-raid alarm and notified the Captain. He and Lieutenant Commander Fuqua came on deck, and the Captain went on up to the bridge. About that time we took a bomb hit on the starboard side of the quarterdeck, just about abreast of Number 4 turret.

We grabbed the men available and started dropping the deck hatches and leading out hoses on the quarterdeck. Then the planes that had made the initial dive-bomb attack strafed the ship. Mr Fuqua and I told all hands to get in the marine compartment. It was reported to us that we had a bomb in the executive officer's office. Just after I stepped in the booth, we took another hit starboard of the quarterdeck, just about frame 88. The Boatswain's mate and I were trapped in the booth by the flames. We started out of the booth, trying to run through the flame aft on the quarterdeck. We couldn't get through so we went over the lifeline into the water. I was conscious of the sweetish, sickening smell to the flame. After I got into the water, my first intention was to go to the quay and then on to the quarterdeck or swim to the gangway and get aboard. But after I took one look at the ship, I decided that it was useless – she had settled down by the bow, and appeared broken in two. The foremast was toppled over – she was a mass of flames from the forecastle to just forward of turret three."

A US warship is devastated by the Japanese attack

FALL OF SINGAPORE

Victory & Despair

The British colony of Malaya, with its rubber and tin, was a tempting prize for the Japanese, who invaded in December 1941 and forced the Allied defenders to retreat down the jungle peninsula to Singapore. The tiny causewayed island was reputed to be impregnable, but by February 1942, its defenders and civilians had little option but to suffer a humiliating surrender

Sergeant William John Mondahl was with the 5th Field Regiment, Royal Artillery, attached to the 11th Indian Division, and fought desperately to reach the relative safety of Singapore.

"We fought all the way down to Singapore. We held certain spots for a certain time to get the infantry downwards, and then we would retire. We were under attack constantly. At times, we were surrounded and had to fight our way out with the infantry. We weren't trained for that type of warfare, whereas the Japanese were. They would send their men out into the wilds with a packet of rice and they would hang on for days.

At times it was frightening because we were being bombed from the air by Japanese aircraft. We had very little defence then from the air. I know that they had asked for a number of aircraft before the war started out, but they didn't get what they asked for. They did get some Spitfires out there, but we saw more Japanese planes than British.

We felt very isolated because even the lowest ranks knew that we would never hold out. We were going down the country so quickly. On the way down we were told to burn things, so where we found a food warehouse, we would stock ourselves up and burn the rest so that the Japanese wouldn't have it.

A British soldier prepares for service in the countryside of the British colony, Malaya

We eventually got across the causeway into Singapore. We put up a good struggle there and we lost a lot of people. Those that died were buried there with a marked grave. The causeway which we had come over was supposed to have been so badly damaged that the Japanese would never get over it. Our engineers had planted dynamite, but the Japanese soon overcame the problem and repaired it very quickly.

Once we were in Singapore proper, we dug trenches, put guns in the gun pits and that was our last stand. We were in action, with our backs to the water, overlooking the town. Raffles Hotel was just across the road.

Morale was not too good, although we didn't have as many casualties as we did coming down country. We did our best, but after a while, when talks had gone ahead with the enemy, we were told to expend all ammunition. We did spike a few guns – in other words, we put a round up and a round down the muzzle, which breaks the barrel.

The men were exhausted – sleeping everywhere. The next morning we were taken over by the Japanese. We were assembled in Singapore and we had to march 15 or 20 miles to Changi jail."

Wee Eng Tang, a clerk at the Singapore Dockyard, had admired the great ships of the British Navy from afar – until their sinking by Japanese air attack.

"'Britannia rules the waves' or so we were innocently taught. We used to sing all these songs at school – but when the Japanese came along, all the bubbles burst. When I heard the *Prince of Wales* and the *Repulse* had been sunk, I thought it was impossible. I was so proud of the *Prince of Wales* when I saw it – all the beautiful modern guns. We really under-rated the Japanese – that's the joke. All our confidence in the British defences was shattered overnight. When we saw the headlines about the *Prince of Wales* I was shattered – morally, physically, mentally, all sorts. Without all that confidence, how could we fight?

There were sailors with oil splashed all over them, angry, tense, shouting and blaming the RAF, because they could not fight back against the waves and waves of kamikaze planes with their fantastic torpedoes. They came right up near the deck to drop their bombs. What chance had they got? That type of bombing had never been read about before in Western books. They meant to sink that boat, the Japanese. They were dying for the Emperor, they sacrificed themselves for their chivalry – Bushido. It was fabulous, fantastic – the Japs really shocked the world, not only us – the whole world was shocked."

Hajimo Sudo was the Lieutenant-Commander leading a flight of land-based bombers of the Japanese No. 1 Air Fleet. He recalls the excitement of the attack on the Repulse.

"The command aircraft waggled its wings – 'All units attack!' The time was exactly 1.48 pm. A host of shells burst in front of us. The whole plane shuddered. 'Calm down', I said to myself, and tried to put some strength into my guts – but my body went stiff and I felt as if my insides were rising up into my gorge. 'This won't do,' I said to myself, to give myself courage, and felt better.

The white wave kicked up by the stern of *Repulse* suddenly seemed to expand. She was changing course! I turn to port, and my No.3 which is just behind turns to port, while banking steeply. But it's only the second ship which is turning inward, the King George V class ship is turning outward. Right, I'll go for *Repulse*!

At this moment, heavy AA MG fire comes up at us as well as the AA shells and literally spatters the fuselage like rain. Star shells which seem to be weightless float up incessantly towards me. The plane backs and judders, but miraculously I'm not hit. If this AA hits me, I can still fix my target before going down. My fish [torpedo] will do 10,000 metres, and there's a high probability of scoring a hit. In this instant of attacking the enemy ship, clenching my teeth and curling my body into a tight ball, all fear of death has gone. If I can swap my life for that enormous ship, I feel absolutely no regrets.

Repulse is making more than 20 knots and listing to port, turning her bows towards my aircraft which is leading the attack. The bearing narrows – I'm so close I can't manoeuvre freely. 'Ready to fire! Fire!'

I feel a slight shock in the plane at the moment the heavy fish leaves it, and at the same time take evasive action, veering to port, almost grazing the sea surface. I've come so close that the big ship's side seems to hang over me, and I can see the flicker of a tense ruddy face beneath a pale helmet, working a machine gun. I can't be more than 150 metres from him, but at the low ceiling at that distance, either they can't depress the guns freely or they feel it's a waste of ammunition because my torpedo has already been fired. Almost nothing comes up at me.

I hear a shout, 'Got her!' I look round and see a weird shape rise up into the air, a huge column of grey water. The one that struck her in the stern, I'm quite sure, that was mine! It was the first torpedo to hit *Repulse*."

Douglas Davis, an Engine Room Artificer, was on HMS Repulse off Singapore when, their position betrayed by a radio broadcast, they were attacked by Japanese aircraft.

"The Japanese attacked us with aircraft in a new style. Instead of coming in at a level where they could attack us and we could set our guns on them, they came in at various heights – it was impossible really for the gunners to decide where to fire.

Soon there was an explosion in the boiler room. The place was dark, there was no shouting – nothing. The men must be dead. I got through an air intake on the top deck, only to find that now I could only just about see with one eye. The other one had been burned.

I had no feelings of pain – the thing was that I felt all alone. I saw men mown down by aircraft coming in at sea level. I found myself flat on the deck, not knowing that I'd also been hit with bullets which had bounced off the deck. I was given morphia – but it didn't work. Why, I'll never know, but it saved my life. I managed to get to my feet and leave the area to climb towards the upper decks. When I reached a porthole, it was at such an angle that it just let in daylight. There was no sign of any water, as it was at an angle of some 30 degrees.

With help I managed to get on the outside of the side of the ship. I was pulling myself down towards the water. I had no lifebelt, and my ability to swim had gone – I just couldn't. Immediately I got into the water, everything went black.

I was pulled up by rope to the quarterdeck of a ship. My clothing had been completely burned off – I was nude. On looking down, I could just see the tops of my shoes – the soles had been burned off. I was severely burned and I had been wounded in the leg.

It was five bullets, according to the doctor at Singapore General Hospital. I was in a very bad condition; I believe I was unconscious for about three days. I had double pneumonia, and degrees of burns which were – I don't know, they used to number them off. I had lost all my fingernails and toenails. My ears had been burned off and my back, feet and legs were burned.

There were complications with my injuries due to the oil that had leaked out of the ship as it sank. It caused septic poisoning, and this had such an effect that the injuries could not be dealt with in the normal way. I found that my hands, legs and neck were being eaten away by maggots – the most horrible feeling.

They gnawed away until all the dead meat that had been burned in my hands, neck and legs was eaten. It took days and weeks for them to do their job, cleaning my hands, then finally the doctors took over and cleaned the maggots away so that they could introduce some skin grafting to cover the injuries. They did a remarkable job."

THE PHILIPPINES

Bataan Death March

The defence of the Philippines seemed an easy option for American troops – until, less than ten hours after the attack on Pearl Harbor, the Japanese took the islands by storm. American and Filipino troops were forced back to the peninsula of Bataan and the island of Corregidor. Thousands of prisoners died on the journey to POW camps – the infamous 'death march'

When General King surrendered on Bataan, Captain Winston Jones of the Philippines Scouts Artillery was one of the 70,000 men who trudged 57 miles to Japanese POW camps; although he had been without food for days, he was beyond hunger. He was about to have his first experience of an unknown enemy.

"I felt very uncertain and afraid. Despite the campaign, this was the first time I had come face to face with the Japanese, and none of us knew what was expected of us as prisoners of war. There were some in our group who were very sick – we helped as best we could, but none of us was strong enough to carry anyone.

We had just come abreast of the dirt airstrip called Cabcaben Field when a battery of Jap heavy artillery opened fire on Corregidor. The island fired back, but its first rounds fell short – they burst along the road and decimated the ranks of the column ahead. Then a Japanese military policeman appeared and motioned our groups off the road into rice stubble. We were made to stand directly in front of the guns, and in plain view of Corregidor. The Japs made us stand there for over an hour, while guns blasted Corregidor. Our boys could see through the range-finders and did not return fire.

When the time came to move on, some of the men were too ill to move. The guards bayoneted them where they lay.

From Cabcaben the road runs north and then straight up the east coast of Bataan. There were artesian wells every kilometre along the roadside. Their pure water had been used to irrigate the rice fields. Now the ground around the wells was littered with the dead, and in some, where we stopped to drink, the Japanese guards would urinate in the water first.

The worst was when a convoy of enemy trucks came down the road. The dust they created was bad enough, but Jap soldiers thought it was great fun to knock our hats off with long bamboo poles as their trucks went past. There were many men in my column who were knocked senseless into the path of oncoming vehicles.

The columns became strung out and frequently we were out of sight of the ones behind and in front. This made our guards very edgy, and they made us march double time to catch up. Some of the men couldn't maintain the pace, so they fell back through the ranks until, alone, behind the column, they were bayoneted. We were one of the later columns, so the road was littered with the dead, who were already being picked over by carrion birds. The smell of the dead is something I shall carry with me to the day I die."

John Spainhower, a lieutenant in the Philippine Scouts, wounded early in the campaign, had barely recovered when the garrison surrendered.

"I marched for two days without water and, on the third, the guards allowed us to drink from a small creek which stank from the decomposing remains that floated in it.

We stayed a night at Orani. The conditions were awful. We were dumped into fields and left until the next morning – there was no food and no sanitary arrangements. The next day, I was questioned by a Japanese officer, who found out that I had been in a Philippine Scout battalion. The Japs hated the Scouts, perhaps because we beat the hell out of them at the Abucay Hacienda. Anyway, they took me outside and I was forced to watch as they buried six of my Scouts alive. They made the men dig their own graves, and then had them kneel down in a pit. The guards hit them over the head with shovels to stun them and piled earth on top. I was made to stand at attention over the graves until eventually I collapsed with sunstroke."

Seiichi Nishida was serving as a Private First Class with a water purification unit in the Japanese 16th Division when the 'Death March' came into view.

"Hundreds of prisoners of war were moving along. When I looked closer, I could see they were, in fact, stumbling along, half-naked, in broken boots. A fiery sun beat down on their heads. From mouth to mouth I could hear a babbling sound, 'Water! Water!' At first I didn't understand what they meant, then I realised what they were asking for, so I filled my mess tin lid with clear water and gave them some to drink. A US soldier, face burned red with the sun, kept repeating, 'Thank you, thank you,' with tears steaming down his face."

Sister Louise Kroeger, a nun in the Maryknoll Order, was in a convent in Baguio. On 23 December she answered the phone to an American businessman from Baguio.

"'Sister', he said, 'we've had a meeting here in the Pines Hotel, and I want to tell you what we're going to do. The Japanese are coming up the mountains and right now are in the outskirts of the city. We've sent a delegation out to meet them. All the troops have left Baguio and we want to surrender. I'm asking all Americans not to offer any resistance. We're civilians, and we'll seek the protection of the Geneva Convention.'

A bird, high in the trees above, gave a shrill cry of alarm, and then suddenly we heard howling and screeching; a horde of Japanese soldiers burst into the courtyard. We all stood quietly calm, but even though we had led sheltered lives, the intent of the soldiers was clear. Both groups stood their ground.

Our gardener and handyman, a quiet and unassumingly devout Filipino, stepped in front of us. At that moment, the soldiers moved aside as an officer strode into the courtyard. Tall for a Japanese, and strikingly handsome, I recognised him as a stallholder from the market in Baguio – we had regularly purchased fish from him, and never been aware of his identity.

Our gardener was a brave man. He begged the officer to explain to his soldiers that nuns were not like other women, and to leave us alone. He did – but they wrecked our convent.

Nobody was sure what they were looking for, but they tore the place apart and spared nothing. Even the beautifully hand-embroidered altar front was slashed by Japanese bayonets. Our priest, a Dominican friar who came from Belgium, was savagely beaten. We could only watch as they beat him to the ground and then kicked him near to death. The Japanese left. I helped carry the priest in and tend his wounds.

Later that evening, when we had repaired as much of the damage

Exhausted American soldiers, their hands tied, face the horrors of the 'Death March'

as possible, I went out to lock the courtyard gate. I found a Japanese soldier standing there, who asked me to take him to the priest. He was humble and subdued – there was no hostility in his manner, so I took him to the bedside. The soldier knelt before the bed and begged forgiveness. I will always remember his words.

'I'm a Catholic, father, and I know how I should treat a priest – but in front of the others, there was nothing for me to do but beat you as I did. I have come back to ask you pardon. If the others find out I came here, they will send me to an infantry assault company, and I will surely die – but I could not live with my conscience and not come and say I'm sorry.'

Our priest gave his blessing; we knelt and prayed. The young man wept unashamedly."

Hidezumi Ima was a member of the No 1 Propaganda Team with the Philippines Expeditionary Force from Japan. His view of their landing on these lush islands belies the violence to follow.

"The island of Luzon was green – so beautiful a green it made you want to cry out. A bright cobalt sky, like something by Fra Angelico, stretched away over receding mountain ranges which seemed to be piled up, one on top of another. By the seashore, clusters of coconut palms, beteen them you could make out, here and there, 'nippa huts', sprouting nippa palm leaves. The sea was totally green, like molten jade, and utterly peaceful.

As far as the eye could reach, bright primary colours. The shore must be about 2,000 metres away, but everything seemed terribly near, as if we could quite happily swim the rest of the way. We were more used to scenery which was like a water colour swathed in mist, rather than a brilliant oil painting – but the island's vivid green was so lustrous that it dazzled.

I was overcome by its unfamiliarity, and quite forgot we were on enemy territory – but as I gazed, leaning over the railing of the starboard side, I saw the shape of a plane glide over the mountains. Then an ear-splitting roar as the AA guns from our ships began to fire.

Tracer shells described a red arc. In the distance another plane, hugging the ground, seeming to be sweeping the landing units with machine-gun fire. From another ship, more AA fire howled up into the sky. In the intervals of all this racket, you could hear bursts of rifle fire. The enemy planes did not seem to be coming for the convoy, which was moving into Lingayen Gulf, but were concentrating on the landing units close into the shore. Like someone passing out lines of red tape, the tracer was cast up into the sky like so many threads trying to trap the enemy planes in their fibres. They sped away, without approaching the convoy. 'You asked for it!' shouts went up from those of us who had been watching.

With that, the battle came to an end. After the enemy planes had beat a retreat, all there was was an innocent, clear morning sky."

CORAL SEA AND MIDWAY

Out of Sight

As 1942 began, the Japanese advance in the Pacific seemed instoppable. But in the naval battles of Coral Sea and Midway, the US fleet – recovered from the shock of Pearl Harbor – used carrier-based bombers to first halt and then repel the Imperial Navy. The tide of the Pacific War had turned

Iyozö Fujita, serving as a Flight Commander on board the Japanese aircraft-carrier Sopryu, was piloting an escorting Zero fighter when the Americans attacked.

"I sighted a formation of 20 torpedo bombers – but this time they had an escort of three fighter planes. I made for the enemy fighters but strangely enough they seemed to have no stomach for a fight and made off. Without pursuing the fighters, I turned and made off for the assault planes. A shell, which I thought came up from our carrier, smacked into my plane – exactly where my fuselage tank was. Smoke began to pour out and the cockpit began to fill with flames.

Next thing, bullets began to spatter from the 7.7 mm magazine. There was going to be no time to make a forced landing on the water, and when I looked down, I saw the cruiser *Jintsu* speeding ahead below me, so I decided to use my parachute. I opened the cockpit windshield and tried to climb out, but my head was pushed against the windshield, and I could not get out.

I could hear the wind scream past in my ears, but the parachute refused to open. The canopy stretched out, but when I saw it was not bellying out with air, I grabbed the chute with both hands and tugged at it. As I did so, I felt a shock go through my whole body, as

I entered the sea. My body was entangled in the cords of the chute, and I tried to free myself. Finally I came to the surface. With amazement, when I looked round, I saw the *Jintsu* making full speed ahead. She hadn't seen me.

On the distant horizon I saw three columns of black smoke. I thought, those must mean that's where our fleet is, and I began to swim towards them. Then I began to worry about sharks. I remembered I'd heard someone say that sharks line up alongside you and measure the length of your body against theirs. If you are

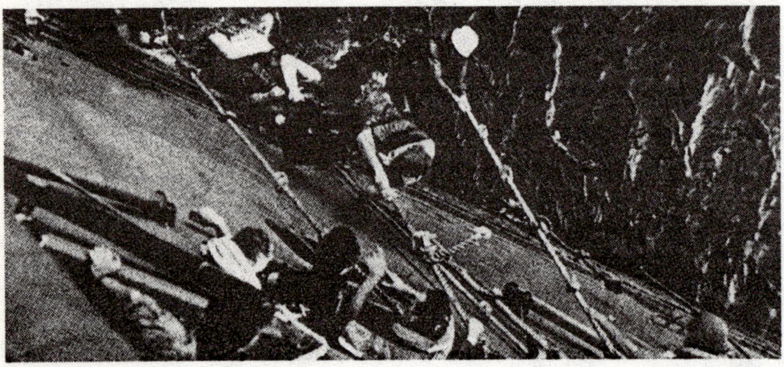

Survivors from the crippled Lexington scramble aboard a US destroyer, 8 May 1942

longer that they are, they don't go for you. So, I began to unwrap the muffler and tied it round my waist to make me look like a long object. But the back of my neck got so cold I couldn't bear it, so I wrapped it round my neck again.

I remembered my long-distance swim from Naval Academy days. I did ten miles, going into the water at seven o'clock and coming out at seven in the evening. Now, as I gazed at the black smoke, I could see it was 20 miles away, and if I kept swimming as I was, it would take 24 hours. I lost all appetite for swimming. In a mood of quiet despair, I spreadeagled myself in the water and lay gazing at the sky.

About four hours must have passed like this, when I heard a noise and opened my eyes. What had been the aircraft-carrier *Akagi*, still burning, had come to within 1,000 metres of where I was. Then one of her escort destroyers came up close. Soon I became aware of something. The muzzle of a gun was pointing at me. My hair was long in those days, and my face, burned by the sun, had turned red. 'They've taken me for an American pilot!' I realised. I trod water and began to semaphore with my arms: 'I am an officer from *Soryu*'. I don't know if they followed this, but the gun muzzle moved up."

Captain Elliott Buckmaster was in command of the US carrier Yorktown as Japanese aircraft attacked – and witness to an astonishing victory of the US navy and aircraft against overwhelming odds, although during the battle he lost his ship.

"The *Yorktown* joined up with other carriers in attacking Jap forces. Our group immediately hit one carrier with torpedoes and bombs. Later it was reported that this carrier sank. About this time, our fighters intercepted a large group of enemy dive-bombers and fighters. The sky was filled with falling Japanese bombers. The AA fire of the supporting ships and the *Yorktown* was magnificent. Our gunners literally chopped the enemy planes apart, but three made hits on us before being destroyed.

I felt that the ship would capsize very soon. Reluctantly I gave the order 'Abandon ship'. The courage displayed by the officers and crew throughout the engagement is beyond my powers of expression. I believed the *Yorktown* was stricken beyond repair. Later, however, I returned with a small salvage party. With the help of the destroyer *Hammond* we were able to right the ship by 2 degrees. We felt sure she would live. Then, suddenly, four torpedoes were fired from an enemy submarine. We were heavily hit and *Hammond* was sunk. As our destroyers were attacking the enemy submarine, our crew was transferred to a small tug to await the arrival of salvage tugs at day-break. However, the next day, from a companion ship, I saw the *Yorktown* slowly sink beneath the waves. The Japanese lost four aircraft carriers in that engagement and many of their best aviators. In the *Yorktown's* four short years, she destroyed more Japanese planes and ships than any other single US ship. Tonight, the *Yorktown* rests on the bottom of the Pacific."

Akira Tendo was special correspondent for the Japanese newspaper Asahi Shimbun and navy correspondent at Wake Island when US aircraft sank his ship – the Shoho – in the Coral Sea.

"I felt the ship give a shudder. What looked like blackened fragments of burned wood swept past our eyes as we stood on the bridge. Then the ship was enveloped in a great noise, like a steel curtain being hit by some great force. That can't be, I thought, nothing can have gone so wrong. 'They're bits of enemy planes', I tried to convince myself. It was no enemy plane, I soon realised, a bomb had done for our rudder.

The enemy pilots must have jumped for joy when they saw our carrier, like a man paralysed from the waist down. They came at us with renewed strength, harrying us, closing up, then dropping bombs. On they came, sweeping over our heads. These were not the American lushes we'd learned about in Japan!

I felt a sensation as if I'd been struck with a whip. 'So, we've had it, at last. That must be the third or fourth bomb that's hit us.' The instant I had time to think 'that's close', something smacked into the deck, and there was the blast of an enormous explosion.

'Bastards!' I turned round in amazement at that voice, ablaze with rage, and saw a petty officer with his cheek torn away. He was holding it with both hands, and from between his fingers the blood was flowing. A sailor was standing close by, his right arm almost torn off. He had a cloth at his waist and, taking the shrapnel fragment between his teeth, he staunched the blood from his right arm, using his left hand. Then he went into the signals cabin. His gait was steady, as if he were not seriously wounded at all. Then, with his left hand, he began to tap on the key of the W/T set.

Another sailor started to his feet, quite near me. I looked at his leg and was aghast. The flesh of his thigh was scooped away, and the white bone was clearly visible. He stood in front of the telescope, trying to support himself. He began to report what he saw. In these conditions, to collapse would be shameful.

The bombs and torpedoes kept coming. When a torpedo hits, the ship does a pitching and tossing movement. They work together, and the result is like an earthquake. The sound's dull, but it makes you feel as if your intestines are being drawn out. Suddenly I had the impression that I was wounded too. I looked down at my leg. Blood was flowing from it. My instinct at first was to go down to the ward-room and have it treated. But what was happening around me stopped me. Men with worse wounds than mine were still at their stations. I stayed.

The ship finally began to settle into the sea, bows first. I hurried from the bridge to the bridge deck. I saw our photographer, Yoshioka, taking pictures of enemy planes coming into the attack.

'You press men, get down below, it's dangerous!' The gunnery

US Grumman TBF Avenger torpedo bombers in formation, Midway, 1942

officer was concerned for us, but we did not listen. An enemy plane released its torpedo. 'Still alive?' We shook hands. 'Let's go!' 'Yes, let's both go together!' But where did I intend to go? Perhaps my mood was, 'If we're going to die, let's die together'. The deck below was already awash, and the waves swirled in front of my eyes....

Although the ship was on the point of sinking, the men were still at their stations. As one man, they had refused to leave. The ship's bows plunged into the sea, and she came up by the stern. By now up in the air, the screw kept turning. The engine room went on doing its job to the end. A petty officer climbed up a mast which was beginning to go under. Someone said he was trying to keep the ship's flag flying. Then, along with the ship, he vanished from sight.

You could still hear the sound of machine-gun fire. It was very odd, as if the firing were coming from the sea bed itself. The gunners were all dead. What happened was that the gunnery officer – the one man left alive – went on firing until the very last. The paymaster crewmen all remained at their stations. From the portholes of the sinking ship, they waved their white caps in a gesture of farewell."

MALTA

Epic Struggle

The small island of Malta in the Mediterranean was of great strategic importance to the Allies as a naval base. The siege of the island by the Axis forces between June 1940 and August 1942 brought the population to the brink of starvation. Yet convoys delivered vital supplies against all odds and the islanders displayed resilience and heroism in the face of more than 2,000 air raids

Sergeant John Mason of the Cheshire Regiment was based at Floriana. While working to clear rubble and help the civilians after air raids, he formed a lasting memory of Maltese fortitude and staying power.

"We used to be a bit over-anxious to try to get out to help. Sometimes we didn't wait for the bombing to finish because by the time we got there, people were already staggering in the streets. If we'd been there five minutes earlier, we would have saved their lives. People were losing limbs unnecessarily because they weren't being attended to soon enough.

One case which I always remember was when the Regal cinema was bombed. It had already been bombed on four occasions, but this time it was particularly bad. The cinema had been crowded, and when we got there, people were making their own way out of the rubble to the nearest hospital in Floriana, with their faces cut away and terrible injuries.

In my regiment alone, we buried 21. In my own company two died, and one of those boys hadn't been out with us long. He was on his way to the dining hall to get a cup of tea. We found him sitting by the railings, not a mark on him, still holding his cup of tea. It was the bomb blast that had sucked the air out of him.

There were very few ambulances in Malta, particularly towards the end, because they were getting worn out. We used the old army ration trucks and 15-hundredweights.

We also did guard duties on the water front against U-boats. We had machine guns sited almost everywhere around the coast. We also helped at Luqa airport, filling the craters in. As the bombers made the craters, we used our 15-hundredweights, containing all the damaged brickwork from the air raids and piled it into the craters to be steam-rollered.

The bombing wasn't perpetual – they would give you a break and then give you a real hammering. They picked meal times, and then the middle of the night. That was how we got the casualties. People would think they were getting a break and leave their homes – then the planes would come over.

People had to go out shopping – they had to go to work. It was impossible for them to stay indoors in the shelters all the time. After about six or twelve months of air raids, there weren't many residential buildings available for them, and what there were were just hovels.

I've never seen people like the Maltese for stamina and fortitude. You would see them weep and wail, but immediately after they were marvellous. Everyone would come out after the raids to see if the neighbours were all right and then they'd get on with their lives."

Maria Gazman was married to a Nationalist Party member – a man dedicated to strengthening Malta's bonds with Italy. Suddenly it is Italy which is bombing their home on Malta.

"The feeling I remember most about the bombing of Malta is the shock and disappointment of being at war with Italy. Before the war, there had been many Italians living on Malta – among them my best friend.

Many Maltese felt the same horror when they realised that the Italians were our enemies. There were British living in Malta too, but most of them kept apart from the Maltese people. I think that what really made us Maltese feel closer to the Italians was our Roman Catholic religion. When you have the same religion as somebody and you go to the same church, it is very hard to think of them as an enemy. Before the bombing the British told the Italians to leave

German bombs burst in the water and on Manoel Island, Malta April 1942

Malta. I remember saying goodbye to my friend and being very, very sad. At that stage, it was very hard to picture what was going to happen to the Maltese.

A lot of British soldiers arrived in Malta by boat and paraded around Valletta in their uniforms. Some of the Maltese boys joined up too, and they were also marching around the city, looking very pleased with themselves. I was glad that my daughter was only nine as a lot of families had problems with their daughters wanting to go out with soldiers. I was also glad that my sons were not old enough to join up.

We were issued with gas masks and told that the Italians would attack us with poisonous gas. My husband and I had four children, and we didn't have enough gas masks for the whole family. We began to get very worried about what we would do if the Italians did drop poison gas on us. Our church was more and more full of people, praying for an end to our problems.

I remember clearly the day of the first air raid. It happened very early one morning in June when I was shopping. I heard a very loud noise, but I didn't know that it was an air-raid siren, although it certainly frightened everybody. When the bombs fell, I was so shocked – I had only thought about gas attacks.

We were very lucky – nobody in our family was hurt. We saw and heard terrible things around us and my husband decided that we should leave our home and stay with cousins in Rabat. We didn't want to leave, but as the bombings got worse, we knew that we had to think of our children.

When the air raids became less frequent, we moved back home. Then, one terrible night in January 1941, hundreds of planes came over – this time it was the Germans. Valletta suffered terribly – there were piles of rubble everywhere, dead animals and dead people in the street.

Again we fled inland. We walked for hours. Although we had left our home behind, we knew that it would not stand up to the attacks for very long. We had left a lot of things behind, but we were glad to have all our children with us, safe."

Robert Porter was a marine on board HMS Aurora, based on Malta. The ship's task was to intercept enemy convoys travelling between Italy and North Africa.

"The Aurora arrived in Malta at the end of October 1941, and the blitzes started in November. There were just two cruisers – us and the *Penelope* – and we were the senior of the two. I remember the *Penelope* became known as 'the Pepperpot' becasue of all her shrapnel holes.

We, along with two destroyers, were the only striking force operating from Malta during the blitz. We would get a message that a convoy had left Italy and was on its way to North Africa, and our job was to intercept. We always seemed to work on a Saturday night – we called it the club run.

The run I remember best occurred when the Admiralty decided to send us a big, heavy cruiser from Alexandria, called the *Neptune*. Her more senior captain took charge of our force. We were told that there was another German or Italian convoy coming from Italy, so we had to leave Malta with the *Neptune* in charge, and go to intercept it. We missed the convoy and somehow ended up within eight or nine miles of Tripoli. We only found out that we were in a minefield when it was announced over the tannoy that we were in a 'tense position' at about two o'clock in the morning.

About ten minutes after that, there was a hell of an explosion. We looked around and realised that we were still all right. It was very, very quiet, and we didn't know what had happened. Then we heard someone shout that HMS *Neptune* had hit a mine and had sunk. There would be no survivors. There were probably a thousand men on board.

Our captain, Captain Agnew, took command again. He talked to us very calmly and said that we were still in the minefield. He sent a light destroyer that was with us to see if they could pick up any survivors. Five minutes later the destroyer blew up. I think that there were some survivors which a submarine picked up. Then there was another explosion – and that was us. The bows were blown off the ship, but nobody was killed.

The ship could now only do about 9 knots, and we had to get out of the minefield and back to Malta before light. We wouldn't have stood a chance in daylight – the Luftwaffe would have picked us off immediately. We did get back before daylight, but we couldn't go out to sea again before the end of March. We had to stay in Malta in the dry dock.

The ruling was that if you were on the ship when a blitz came over, you had to leave and go into the underground shelters in the rocks. The shelters were only yards away from the ship, but me and my friend, Johnny, would never go into them. I think we thought it was sissy. I remember one particular afternoon when I was walking past the turret, and I heard 'All men to blitz stations'. People ran to their guns or left the ship. I thought to myself that I would have a little sleep on deck. It was a lovely hot day. I didn't worry – I was young, I suppose. Our Sergeant-Major was on top of the turret, firing at the Stukas. He happened to notice me and called out, 'Marine Porter, you get in that shelter. That is your duty!' All the time, he was facing the enemy, firing at them. I have never seen coolness like that in a man. I felt very sheepish going into the shelter.

I used to go ashore whenever possible. You could get a little bed and breakfast hotel for sixpence a night. I stayed on the seafront on one particular night in a little place called 'The First and Last'. The seafront hadn't been bombed then. It had been one of those days when the Germans had followed a convoy and sunk practically all the ships. I was the only marine ashore that night.

I fell asleep and in the morning, there was only my hotel and two other buildings on the front still standing. The Germans had blitzed the lot. Everything else was rubble."

TOBRUK

Desert Furnace

The deep-water port of Tobruk in Libya had fallen to the Allies in January 1941. At the end of the year, however, the town was subjected to a two-month siege by Axis forces. A new German commander had arrived who threatened to turn the tide of the battle for North Africa – Erwin Rommel. In June 1942, Rommel's Afrikakorps finally recaptured the vital base

Ian Quarrie was a Sub-Lieutenant RNVR commanding an experimental boat in October 1940, when he was given an order which seemed nothing short of suicidal. It was to be the first incident in an uncanny coincidence which concluded in the sea off Tobruk.

"In 1940 I was a Sub-Lieutenant, commanding HMMTB 106 – an experimental boat with one torpedo and a speed of over 45 knots. On a dull, cold October morning I was suddenly ordered to take her to sea to explode an enemy mine by going over it! Off Southend, a convoy was waiting to sail with cargoes desperately needed up the east coast. The Germans had just begun laying acoustic mines, and that night an aircraft had dropped one in the narrow channel the convoy had to take. There was no known antidote and it was considered worth risking us to get the convoy away, hoping our speed would carry us clear of the explosion.

We managed to pass directly over the mine. The reaction was instant, and we were blown out of the water. The launch sent to pick us up in this eventuality had stopped and couldn't restart her engine – and we had a long swim waiting for MTB 107 to come and rescue us. Her First Lieutenant, Sub-Lieutenant Johnny Wolfe RNVR pulled me out of the water.

Four months later, my father's ship, HMS *Rosaura*, an armed boarding vessel, was also sunk by mine, close to Tobruk. A strong swimmer, he too survived.

In the spring of 1942, I also found myself in Tobruk, commanding a new boat, MTB 312. Our flotilla spent some months there, carrying out offensive sweeps up the enemy coast, landing agents behind the lines and so on. We were a well-knit, happy unit but oh, how we hated Tobruk! Stukas by day and night were bad enough, but my own pet hate was the appalling water supplied – too brackish even to brew a drinkable cup of tea. We left just before the town fell to the enemy. I hoped never to see the place again.

I was back again on 14 September, MTB 312 being part of a Combined Operation intended to hold Tobruk for a day and destroy the enemy's ammunition, fuel and other military targets. Unfortunately our operation failed, and our losses were high.

The attack was abandoned shortly after dawn, and soon after setting course for home, we were attacked by several Italian Macchi fighter planes. Despite our manoeuvrability and fire-power, augmented by the Bren guns of the soldiers we were carrying, we were eventually set alight from end to end by incendiary bullets. The boat burned long enough to enable us to take to our collapsible boats or jump into the sea and swim some distance away before our ammunition, 3,000 gallons of petrol and four torpedoes, blew up with quite a bang. And there I was, swimming for my life again.

To my relief, two MTBs came across and took us all aboard, though not all were to survive the running battle back to Alexandria. As I was hauled aboard MTB 265, her captain looked down from the bridge and said with a wry smile, 'Haven't we done this before?' His name was Lieutenant Johnny Wolfe – and I later confirmed my suspicion that we had been sunk within yards of where my father had swum for his life too, ten months earlier."

Hauptmann Adalbert von Taysen was Company Leader of the 3rd Company Machine-Gun Battalion Tank Grenadier Regiment 104 as his men went to retake Tobruk.

"We crouched in the dark, the tension enormous. You could only detect the presence of the next man by the cigarette behind his hand. The question was, 'Would it work this time?' We had maps of the fortress, but would we be able to spot the bunkers, machine guns and gun emplacements quickly enough?

There was an eerie silence in the battle zone. Time passed too slowly – it seemed like an eternity until the first glimmers of dawn appeared. A light ground mist blinded us, but the British were in the same boat. Five minutes later there was an ear-splitting roar. Stukas flew in, dropping their bombs on the fortifications about 100 metres in front of us. The last machine had scarcely turned away when there was an almighty bombardment of shells raining down on the British positions. Before us was an almost impenetrable wall of mist, dust and smoke.

The commanders and platoon leaders gave the signal to attack. We shot up and stormed through the barbed-wire and minefields ahead. In front of us were tank traps – we jumped in and climbed up the opposite wall. Anti-tank gunners raced through a sloping passage, intended for the British reconnaissance trucks. The men worked their way through under the protective fire of the machine guns, threw hand-grenades and took the combat positions. Then came the first British, running towards us, their hands in the air."

South African Sapper Wesson was with the 5th Field Engineers when, after a battle at Sidi Rezegh, the survivors of his unit were left to try to join up with any other group they could find.

"Our company found itself right in the thick of it, with Jerry tanks and armoured cars everywhere. The only protection we had was under our trucks. Having spent all our ammo, trying to shoot Jerry heads as they appeared from tank turrets, we found our shallow slit trenches were of no use, as the tanks and armoured cars rode over them, firing at random.

At dusk, an officer shouted, 'Into your trucks, and join the convoy to the east'. Most of our trucks had been destroyed, so we got on anything that moved and headed east. I think the driver went over every shell slit in the desert that night, while we were bashed around in the back. As soon as we found the convoy we tagged on. A German armoured car came up, not certain where it was.

When they realised they were in our convoy, they opened up with everything they had, but fortunately all went high and through the canvas of our truck. It was late afternoon, and we were still under our trucks, when I saw General Erwin Rommel. A line of German tanks came straight past our position. In the middle tank, with the hatch open, stood Rommel himself. The battle was over, and he knew it. He was right out of the turret, saluting to both sides."

Flying Officer James Hepburn, an air-gunner with 216 Squadron of the RAF, arrived in the desert in 1940, but his navigational skills soon came to the fore in the featureless terrain, and it was as a navigator that, in 1941, he operated in the 'Maid of All Work', from a base near Cairo in support of ground troops.

When I first went out we were at Heliopolis, which is on the outskirts of Cairo. Of course we were always operating in the forward areas from wherever we happened to be. There is no doubt that there are problems, because you get these sandstorms which blow up quite unexpectedly. They are more likely to happen at certain times of the year, of course. You get the Khamseen wind blowing, which goes over the desert at about 80 mph – you can imagine what conditions that produces. There is sand everywhere. One doesn't know whether one is in the air or on the ground.

It was a marvellous war, really. It was more like a naval situation. We were operating on a completely open flank. You had the Quattara Depression, through which not even tanks could operate, and then you had the sea on the other side. You had these vast open spaces in between, with a couple of oases where the Long-Range Desert Group used to operate. You've probably heard of them – they were commandos really, the beginning of the SAS.

Cairo was great. One had the Turf Club and the Ghezira, which was the most marvellous country club in the world, really. One had Tommy's Bar – one even had an air-conditioned cinema. You see, this was when we were operating from a landing ground. It was uncomfortable when you were there, but one always had to bring the aeroplanes back after 30 hours' flying. You might only come back for a day and a half, but then when we brought them back for major maintenance, one might be back for a week. Then you could stay at the Continental Hotel overnight – and arrive in the barber's shop to get rid of your seven-day stubble. Operating from an airfield, water was very short – one certainly didn't have enough water to shave, and

A truck-load of British troops crosses from Egypt into Libya

what water there was was very salty. It actually used to spoil the taste of the whisky, so the problem was to get some decent drinking water up from the delta to put in one's evening libation – which was very necessary in that climate. One didn't, literally, take a drink until the sun was on the way down, and then a little whisky was very helpful!"

U-BOAT WAR

Fire & Ice

After the sinking of the Bismarck in May 1941 marked the end of the era of great battleships, the Atlantic war continued unabated as German submarines preyed on Allied merchantmen. The following month, the British began a series of Arctic convoys through the icy northern ocean to send aid to their Soviet allies. In forbidding conditions, the vulnerable crews suffered terrible losses

Otto Kretschmer was commander of U-99, on patrol in the North Atlantic in March 1941, when his submarine came under attack by depth-charge. Apart from the memory of the struggle to survive the wreck, he remembers the horror with which U-boat men were viewed by Allied seamen.

"Knowledge, of course, is the basis of everything – and in peacetime training in seamanship tactics or whatever it is, you must know your job. You must also be in a position to know what's going on on the battlefield – and that which you don't see – or which you see only at a glance, either when you're submerged or when you are on the surface. You must try to find out what your adversary, say the aircraft commander, for instance, is thinking, and what the crews of the ships are thinking, and what the crews of the ships are doing – whether they have come from America with a long sea voyage behind them, or from England to the west of Ireland, when they are waiting for the change of the watch, and what the weather is like – if the lookouts have got the wind in their faces, or the moon is shining at night. You must think about all these little things and store them in your mind, so that you have everything ready when you have to make a decision.

It's a bit difficult for us now, trying to get some insight into what was going on in the battle of the Atlantic, because during the war the role of the U-boat sailor was a much despised one. They were thought of as pirates and that sort of thing, but when we talk to people on both sides now, naval officers on both sides, I mean, it's almost as if they were talking about a football match. Everything's very jolly and very friendly, and they're all marvellous chaps together. It's hard to realise that all those years ago these same people were at sea trying to kill each other.

Oddly enough there was no hatred on our side – at least on my side – and it was a pity to sink those ships. They were, some of them, very beautiful – but we never worried so much about the men because, well, I always thought they had time enough to go into the boats, and on many occasions, I helped them.

When I found a sailor on a raft, I took them aboard and put them into a lifeboat to go and get safely home, and told them which course to steer and so on. I gave them food and what they wanted, so we didn't worry so much about the men. It was the ships we had to go after, and the most precious ships first of all – the tankers, to create a bottleneck, then the fuel – then that was that.

Well, when I was depth-charged, I had to go to the surface because the water was coming into the boat. I couldn't move and was lying in a large oil patch, listing to starboard and being fired at by two destroyers from portside (without success, I must say), so water spouts were coming up all around the boat – however, their 40-mm poms-poms had fuses against aircraft, so they didn't harm the boat very much. Only the paint was off, that was all, but still the aft part of my boat went under.

The boat was sinking by the stern and that part of my crew which was on the afterdeck was thrown into the water. I couldn't do anything about them. My own thinking was for the crew – I wanted to give them every chance to be picked up and get into captivity, and this I could only do by asking the one destroyer which was in the vicinity (the commander, Donald McIntyre, would later become my friend). Passing through at about four o'clock in the morning, my morse lamp was getting the signal that part of my crew was floating in the water and I asked him to pick them up. I couldn't do anything about them and afterwards he drew alongside the people in the water and put on his search lights so I could see their heads through my glasses, how they got aboard. At least half the crew got to safety.

Three were completely lost. One officer went down with the boat. He didn't get out in time – and two were lost in the water. I don't know why or how. One sick man we got safely aboard the destroyer.

He had concussion and when I went aboard the destroyer which saved us, I couldn't see anybody left in the water. I was told on board that they couldn't see any more either."

Leading Signalman Bert Wade joined the Navy as a scout and took over from regular Navy staff who had been allocated to commodores of convoy. It was on Convoy PQ17 that his luck ran out.

"I was on the bridge, fortunately, when the torpedo hit us. I'd just come on watch about an hour before, and it was about six o'clock in the morning. The torpedo hit the after end, where the men were accommodated – the gunners, naval personnel who were on the ship. The lifeboats had moved away on one side, because the ship couldn't stop – the engines' special stopping valves were all jammed and she was travelling at about 8 knots, sitting down at the stern. Two of us managed to get off on the port side in a small boat, which was lowered by the gunnery officer. As he lowered it down, he let go of the rope and the thing hit the water and filled up. We slid down and managed to get in. I fell in the water alongside the boat, but my friend pulled me in. The other signalman jumped over from the deck. He'd managed to get out from below where he was trapped – but he was covered in smoke and tar. In his hurry to get over the edge, he'd caught his legs and thighs on the hooks of the rails – but fortunately the blood froze.

Then the submarine came up and came alongside us, filming all the time. The captain ordered us to join the other boat, which looked to us to be about a mile away. There was an argument about who was captain and who the people in uniform were. They settled it by taking the army cipher chap off the boat. He went in the submarine and we didn't see him again. The Captain, who was sitting in ordinary clothes, everyone said had gone down in the ship. We scrambled aboard two boats, about 60 of us, and we were there five and a half to six days. The Arctic is unbelievable. In the cold, there was the rumbling of icebergs – the colour is unbelievable and, to a young bloke, of my age, is fascinating. You didn't think what the problems were. When I went into the water, I had a big overcoat on, which was drenched. The people who had been in the water, in waterproof suits, which were supposed to be the essence of survival – they were the worst off. There were two stokers in these suits, and

A convoy crew, their gun completely frozen, brave the ferocious seas of the Arctic

they weren't too well at all.

They used to row an hour on and two hours off, but no-one was quite sure where they were rowing to. The corvette picked us up on what was, more or less, my 21st birthday. In the open boat there was water collected from what was left from each of the three boats. Most of the water was mucky stuff, but there was pemmican and biscuits. They rationed us to two ounces of water every eight hours.

I remember it now, there were 30 people sitting in a boat, passing a beaker down to the other end with two ounces of water – and passing the same beaker back through the boat. It was unbelievable. Everybody tips it up on the way back and it's ages before it comes out with the next two ounces. I made up my mind never to be thirsty or wanting again.

I don't remember, as a 20-year-old, being very cold or tired – I think it was excitement more than anything. The chap alongside me kept on about what it was like to die – and in trying to make him change his mind I obviously managed to change mine. Most of them were quite happy. Two or three of them died – because as soon as you got very cold, there was no way of recovery. You had to try sitting on people to recover them. We held a church service for two or three of them, and there were two boats together trying to sing 'Abide with me'. It still sends shivers down my spine if I hear it now. It was a young kid of about 18 – a wireless operator – who had died, and the captain decided to have this service. We couldn't clothe the bodies, they went over as they were.

Rowing, I suppose, took most of the time, and a lot of them didn't want to sleep – they thought that if they went to sleep they wouldn't wake up.

Captain Wharton had the idea that if you rubbed some whale oil on to your feet, it protected you against frostbite. But we only proved then that it was the wrong thing to do. I took my left shoe off and couldn't get it back on again. Frostbite made it swell up like a sprain, and you find you're walking on a lump.

When we went into Archangel the reception from the Russians was more or less negligible. We hadn't brought them anything, and they didn't want to know."

Arctic convoys were run to deliver weapons such as these new Valentine Mark II tanks

NEW GUINEA

The Fittest Survive

Guadalcanal, a double chain of lush tropical islands in the Solomons, to the east of New Guinea, was the scene of some of the worst carnage of the war. US Marines landed in August 1942, triggering a series of battles on land and sea, while Australian troops and raw GIs struggled through the dense rain forests of New Guinea to drive the Japanese back to the sea

Joshu Otomo entered the Japanese 24th Infantry Division as a 24-year-old graduate. It was after landing on Guadalcanal that his group became part of the Battle of the Ridge, the subsequent attacks and the eventual ignominious retreat. He recalls their gradual collapse.

"We'd been involved in operations one after another, morning and night, on the principle that if we attack we take. We took whatever we attacked, and we felt we could do it with a single blow. So we only took one week's rice ration with us. From the experience of war we'd had until then, we felt one week was enough to win, and then we could have the Americans' supplies.

The night of 13 September was pitch dark. To tell you the truth, there was an interval of about a day before the general attack began, and the intention of our attack unit was to recce the enemy situation. However in the initial arrangement, the Navy was to support us from the sea by gunfire, and aircraft were to coincide with a bombing raid, so it was impossible to alter the anticipated time of attack.

It was a flop. We withdrew without having taken the airfield. Our unit looped immediately round to the south and all returned to Oka's positions with the regimental HQ. Here again we made preparations for a second attack.

We were at a point where, if you climbed the hill, you could see the runway and aircraft moving along and taking off. However, I thought a second general attack would be a flop. Not completely – but the enemy had stiffened his defences, and if we put in an attack, the gunfire would be so terrific that we wouldn't be able to lift our heads. Really. And in fact, on one night, in the first position, I remained stuck in one place, unable to move. At the closest we were about 50 metres from the enemy. Then the second attack failed and we made a third and fourth.

There was no good, honest food, so we ate whatever seemed edible – grass roots, tree roots. In that area there were monkeys, so on the reasoning that whatever monkeys ate, we should be able to eat too, we ate the pith from betel-nut palm trees, a grass that looked like parsley and so on. There wasn't a grain of rice. Since we couldn't move around midday, we went into our trenches and sat tight.

It helped that the American troops did not fight at night. The sun would go down and the Americans would draw back, so we were able to take our time and put water in our mess tins, mix it with what looked like edible grasses and make a sort of soup out of it. If there

An American Grumman TBF Avenger torpedo bomber about to take off from a carrier

had been some salt it wouldn't have been so bad, but we had nothing like that – we just had to force it into our stomachs. We did have matches, but in the end we used to take the gunpowder out of rifle cartridges and explode it to make kindling. Then we ate lizards – sometimes they were even a metre long. We boiled them and ate them, and they were just like the white meat of chicken. They were like the lizards you see in Japan. When they came out, everyone grabbed a stick and beat them, and we ate them on skewers. They didn't taste of anything, but we knew that if we didn't eat something we'd die.

However, because we got tired when we moved, we used to sleep a lot. When we stood up, everything went black in front of our eyes, and we'd feel dizzy. Even so, we survived, moving about a bit, collecting grubs, boiling up soup or something. When orders came to move, we could not stand on our feet – we couldn't walk. Lending a hand to a comrade – that didn't happen on Guadalcanal.

As we went along that coast for the last time, there were groups of men, here, there and everywhere, without the strength to walk. There were men who looked as if they'd fallen out and become separated from their units. Those men must all have died, or been taken prisoner. They were sick with malaria or amoebic dysentry, and many of them must have been on the point of death. They were given hand-grenades to kill themselves with.

There were Japanese soldiers like living skeletons, moving along and then collapsing on the verge of death. Starvation, malaria, malnutrition – they just lay there, staring with drooping heads. They didn't look like human beings any more."

Lieutenant John Gray, flying with fighter unit VF-5 from the carrier Yorktown, recorded a clash with Japanese 'Betty' bombers over the northern coast of New Guinea.

"My wingman and I started diving down to the east and dropped our bombs. Damned if I know where they landed. Then we dropped our belly tanks and we were really going like hell.

Anyway, we sighted these two Jap twin-engine jobs tearing along close to the water, hugging the shore so nobody would see them. I went down around and came up on their tails. They were in position one ahead of the other.

The back one was smoking already, so somebody must have hit him before I did. Anyway, I hit his other engine and he went in. I guess I get a 'half' for that. I pulled up right over him and tailed after the other one ahead. I got so close that he didn't just fill the sight – he filled up my whole windshield. He wasn't more than, well, 100 feet away – I couldn't miss.

I could see the bullets going in all over, riddling him. He was burning everywhere but there wasn't any explosion. He just bounced on the water once, twice, and then turned over and sank. I'm sure I killed the pilots. I hope they got my pictures developed... "

Lieutenant Chikanori Moji was an officer of the Japanese Special Landing Force, involved in the battle of Milne Bay on New Guinea. This was a crucial battle for the Japanese, but as the tide turned against them, some surviving officers met near the evacuation site towards the end of August.

"As the cutter withdrew with the wounded, we felt left alone at last, and sure that those remaining would die within the next few days, more or less. We could not imagine being able to hold out until the army came with reinforcements.

It was not that death was staring us in the face, but rather that we still had a few hours' or days' leeway, which made us think even more intensely about death. My life would be reaching its final showdown within three or four days. Reflecting on my life, wondering about the meaning it may have had, I felt that I had done nothing at all – that it was completely meaningless. I had neither core nor content – no real self. My life of 20 or so years amounted to nothing. It might be described as empty or vacuous.

The next night we moved to the evacuation point and waited. A launch with two or three cutters arrived at the shore. The wounded were taken aboard and they left. We waited as patiently as we could, not knowing how many warships were at sea, but knowing that at least by leaving the land we were escaping a death-trap. To us, this peninsula at the east end of New Guinea was a nightmare of a place. After waiting patiently we boarded the boats.

The pace was slow as the launch towed the cutters and we moved out over the black seas. They finally reached the *Tenryu* and I grasped a hand extended from the side of the ship and was dragged up on to the deck, where the previously evacuated were waiting, some lying and some seated. They were silently grouped in the darkness as if suddenly overtaken by exhaustion – they had the air of a defeated force."

Private Bob Swanborough of 2/3 Infantry Battalion was a veteran of the Middle East and, like many other Australian soldiers, had to make a swift transition to jungle fighting. He recalls the trail from the roadhead to Port Moresby.

"I would have had more than 50 lb on my back at the time because I carried a Thompson and 650 rounds of ammunition. I carried four tins of bully beef, a couple of packets of biscuits, a blanket and 24 two-inch mortar bombs strapped around my belt. We had our shaving gear and most of us tried to carry an extra pair of socks – not that it meant anything after a day or so in the wet conditions.

As far as the general mood of the fellers was concerned, their morale was very high and there was a sort of anticipation because we had heard a lot of tales about the Japs. We didn't have a bloody clue as to what was in front of us, but we were in high spirits and the Battalion was really quite looking forward to tangling with these blokes.

As an Infantry Forward Scout, you were living on your nerves all the time and it was a relief when it was time to come back to your company positions. Each bloke would have about two hours as the Forward Scout and then he'd change with his Number Two. You'd be edgy, expecting at any time for someone to come out of the foliage and cop you. All the time you were on the look-out for snipers – they were very difficult to see. The first indication you'd get of a sniper was when a shot was fired, and nine times out of ten, they got their target first go.

One thing I always remember about scouting. You tended to be able to segregate noises – you developed animal cunning and if something moved, you would immediately assume that there was someone out there.

For months after I came back, I used to sit up in bed with nightmares, sweating like blazes and mainly I was on the track, going through scrub and a Japanese opened up on me. It was a devastating sort of experience that we all went through there."

DIEPPE

Blood Beach

The German occupation of Europe was at its height in 1942. Following the disaster of Dunkirk, and encouraged by Commando success in lightning strikes, the Allies launched an assault on Dieppe in August intended to be a large-scale test of the German response to an invasion. The resulting massacre left the beaches drenched in blood. Only the lucky ones survived the carnage

Hans Muller-Baule was a gunner in the 1st Armour Reconnaissance Company, Reconnaissance Section 10 of the 10th Panzer Division. Having been on the Eastern Front, they had been posted to Amiens, they believed, to freshen up and take a well-earned rest. Then 19 August dawned.

"A piercing signal, normally so familiar – the whistle of the duty NCO rang out through the high corridors of the barracks. We woke with a start, still a little drowsy. In our wire-mesh beds we – the six-man crew of the 1st Heavy Armoured Reconnaissance Unit – didn't know what was going on. We had been pulled out of Russia so that we could freshen up and take reinforcements far away from the front.

And then, this incredibly piercing whistle again – interrupted for a moment by shouts of 'Alarm! Alarm!' To reinforce the effect of our signal, the door to our room was flung open. Quick as a flash, we were out of our beds, everyone diving on to his carefully arranged bundle of clothes and throwing on clothing out of a kind of instinct, cursing as we pulled on our boots and ran, as we had practised so often, out of the room, down the corridor, on to the courtyard and into the scouting truck.

The commander of the reconnaissance troop was standing impatiently waiting by the radio-scouting truck, gesturing us to get a

Survivors compare experiences on their return from Dieppe, 19 August 1942

move on with the most frantic hand movements. We had never seen him so animated – he usually radiated such calm. Seeing him like this woke us up to the fact that this was a serious alarm. Dawn was just breaking, but every one of us, the driver, commandant, rear passenger and myself (the gunner) had practised this many times over and took our places quickly.

The rear passenger and radio operator was having problems as usual getting his uniform and radio equipment in order. The commandant, as always, radiated calm and level-headedness. I was, to be honest, thinking about how to operate the 2 cm cannon. In no time we were on the arterial road out of Amiens, heading for the coast, after our radio had picked up the news that an enemy landing was under way at Dieppe.

Bombers and fighters cut through the sky. We took cover for a moment under the trees at the side of the road, then set off again at top speed for the coast. There was a tense calm in the scouting truck. All my senses were on the alert and everyone was deeply immersed in his own thoughts. The nearer we got to Dieppe, the muffled rumble which we had been hearing at intervals on the way eased off – the unmistakable sound of ships' artillery fire.

About 20 km from Dieppe we were stopped by military police. They told us there had been a failed landing operation – mostly Canadian soldiers. It had been beaten back for the most part, but we were told to proceed cautiously. When we arrived in Dieppe, fires were still smouldering in ruined houses. The two reconnaissance trucks headed for the coast and there, on the beach, in view of our coastal fortress, we could see the aftermath of an obviously brief but intense and ruthless battle. In the water were the remains of landing craft, some totally destroyed. The beach was littered with corpses."

Trained up as a member of the Special Sea Service, Jack Brewin and his group are informed by Lord Louis Mountbatten that they would man new craft – the brainchild of Churchill – in heading an assault on France.

"On the afternoon of 18 August, things really began to take shape. I think our own force left Newhaven at about 0100 hours. I recall it to have been a very dark night, the sea was swelly and no lights were visible. We were under strict orders not to fire, even at suspicious targets. There were several near collisions between craft and we ourselves missed hitting an LCT which actually was beam on to our approach. Movement was very hazardous in the dark.

Naturally we were at action stations and I was gun-layer on No. 2 pom-pom. I now have the impression of feeling very lonely when I cast my mind back to that stage of the operation. I was not afraid of the events which would undoubtedly lie ahead. I do not think any of us were, but we had time to think and contemplate on what might be in wait for us. The average age of the ship's company was 19 to 20 years, and none of us had seen previous active service. I myself was just 19 and a half years of age.

At about 0300 hours, the sky suddenly filled with tracer shot and it was obvious that some attack was taking place. I now know that this event was the unfortunate chance meeting with a small German convoy. We did not participate in any way, neither did I realise that this encounter had already contributed towards the terrible outcome of the operation. As dawn broke, we had our first glimpse of a hostile shore. Strangely at this stage, it appeared quite normal – not at all like I had envisaged. I saw some white cliffs and a town, and apart from some distant thuds, nothing seemed other than commonplace. However, as the morning light grew I began to see the magnitude of the operation. The foreshore was obliterated by many craft, the sea around us occupied by many ships.

Maybe it was not actually like I now imagine it, but it now seems that with the coming of full light, the scene changed. The air was suddenly filled with aircraft and we fired madly at them. We were about half a mile from the shore, and so occupied with our fire that whatever was happening on the beach escaped us.

I estimate that we were so engaged for about two hours. There appeared to be hundreds of planes swarming everywhere, and identification was difficult. We just fired at everything that came near. When a plane was shot down, we all cheered and claimed responsibility. That day the RAF were operating Mustang fighters for the first time, and the resemblance of this aircraft to the German Me-109 was such that we almost certainly shot one of these down.

It was about 0830 hours when there appeared to be a change in our role. We began to steam closer to the shore and whatever we had already experienced under air attack was nothing to the holocaust which now presented itself. It now all seems to be one mixed impression of terror and nightmare. I can but try and describe that impression en bloc, so to speak.

Withdrawal of the landing was now taking place and landing craft were streaming from the beach filled beyond normal capacity with badly wounded men. Our own craft lay all but on the beach, and it seemed that every gun, light and heavy, was directed on us from the shore. I seemed rooted to the gun platform, possibly because I imagined the shield would give some protection. Tracer flew in all directions, and a great piece of metal from the ship's side landed at my feet. I heard terrible screams all around me. The wounded were being lifted aboard from the shore. The sights were ghastly – a Canadian minus an arm climbed aboard unaided, calmly smoking a cigarette. I wouldn't have believed such courage. Terribly mutilated bodies all around, the sea full of debris and floating dead, tremendous noise and the air full of stinking smoke. I remember looking towards the bridge seeking some renewal of strength from our officers – and seeing nothing but white faces that were as frightened as my own.

The officers' mess deck was being used as a sick bay and the orderlies were almost throwing the wounded down to the surgeon, who was doing an impossible task of mercy that day. Almost as continuously, the dead were being arranged on the deck.

I have no idea how long this terrible episode lasted – it must have been several hours. This ship's guns were now all out of action and our only purpose was as some misplaced haven for those returning from the beaches. A Canadian tumbled aboard, cursing and screaming before he turned around and dived back into the dead. I remember a dead Canadian being eased with my foot over the side to make further room aboard. It all added to the general impression of noise, smoke and utter disaster.

Orders were eventually given for our withdrawal. I have no idea of the actual time, but I do know that we were among the very last to leave. The skies were by now clear of enemy planes, but the fire from the shore was still active until we were out of their range. A heavy cloud of smoke enveloped the town, the beach filled with immobilised tanks and landing craft.

The returning force must have looked a sorry sight. We were all bearing the scars of battle and even now I noticed craft sinking or being abandoned. A steam gun boat slid alongside us and transferred to our keeping a German pilot picked out of the sea. I remember him to be naked apart from a blanket, and some of the Canadian survivors attempting to kill him before being restrained. He was to be confined in a paint-store, little larger than a cupboard, for his own safety. No-one was in the mood to respect conventions.

The journey back was one of utter misery. The mess deck was crowded with survivors and wounded lay everywhere – a stench of mutilated humanity prevailed. I was in a state of shock. I lay on the deck and tried to gather my shattered wits together. I had no knowledge of what our role had been. I knew even less of what, if anything, we had achieved. I suppose someone, somewhere was able to make a pattern of the day's events – I couldn't.

Later a war correspondent came aboard and approached me. 'What did you think of Dieppe?' he asked me. 'So that's where we've been', I replied. How ridiculous that must have sounded to him – but the name meant nothing to me."

EL ALAMEIN

The Final Onslaught

In June 1942, as Rommel's Afrikakorps headed towards Egypt, the Allies finally broke their advance at the last defensive position, west of the Suez Canal and less than a day's march from Alexandria – El Alamein. Over the next five months, Montgomery's Desert Rats brought new hope for the Allies in this, the toughest battle of the Desert War, which saw the German troops finally retreat

Major Tom Bird MC commanded the six-pounder anti-tank company of the Rifle Brigade in the 'Snipe' action on 26 and 27 October, earning him the DSO. He tells of the courage of other members of his company.

"The battle for Alamein had come to an impasse – neither side was winning. We, a motor battalion of three rifle companies and one anti-tank company, were instructed to carry out a night attack and take what was thought to be a ridge, some 2,000 yards in front of our line. As we met almost no enemy resistance, the rifle companies' attack succeeded and the anti-tank guns were sent for and dug in during the night. But at dawn, to improve their field of fire, some had to be resited. I think the majority of our casualties were at that moment, and it's always one of the remarkable things in the desert, that if you were just below ground in a slit trench, you could have a fantastic amount of bombing and shelling and not come to a great deal of harm – unless they actually hit you.

All day we found ourselves under fire from our own men. As far as they were concerned, we were 2,000 yards ahead of where they thought there were any of their own troops. Added to this, during the night, various German tanks and guns had come through our positions, and we'd knocked them out. Looking through the haze from quite a long way away, all they could see were some jeeps and some enemy tanks, so they assumed that we were the enemy.

The most memorable occasion was when we were being attacked by nine Italian tanks – but only one of our guns could fire at them. They'd shot six when they ran out of ammunition. Jack Toms got in his jeep and drove to one of the other guns. Tanks which were still coming on were shooting, and everyone else was shooting at us, so he drove through very heavy fire. Then he loaded the ammunition from one of the other guns on to his jeep and as he drove back, his jeep was hit and caught fire. But he managed to drive as far as the gun and he and the colonel unloaded the ammunition – and of course, with the fire, this was liable to go off at any moment – and managed to get the ammunition to the gun. Calistan then hit all the rest of the tanks and knocked them out.

I was hit in the back of the head but was more or less *compos mentis*. Vic Turner and I were more or less knocked out. Two German tanks got within about 100 yards from where we were. There was one gun in a position to fire but the gun crew were in a trench a little bit away from the gun, and they couldn't get to it because every time they made the slightest movement, there was a huge burst of machine-gun fire. The platoon sergeant managed, by using dead ground, to creep up to the gun to shoot at the tanks. They were within such short range that one exploded, more or less. I can remember the cheer which went up – it was a very, very brave effort.

Monty came to give the battalion a talk – I suppose it was before Alamein. I remember him telling the men that they were a 'fine body of men' – which was such a cliché, if I'd said it to my company, they would have roared with laughter and they'd have known that I was pulling their leg. However, it seemed to go down quite well. It didn't seem to matter that he talked in clichés."

Henry Byrne, 18, a gunner with 154th (Leicestershire Yeomanry) Field Regiment, Royal Artillery found himself among complete strangers – on the way to fight in the desert.

"Where was I going? What was I doing on this troop ship, risking my life at sea, manning a Lewis gun, watching the sky on August Bank Holiday and remembering my picnic in the Dublin Mountains only a year before? Last year a junior salesman – now a highly trained field gunner. Is it fate or madness? My comrades must have thought the latter, since compared with these men of a pre-war yeomanry regiment, I was only a boy. Gibes abounded and for the first time in my life I felt isolated and at times near to tears.

Three days before the battle, our regiment moved up to the front. The sun disappeared and we were faced with a dull, dreary and eerie scene, our faces grey with dust in an empty, cold wasteland. Here and there were the burnt-out remains of vehicles and the odd crane. The rumble of gun and machine-gun fire told us we were near the front. In the distance we could see Stukas dive-bombing our lines – our war had begun. We had to wait until dark to take up our positions, so we ate our 'desert chicken', otherwise known as bully beef, and waited. No fires – no tea. I shall always remember, in the dusk of that day, feeling I would never come out of this.

On the afternoon of 23 October leaflets were distributed, giving Monty's eve-of battle message. 'Fight as long as you have breath in your body'. It seemed unreal in the quiet afternoon. Where were the tanks, infantry, planes and guns?

At 2140 hours, the desert shook like an earthquake. For as far as we could see, the sky was ablaze from the guns. Such was the deafening noise that we could see enemy shells exploding on our positions, but could not hear them. Our gaunt stares said it all – we were scared stiff, but oddly enough, not frightened. In the hours that followed, the tension eased. Our barrage was having the desired effect, but the infantry and engineers had it rough. In the glare of the guns, men could be seen falling and groups being blown up by mines. Cameramen were moving forward with the infantry, but to no avail. Jerry held a strongly fortified line.

By morning we were veterans, or so it seemed. Gippy tummy reared its head, and though painful and distressing, it provided a comic relief watching each other going back and forth with a shovel to dig a loo. We got our bottle of water in the morning and each put some in a petrol can for washing. We then got another tin, pierced holes in the bottom, put some stones in and sifted the water after every wash. After two days, one of my quips was 'It's cleaner to stay dirty'. Most of us went for bald heads because of the sand lice.

The cook-wagon, when it could provide a hot meal, did wonders with bully stew, bully fritters, cold bully (which melted in the tin), biscuit porridge, biscuit date pudding and good old cocoa. They were few and far between, but most welcome! They occasionally gave us Carnation milk, tea, sugar when they couldn't cook and, thanks to the petrol can, we made the famous 'Benghazi' fire, made by cutting the can in half, filling it with sand and piercing holes in the sides. We then poured petrol on the sand and lit it. Our shirts and shorts were dropped into a petrol can, dipped, and dried in minutes in the sand.

Of course the war was in full swing though static, and with all the above, the shocks of the 23rd became a bad dream. Stukas came over and we came out of our holes and fired rifles at them. Although no advance was possible yet, the whole picture of war changed. Morale was high, and as the days passed with the endless bombardment, the warning came that if we didn't break through soon, we may have to withdraw into Palestine. None of us accepted this – we had been too stirred by Monty's message.

On the tenth day, the Axis collapsed and the breakthrough came. We were on the chase, moving up and down the line of advance to give support. Soon we caught our first glimpse of POWs. Thousands of Hitler's supermen, dishevelled, dirty, some in stockinged feet, all thoroughly dejected and apparently starving, were taken. This is what we waited for – a victory, finally breaching Hitler's master-race.

In the event, I couldn't hate. We stopped and watched these men pass by. I thought what heroes these men were to have stood this bombardment from land, sea and air for ten days. I wished I could be sure I would be so brave. For a moment I imagined they were British and I was one of them. I thought of my family at home, and I'm proud to say it brought a tear to my eye. I was to see more of the Nazi element of Hitler's men in Italy, which did fill me with hatred – and a determination to destroy that evil empire. However, remembering Alamein, and I often do, I feel there is a certain affection between the *Afrika Korps* and the Eighth Army.

It was man's war and I had become a man. We fought soldier to soldier, no civilians involved, and although we all lost friends, I feel sure we will always have a healthy respect for each other for the manner in which we conducted ourselves in that war."

Heinz Erdmann volunteered for the 'Sonder-Stab F', a special staff unit, and set up Special Unit 288, in which he served in the medical unit, during the early part of 1943.

"We had erected a first-aid post between the coast and the road, marked with a huge red cross. As a medical unit, we had relatively

The makeshift grave of a British tank crew, casualties of the fighting at Alamein, 1942

little to do. Then we were woken in the night of 23 October. We suddenly heard ahead of us at the front a terrible roar and rumbling and crashing over a broad area, and saw a long, wide flickering gleam of light in the background, from the sea right over into the desert. It went on and on. And this rumbling went on for days and nights, sometimes further away from us, sometimes nearer.

Now we had more than enough to do from the medical point of view. The first returning vehicles and smaller units were blocking the road and tracks. It became difficult for us to get our wounded back to the post. Sometimes we had to force our way through.

On 3 November the front collapsed and we began to retreat. This was definitely the worst for us, the sand blowing in our eyes, the fighter/bombers, to say nothing of the artillery and tank fire. Everything blocked up, terrible chaos, screaming, cursing, running about, burning vehicles, rescuing the wounded between them, treating them and carrying them off, and burying the dead. All this went on for about tendays and nights. Then, at Sollum, things got more or less back to normal (for us at least). I was, and still am, grateful that my unit and myself got ourselves through this period relatively well."

TUNIS

Final Act

After their defeat of the Afrikakorps at El Alamein, the Eighth Army drove Rommel back to the west. But Allied landings were already underway further west still, where American troops invaded French North Africa with little opposition. Rommel, trapped between the two forces in Tunisia, retreated to the capital, Tunis, and evacuated his troops in May 1943. The war in North Africa was over

After the Malta campaign, Royal Marine Robert Porter trained in West Africa at Freetown to carry out bombardments. Unbeknown to him, this was in preparation for Operation Torch, to which his ship, the Aurora, took a large number of US troops.

"While we were docked at Gibraltar, massive troop ships, two or three thousand on each, arrived. Most of the men on the ships were American – the general idea seemed to be to make the campaign appear to be American, so as not to offend the French.

The day before the invasion, we got hundreds and hundreds of American Rangers on our ship. They were wearing enormous armbands showing the Stars and Stripes, so that they would be easily identified as Americans. It got very crowded, but we didn't mind as we were used to not having much space. They slept on the deck, like the rest of us. You didn't have bunks in those days.

These American Rangers were the crack force of the American Army. They were all armed with guns and bullets – we weren't, of course, because we weren't going ashore. There was one Ranger there, a real comedian – we all took to him. His name was Dizzy. He was showing his guns off to us, and we were all fascinated, looking at these American weapons. He was getting very excited – you have to remember that these men were full of tension because they knew they were landing the next day. Unfortunately there was a live bullet up the spout of his gun, and it went off as he was showing it to us, and hit the deck-head. The incident caused a terrible commotion and he got a real telling off from his sergeant.

In the evening, just before it got dark, the troop ships sailed right into the Mediterranean. Our destination was Oran, but we sailed right past it, as if we were heading for Alexandria. The idea was to give any spies the impression that the invasion wasn't going to be in French North Africa. When it got really dark – at about two or three in the morning – we turned around and went back towards Oran.

There were some coastal guns in Oran harbor, and some Vichy French destroyers. We had some trouble breaking the boom, which is the gateway into the harbor. There were two little ships in our force, rather like frigates. They were sent in first to break the boom, but both got hit and most of the American troops on board were lost. From the 6-inch gun turret and looking through the cabinet, which was like a spy hole, I could see a searchlight from the shore that was shining directly at us. We immediately got the order to fire, and the light disappeared – we must have hit it.

Three of the French destroyers that were in the harbour tried to get out. The captain of the first one decided not to fight us, and instead of firing, he ran it aground. We left them alone then, because they had surrendered. The second destroyer managed to get out of the harbour and escape. Then another destroyer came out and we sank it. I don't know if there were any survivors, because we started firing at the coastal batteries immediately after that had happened.

There was little opposition to the actual landings. There didn't seem to be much heart in it, and we were on shore a day or two later, in the town enjoying ourselves. It was like a real holiday for us – it was like going to a fantasy land, seeing the old market place and the buildings and the young French girls. It took my breath away."

Peter Allebury, a pilot with the Fleet Air Arm, was catapulted from the deck of HMS Renown in his Walrus, with a crew of two, to carry out an anti-submarine patrol and protect the invasion fleet attacking Algiers.

"We had our British markings painted out with American ones, because it was thought that the French would give the Americans a better welcome than they would the British. When we got to the end of our patrol, we were told to 'proceed ashore' as the ship was not in a position to recover us. We found an airfield at Maison Blanche, about 20 miles to the east of Algiers. The place was well supplied with French fighters, but to our pained surprise there was a German Ju-88 and an Italian Savoia Marchetti three-engined transport too. The petrol situation was now critical, so we had no option but to land there and hope for the best.

No-one came out to greet us – but it was about 6.00 am so we assumed that everyone was still abed. We could see an estaminet down the road and wandered off to see if they were serving breakfast. Much to our surprise, a lot of people were gathered there and we were right royally received. The breakfast became more liquid than solid and we eventually staggered back to the airfield to find hundreds of American soldiers. They were astounded to find that we spoke English, and more so when we explained that we were British Fleet Air Arm aircrew. They were not keen to let us back on to the airfield, as they had come to capture it.

We stayed at Maison Blanche for a few days, and the place filled up with RAF personnel. We took it upon ourselves to do dawn anti-submarine patrols, until a British Army major asked if we would do tactical reconnaissance for the army. We were delighted to help and flew him about 20 miles east to the town of Bougie, hoping that it had been captured, so that he could see how things were going with the army – especially the tanks. This meant flying very low, and zooming down wadies in the hills, to see if there was any opposition waiting for Allied tanks around the next corner. We had great difficulty in establishing good relations with the RAF and consequently had basically to steal petrol to keep us going in our more-or-less freelance operations. When we were joined by other Walrus crews which had 'lost' their ships, we moved to Algiers and arranged to take over the Air France base. Our army had always been most cooperative and provided us with clothing and other necessities. The army Base Ordnance Dump was to be found in an area shown on the maps as the 'Ravine des Femmes Sauvages'–there was great competition to go there in the first place, but no-one was lucky enough to discover any wild women there.We also found that during an air raid, we were able to pillage the heaps of supplies being unloaded from the ships, especially boxes of rations, while others were in air-raid shelters.

We lived in this very unorthodox way for some time before we came under the control of Allied Supreme Headquarters in Algiers. By then we had carried out 176 sorties and flown 388 hours, attacked two U-boats and rescued 19 people on air-sea rescue duties."

Hans Teske, a lance-corporal in the German 5th Parachute Regiment – a trouble-shooting unit – was 18 years old when he was dropped into Tunis. The controlling French forces in Tunis remained neutral for the first few weeks, but this would soon change as the Allies progressed.

British soldiers run to take up positions along the cliffs, close to the Mareth Line

"We arrived in Tunisia in November 1942 from France via Italy. Our purpose was to provide a secure back-up for Rommel's forces fighting in North Africa. We were told that, apart from the native Arab population, part of the inhabitants were French, and some were Italian. We were told not to alienate the French population, with whom we had had a good working relationship when we were in France. We did not know how sincere the offer by the French government was to allow us into Tunisia. We found this out once we landed. The French had tanks and fighter aircraft there, but they did not hinder us. They let us use all their facilities. In fact, when it came to setting up on the outskirts of the city we could use the local trams, and the French Army agreed with the local police force to give us a gendarme as protection on our journey there.

British Indian troops fire a 6 pounder anti-tank gun during the advance on Tunis

The French forces remained neutral for the first few weeks, then sided with the Americans and British, though most of the French population of Tunisia remained friendly to the German soldiers. Most farms were owned by Frenchmen, some by local people of Italian origin. The local Arab population remained friendly with the Germans right until the end of the Tunisian campaign.

When we first arrived in Tunisia we were surprised to find how European the climate was, and the temperature was like a European spring. It was very peaceful, and the French and Arabs were trying to outdo each other in hospitality. By 21 November, there were about 400 of us there.

From our provisional frontline we made further advances towards contacting the enemy, but normally the smaller party would give way to the larger party from either side. One example: we had a standing patrol near Bir Arada, and we were sent to pick them up. We had about six motor-cycle combinations, each with a machine-gun mounted on it, but we were ordered not to fire, because we did not want to give away the position of our standing outpost, as we wanted to use that position again. At this point the enemy troops were about 30 miles away. While we were travelling down the main road we saw a British motorcyclist coming in the opposite direction. He spotted us and threw himself down immediately into the ditch. We drove past him, ignoring him, and he lay there hiding from us. We looked back and he continued on his way, flogging the guts out of his machine."

STALINGRAD

Frozen Hell

Ordered to take the tank factories of Stalingrad and the Caucasian oilfields, German troops continued their advance. As another brutal winter ravaged the besieged city, cold and hunger attacked the health and morale of both the opposing forces. Yet Soviet resolve was stronger than ever – every house in every street was defended in close-quarter fighting known as 'the war of the Rats'

L Ovchinnikova was only a young girl during the battle for Stalingrad. With three women and three other children, she hid out in a cellar for 163 days, not far from the ravine which divided the city.

"That day I had to go into the ravine for bread or soup. Mother and my little sister were completely laid out by hunger. I had to walk, run and crawl about 200 metres over open ground. The snow was coated with ash because the factory had burned for several days. The flames swallowed the wooden houses with their wooden carvings, the apple and cherry orchards and the tree stumps and fences on which samovars used to simmer on summer evenings.

The wind blew snow between the still-standing factory chimneys. Along the way to the ravine I knew all the craters where I could shelter during a shelling. It was terrifying, crawling past the body of Nastya, the old woman who was our neighbour, lying not far from a scorched pear tree where the children of our street used to play.

I crawled through deep snow towards the Volga. Somewhere behind were the enemy trenches. The snow covered me from the head downward... this snow was my salvation. If the Germans spotted anything moving, there would be a bang and the slash of a bullet.

I trod past a field kitchen. There was an unusually tasty smell in the air. Pea soup, probably, made from concentrates. I couldn't make up my mind to knock on the door of the dugout. We knew that soldiers' rations had been cut from day to day.

'Where have you come from, little girl?' In front of me stood a soldier in a white sheepskin coat and fur cap. I was used to that question. What was there to say? Our story was quite ordinary – we hadn't had time to get across the Volga. Where was our cellar? On a tiny patch beyond the ravine. The captain took my small, empty bucket. We made our way up a steep climb, with me crawling on all fours, gripping heaps of soil and bunches of dried grass.

It was warm in the dug-out. It seemed I had already forgotten what this kind of warmth was like. I suddenly grew happy. I saw the captain take a string bag off a nail in the wall and put out some ration concentrates – gruel, pea soup. What riches there were on the table! The officer slid the food cubes into my bucket. I looked at this and suddenly understood. He knew how cold I had been when I was crawling to the ravine. At first I wanted to cry, but in our cellar there had been a kind of unwritten law against crying....

In exposed places, even a ruined house seemed reliable armour. I lifted a board so as to make my way to the cellar, and suddenly saw

German engineers construct a fairly sophisticated bridge over the bed of a stream

a machine gun over the entrance. Two soldiers were taking machine-gun belts out of a box. The gun was one of ours, its muzzle turned towards the fascist positions. They were our soldiers – they stayed silent and I, silent as well, went down into the cellar.

Above us the machine gun was firing. Cartridge cases flashed past. The empty saucepan on the stove trembled and the pipe leading to the window was whistling. Silently, and not taking our eyes away, we all watched the door. If the fascists broke the house, they'd throw grenades into the cellar without warning. Many families in our district had perished that way.

The machine gun fired away. We knew that so long as the machine-gunners stayed alive they wouldn't go away – wouldn't leave our cellar unprotected. I was convinced of that, in the same way as I believed in goodness and truth. Everything depended on one single thing – the thudding of that machine gun above us."

Sergeant Ivan Ivanovich Morotskii commanded a mortar detachment of the 277th Infantry Division, one of the units taking part in the encirclement of the Germans besieging Stalingrad.

"On 3 December, while repelling an attack, our mortar company cut off some German sub-machine gunners from their tanks. They opened up with a storm of fire. Shrapnel sang through the air and a mortar bomb exploded near us. Vanya Bochkov, a mortar layer, and Galib Setulaev, an ammunition carrier were wounded. I merely had my greatcoat lapel torn off. I rushed to help them, but was then knocked down by two automatic-rifle bullets in my rib on the right side. Bochkov was carried off on a groundsheet and Galib and myself crawled our own way to the first-aid point, which was quite close. This consisted of a kind of tent whose corners rested on the heads of the people holding it up. Hasty bandaging was done here, under the illumination of lanterns. One felt sorry for the nurses...

I remember meeting along the way some local women. 'We don't need anything', they said, 'except something to eat. The Germans here have eaten every last cat and dog.' It was painful to look at these worn-out and exhausted victims. We gave them our last crusts of bread – but there was no more we could do for them.

The surrounded units of Paulus tried to break out of their encirclement at various points, but they were mercilessly crushed.

One dawn we saw German aircraft flying low, and they mistook us for their own troops. They dropped provisions by parachute and this 'manna from heaven' was just what we wanted.

Along the road, broken and holed, stood enemy equipment, and piles of abandoned belongings. The one-time immaculate all-conquering Hitlerite army was in retreat. On the way in we often met columns of prisoners, escorted by our men. It was quite a sight, how they looked. Some wore women's dresses and blouses and substitute over-boots made of straw. They were dirty, with frozen faces, and without the slightest spark of life shining in their eyes."

Siegfried Melinkat, age 18, was a corporal (Untererscharführer) in 2nd Company, 5th SS Panzer Regiment, Wiking. Late in 1942, his regiment was advancing towards Stalingrad through the grim winter landscape.

"We were set down in Proletarskaya. This was a chaotic scene – abandoned trucks and weapons, scattered soldiers wending their way back, Romanian soldiers in a pitiful state. Fighter bombers hung in the sky and attacked everything that moved below. Our armoured column was the only formation which was heading north. We felt lonely and deserted. The company rolled on into the gathering darkness, in the endless, undulating, snow-covered plain, treeless and shrubless. Suddenly the engine started to sputter. The tank jolted, then jolted again several times and came to a halt.

In the pale moonlight, our tank stood out like a silhouette against the steppes. An icy wind was blowing from the east and brought snow with it. In a northerly direction, where Stalingrad must have been, I could hear the rumble of fire and the staccato sound of machine guns. Balls of light shot up in the air and fell slowly to the ground. What would happen to us if the Russians advanced further and were suddenly here? I couldn't get this thought out of my mind. If only the night was over, the terrifying moonlight in this white wilderness.

The fire was crackling in the stove – the smell of toasted bread and sunflower oil filled my nostrils. I now had four hours to get some sleep until the next change of guard. Someone shook me by my shoulders. I leapt up, looked around and breathed out, relieved. It was only a dream, which had made me start. But there was no time to ponder this anymore, it was time for my guard duty. I got dressed, forced on my winter gear and shoved my loaded 08 pistol, tied by a strap to my belt, into my trouser pocket. Then I reported for duty and went outside. A howling wind blew snow into my face. I pulled my head guard over my mouth, nose and eyes and pulled my fur cap lower down my forehead."

Pavel Ivanovich Doronin was one of the multitude of Communist Party propagandists mobilised to become the political officers attached to all Red Army units. He saw his role as strengthening the troops' morale and from September 1942, as a major-general, he headed the political department of the army group defending Stalingrad.

"The nature of street fighting determined the form of our mass propaganda work. Usually it was carried on after dark in cellars, trenches and shelters. Leaflets, dropped into dug-outs and buildings, were the most common medium. Sometimes these leaflets were the only form of political information, telling the soldiers about the most important events on the fronts, about military activity in their neighbourhood or by their own formations.

Often our soldiers were only a few metres from the enemy, and there were houses in which Germans and Russians were on different floors. In these conditions, the political officers kept our troops informed by means of powerful loudspeakers, and care was taken to ensure that these transmissions were carried with war songs, poetry reading and excerpts from front newspapers.

Special attention was paid to developing the sniper movement, which became very widespread with the fighting in the city. The army groups, as well as the political instructors, busied themselves with the selection of snipers and the organisation of their training. Armies, divisions and regiments held sniper conferences for the exchange of experience and activities involving the study of the optical sight, the theory of rifle fire, practice in camouflage and observation. The best snipers trained their pupils to become masters of rifle fire, without, as soldiers joked, 'taking time off work'.

The most popular sniper of the army group was Sergeant First-Class Vasili Zaitsev, about whom legends abounded. One claimed that, on hearing the Germans were bringing up reinforcements in the factory-zone, Zaitsev took six of his pupils and went to meet them. He killed 11, and in total they killed 40 of the fascists."

BOMBING GERMANY

Fear in the Dark

In answer to the fierce bombing of Britain, the RAF's strategic night-bombing of the towns and cities of the Reich inflicted similar suffering on German civilians. Hamburg, in particular, was completely devastated, with 30 per cent of its buildings destroyed and more than 44,000 of its inhabitants killed

Angelica Roms, née Söhn, was a girl of only 11, living in Düsseldorf, when war broke out. The bombing of her home town was so traumatic that it has left permanent scars – she says that she still can't hear a thunderstorm without the old war-time fear returning.

"Düsseldorf was not made up of little houses – it was high flats. One cellar was made into an air-raid shelter and fortified – they made a soft wall in them so that if something happened, you could knock through to next door, or the other way around.

It wasn't so bad until 1942 – then it really started. Don't forget, we had three enemies, the Americans in the daytime, the British at night and the Gestapo every day. If you saw a stranger, you treated him with mistrust – say even someone who came from a different part of Düsseldorf. You never knew, if you said, 'This damn war,' if they would report you. People had been arrested for showing a bit of light in the blackout. They were accused of guiding the RAF in – but we didn't need to tell them – they knew where we were. All they had to do was find the cathedral of Cologne, go up the Rhine, and there they were. Everything you said was picked up – even if you had grumbled about the food. You had to be careful – you were really afraid. In the factories they put Gestapo in among the workers in

For watchers on British bases, the wait for returning bombers was an axious time

boiler suits. If there was a meeting, if someone voiced a wrong opinion, they were arrested.

Within yourself you felt resentful about having to suffer the war, but you could only talk to the family – but sometimes you couldn't even trust them. There were no squeakers in my family, but there were occasions when children reported their parents. The drive to recruit young people was towards the end of the war. I was involved in that. I learned to shoot – after the war I could go to the fairground and win prizes – and I taught my children to shoot with air rifles. But I never fired a shot in anger.

The difference between our two countries was not hate. You see, the British always classed the army as the Nazi Army – but we looked on the Nazi Army as the SS. Even the Germans were afraid of them. The *Wehrmacht* was just the same as your army – conscripted people. You would hear old soldiers after the war saying that the SS stood behind them and pushed them into the front line. Officers had been shot for disobeying orders from the SS. You nursed the myth that all Germans were bad – but we didn't want the war. I didn't want to lose my friends. My school was bombed – in my street there were 144 houses, and after the war there were just three shells left.

I had no hate, even in those days, and I have none now. We knew that someone had been given a job to do, and they were doing it. The Americans came over during the day at the sort of height that you see aeroplanes flying over now. They always did carpet bombing – never target bombing. In the winter you would see a great vapour trail – then you knew there was a load coming towards you. If you heard something whistling while they were coming towards you, you ducked – if they were passing you, you knew you were safe. The RAF tried to hit the target, but in our street there were just the three houses left standing. Two streets further down it was the barracks, but it was our street which was obliterated. We all said we thought it was the bomb-aimer's fault. It's an easy mistake, at night in a wind. We put it down as a mistake.

When you came out after a raid, the first thing you did was make sure who was underneath, and you counted your friends – so and so had not come out – they must be under the rubble. The soldiers in the barracks came and helped – an elephant from the zoo came and helped – and the zoo was bombed too. Police, air-raid wardens, army, civilians, anybody who could possibly help, helped. If a dog heard a knocking, you'd dig until you found where that knocking was coming from. Quite a few got killed, but you tried to get out as many as you possibly could."

Michal Leszkiewicz, a Polish pilot, escaped with his aircraft from Poland, went to Romania and was a POW before finally reaching Britain, where he completed two full bombing tours with 300 Polish Squadron.

"First of all, we'd usually have about 15 operational aircraft in one squadron, but after operations you came back absolutely riddled with bullets. Goodness gracious – I was terrified of moonlight because of the German fighters. At first they were not night operational, but eventually they picked up night flying skills and got quite good. They could spot you – and they were so much faster. We had only about 210 knots – they had about 400 and could outmanoeuvre you. We would try to go as high as 20,000 feet, but when you lost your height, you went down into searchlights and anti-aircraft fire. You had to throw your aircraft this way and that and dive.

I started my operation flying in 1941 and finished in 1943 after 53 missions. I had such adrenalin while I was up there, so after the first tour of 30 missions and the second of 20, they let me do another two trips. A squadron leader debriefing us at headquarters was very impressed with my knowledge and asked me, 'How many sorties have you done?' I told him 52, and he said, 'That's impossible'. I was a warrant officer – not even commissioned.

Coming back from a mission there was this wonderful elation – 'I've done it' – and that's when the danger came, you cannot help but relax. You were tensed up going over the target, then you'd done it and you relaxed – and by Jove, that was the danger.

I had a nervous breakdown when I went out of the squadron. I lived with no tomorrow. I watched all these people disappearing – my friends. You thought to yourself, 'You may be lucky to make another trip, but your time must come'. So you were not quite yourself – it was as if you were on drugs. I didn't sleep at all. When you finished, you went to bed and you lived though it all again in your mind. I never felt I was killing people – all Germans were sworn enemies of the Poles. They started it all, and it was so unnecessary.

On 1 September [1939] we just heard that this airfield was bombed and so on. We couldn't believe it – it was without warning or a declaration of war. They jumped on us like an animal in the jungle which you don't see and which lands on you. All this is with me deep down, it is my personality. I want to run away from it because it completely ruined my life. I am a war casualty. The things which happen to me at night. I lived so much, it had ruined me, squeezed me out – drained every bit of juice out of me."

Flight-Lieutenant Frederick Saunders, at the time a Flying Officer, was with 627 Pathfinder Squadron, flying Mosquitoes on vital missions to locate and mark targets for bombers. He describes the form of operations.

"When our briefing was over, the duty aircrews would know their specific role, who was to wind-find and who was to mark, and so on, and what the target was to be. Later in the morning, the duty air crews would assemble in the operations room, and there learn of the specific routes we were to take, code call signs, radio frequencies and timing of the events that comprised the operation.

The route out for us would be different from the main force and the pattern would also be different. For instance, neither we nor the main force would fly the direct route to the target. A number of 'dog legs' would be flown to keep the enemy guessing.

Of particular interest would be our final run-in route at low level, on which would be marked various prominent land marks, like a particular chimney stack, stretch of water, railway line, church tower etc. Often, there would be blown-up photographs of these taken from reconnaissance aircraft at the heights we would be flying at.

We would not be able to make notes of these, but they had to be committed to memory, and you could visit the ops room any number of times from now until the final briefing time to refresh your memory. At the final briefing, all the latest information would be given, like where to expect opposition, and in what form, and so on. Times of take-offs, what petrol load, what colours of TIs (Target Indicators) and dozens of other important details.

When the final briefing was over, the next main event would be the 'Op supper'. For some aircrews it would be their last supper. The op supper never varied – it was always egg and chips. The medics said it was a substantial enough meal for a tensed up stomach to absorb, yet not too substantial that a fluttering stomach would reject it. Bomber Command fought its war on egg and chips, and I truly believe, somewhere in our battle honours, there should be a reference to the chicken and the egg.

Very often we would witness the forming up and departure of anything up to 800 heavy bombers in the Lincolnshire skies. Then we would take off and fly our devious routes, overtake the main bombers and reach the target 12 minutes before the first bomber was due to arrive.

Simultaneous with our low-level arrival in our Mossies, would be a number of high-flying Lancs and/or Halifaxes (Halibags) also of the PFF (Pathfinder Force) Group. Their purpose was to release 'candles'. These were highpowered flares, descending on parachutes, which burned for about five or six minutes. The purpose of this was to illuminate the countryside and to keep it illuminated until we, the low-fliers, could sight and properly mark the target.

This part of the operation would be controlled by the Master Bomber watching the progress. When he was satisfied with the marking, he would call both us and the high-flying Lancs/Bags off away home."

SICILY

Rugged Test

In July 1943, Axis forces found themselves defending their own territory for the first time as Allied troops, fresh from victory in Africa, landed on the Italian island of Sicily. Fighting in the shadow of Mount Etna, the US infantry of General George Patton won the race to Messina, next to the mainland, as the Germans evacuated and Mussolini was ousted and subsequently arrested

Sergeant Joe Hardy had returned from Dunkirk then trained for a mountain campaign in Norway – only to be told that he was to retrain for airborne work. After training, victory in the desert seemed secure, so his first mission was to Sicily as Acting Lance Corporal, 1st Bn, Border Regiment, 1st Airlanding Brigade.

"After training, Sicily was our first major mission. Getting into the glider, I dropped my torch just inside the door. It went straight though the canvas and on to the ground below – I remember thinking that if all the Italian Army is laying on a reception committee, I will still be very glad to get back on to the ground.

As we approached Syracuse, it seemed that all the Italian Army was trying to blast us out of the sky. The slow curve the tracer formed as it came up was almost nice to watch – but the speed at which it flew past the window was apt to make one wish the flying part of the affair was over. We were supposed to land a few hundred yards in from the sea, but most of us found that we were gliding some long time before we should have been. The moment that a glider releases the tow-rope, it must necessarily head downward. Whether my glider pilot hit the release switch or whether it was the tug aircraft that cast us off, I shall never know. The tugs naturally wanted to get away from that flak as quickly as possible. It was decidedly unhealthy. Who was to blame, I do not know – I do know that the 1st Airlanding Brigade lost a terrible amount of its men through drowning.

My glider hit the water about 200 yards from the shoreline, the complete fuselage sank below water level, but the wings kept the framework from sinking altogether. My seat was near the door at the rear, and a split second found me completely in the drink. The tail end was completely submerged. An air-lock in the part of the fuselage connected to the wings left just enough room for most of the men to get a gulp of air. I managed to get the door open somehow, managed to get my fingers round the steel on the upper side of the fuselage, release my equipment and pull myself out.

I immediately heard the voices of those trapped in the forward part of the fuselage, so I kicked my way along the top, tearing the canvas with each kick. Two or three heads popped out, then the men started to tear at the canvas from the inside. To crash in the drink in the very early morning, black dark, is not a nice experience. If we ducked, there was a fair chance of getting drowned. If we didn't, there was a very fair chance of getting shot.

It was a fairly long swim to the shore, so I asked for volunteers to swim in with the object of trying to do something about the machine guns. I was wearing a brand new pair of boots at the time, so I took them off, tied the laces together and hung them round my neck, dumped all my gear except my revolver, and three of us slid quietly into the water. (In fact I lost the boots in the water.) To swim in the Mediterranean in the dark is an unbelievable experience. The phosphorus in the water is so concentrated that the arm movements caused what to us seemed like a million lights with each stroke.

When we made it to the shore, we found ourselves at the foot of a perpendicular cliff that was impossible to climb in the dark. When it became light enough for us to scale the cliff, up we went, looking absolutely ridiculous. On arrival at the top we ran straight into three Italian machine-gunners. They were so surprised to see us appear a few yards in front of them, that they just couldn't decide what was best to do. I shouted in my very best mixture of obscene English, French and Italian, that *'La guerra finito. Mussolini kaput!'* They were very willing to agree to that suggestion, so I immediately relieved one of them of his boots and then demanded that the rest of them should show us how to use their weapons. We took the weapons, explained to them that they were prisoners, to stay exactly where they were and they would come to no further harm. As to whom they

Troops of the Royal Marines hurry through ruins in war-torn Sicily

were the prisoners of – they were perfectly happy with the *guerra finito* story, so that was good enough.

By this time, the CO had joined us and he suggested to me that he must get to where the regiment was supposed to be, to get command of whatever troops were available, so he and I set off. As the pair of us had to go through perhaps a mile and half of what we presumed was enemy-held territory, I thought that his idea was extremely unfunny, but one does not argue with one's CO. Off we went. Progressing down a hillside, I looked over a wall on the lower side of the land and found myself looking directly into a quarry in

British airborne troops train for a night-drop

which there were something like 80 people, about 20 of them female. The remainder of them were Italian soldiers, all fully armed. I gave them the *guerra finito* business, and was then left with no other option but to go further down the lane, turn into the quarry, and walk up to the soldiers as though I was leading a thousand men, and explain that Mussolini was *kaput*.

I then got hold of one of the soldiers, made him lean his rifle against a very large rock, raise another rock above his head, and throw it down on to the rifle. The ladies and soldiers began to cheer. As soon as it seemed to me that they had accepted the idea of destroying everything, I turned to walk out of the quarry. For the 20 or so paces that I had to take to get into the lane, I felt that my back was at least four yards wide, and that it was due to get an Italian bullet at any second. I was terribly pleased to get to the corner."

Fred Jordan was serving as a medic with the 217 Field Ambulance, attached to the Royal West Kent regiment and was involved in action at Bronte in Sicily.

"We landed in Sicily in July 1943, arriving by boat from Algiers. It was a quiet landing with no opposition. We marched up towards Mount Etna, where the terrain was very hilly. The Germans were already there, dug into the hillsides. We had a lot of casualties because the Germans, being higher up than us, had the advantage, and our men had no protection. Their mortars were deadly accurate, and they were just hailing down on to the infantry.

We were attached to the infantry, so that wherever they went, we went with them. On Sicily we were doing the attacking, so the infantry would go in first, and then we would follow up behind and pick up the men as they got wounded. We would evacuate them on stretchers to the next post down.

Out of all my experiences on Sicily, the incident I remember most vividly happened in a town called Bronte, which had been badly shelled by the Germans. They were mortaring the town and casualties were occurring. We moved up into a railway tunnel where the civilians were taking refuge.

Our Corporal was called Bill Lea – a very good man, very well liked. He said to us, 'You stay here and I'll just go up a wee bit and see what's happening.' He went up and there was an almighty bang. We ran out, and he'd been hit. We picked him up on a stretcher and managed to get him back to the ambulance.

After the Germans had moved out, we went to the hospital that he was in and asked for him. They said, 'He's there'. There was a blanket covering him! By all accounts, the blast from the mortar bomb had burst his lungs. When you get a blast, it doesn't blow in, it sucks out, and he'd simply died.

The sad thing was that a chap that was with us was a big friend of Bill Lea. Whoever had covered the Corporal up had left his feet outside. It's a simple little thing, but when you cover a body up with a blanket, all parts of the body should be concealed. This poor chap went absolutely beserk – almost hysterical – when this happened."

THE FALL OF ITALY

War on the Rocks

From Sicily, the Allies moved on to the Italian mainland, landing at Reggio, Taranto and Salerno in September 1943. Meanwhile, the Italians had lost heart and surrendered, leaving the defence of the peninsula to the Germans. But the Allies' planned advance on Rome still took months of bitter fighting amid the inhospitable landscape of southern Italy

William Ernest Wright, a private with the Royal Irish Fusiliers, landed in Taranto from Sicily. His platoon marched to Bari, then went to Termoli by landing craft – an awesome experience.

"I was the commanding officer's company runner, carrying messages. The life expectancy of a runner was six weeks, though I didn't know that at the time. If a message had to be got from here to there, and the area between was being swept by machine-gun fire, you still had to go. Most messages would be verbal, but sometimes they were written – and sometimes they were people.

In Sicily I once marched a German major with a lump of his brain hanging off for three miles, to take him to the Intelligence Officer. He never got there – he died on the way. I had to ask for a receipt for the body – I couldn't just go back to my company commander and say the prisoner had died on the way – he would only have thought that I had taken the German around the corner and killed him for an easy afternoon.

The landings at Taranto were quite peaceful. All the gay Italian matelots came out and waved at us. This was something really new to us. They asked us if we were looking for boyfriends. This young matelot came up to me and asked if he could buy me a drink. I had been through all that fighting and yet that young boy had really frightened me!

We were at Taranto very briefly. We more or less marched up to Bari with troop carriers, lorries, everything. Then we hopped two landing barges up to Termoli. They were Yankee craft and, although they were good, they had been thrown together.

We got on board these troop landing craft. They were launched sideways – like tins. The crossing took a matter of hours, from dusk to dawn.

It was a terrible experience. Some of the things I remember are best forgotten really. We came under fire and these blinking landing craft were like tins. The caps were coming through the sides and killing people and those on the outside were being blown apart. You couldn't get out because they had locked the hatches on us – they didn't want a load of panicky soldiers on deck. What went on in that landing craft, I'm ashamed to think of. People were fighting with each other to get out and treading on top of each other. You can imagine being under fire in the dark, in the middle of the sea, and they won't let you out – it was like the end of the world.

Once we landed at Termoli, the commandos had already got a foothold. We were only there for 48 hours, but it was very bloody. It was the big breakthrough for the north."

Sergeant George Rhodes, 277 Battery, 70th Field Regiment, Royal Artillery, 46th Infantry Division and his gun crew had landed in Italy and were ready for action on D-Day Plus One – 10 September 1943.

"That night, hordes of giant mosquitoes decended on us in the orchard. They settled everywhere, on the dead bodies, excreta – and on our biscuits. They even ate the cream we had rubbed on our arms, legs and faces to keep the blighters away.

Dozens of men were, by now, incapacitated by violent diarrhoea, because, during the day they had been eating fruit from the trees and bushes. I had taken my mepacrine tablets in the usual way.
As I cannot swallow tablets, I used to eat them like sweets or pop them in my tea.

That night, General McCreery reported to Clark that, even though we in the X Corps had not taken all the objectives, we had established a bridgehead and were holding firm. The Yanks, on the other hand,

Soldiers and vehicles come ashore from their landing ship at Salerno

farther south, wanted to go back to North Africa. Once again, the British had to face the blunt end of the German might. As soon as Jerry fired a few shells at them, the Yanks wanted to be taken back to England. (We had by now no confidence in either the Yanks or their officers, so we had the tendency to carry on the fight without them.)

On my side, we had by now dug our slit trenches on the shore side of the trees to give us extra protection from the shells which kept coming over all that night. I had told my men to get some shut-eye if they could, and to put their tin hats over their faces for protection from the shrapnel and the bullets from the *Schmeisser* machine guns. The Durham Light Infantry had moved to a position just in front of us, so we left it to them to protect us for the night so that we would be fresh for the dawn offensive.

I sat there under the tree and brewed up again. As I sat there, with my gun resting on my knees, my thoughts turned to home and the Pennines that I had often walked and cycled, and to the odd girlfriend or two.

Everyone was agreeing that the Yanks should never have been allowed to be in charge of this invasion. Even the big-wigs were having second thoughts. Major-General J F C Fuller said, 'The war in Italy was strategically the most useless campaign in the whole war. It prolonged the war, wrecked Italy and wasted thousands of American and British lives'. Even Field Marshal Alexander asked, 'Who is containing whom?' Another factor of this brilliant cock-up was that Eisenhower kept us short of landing craft and, indeed, wanted back those that we already had.

At six o'clock in the morning, Number Ones were called to the Command Post, where Captain Haslam briefed us on the plan of attack for D-Day Plus One. We Number Ones had map cases which we slung round our necks. Inside the case we had Chinagraph pencils so we could draw both ours and the German positions.

Our object was to advance and drive Jerry off Hospital Hill and hold for the Durhams to come through – but Jerry had other ideas. He had orders to push us into the sea – and he nearly succeeded. We had to call on the navy for quick and accurate gunfire. They were simply marvellous. They broke up the German tank attacks and silenced the German gun batteries. We couldn't praise the navy enough – they were the tops.

Over on our right, the 9th Battalion of the Royal Fusiliers were having a hard time trying to capture the tobacco factory at Battipaglia. The 3rd Battalion Coldstream Guards, the 201st Guards Brigade, plus the Grenadiers and the Scots Guards, were on the other side of the factory. They had been shelled all during the night, and when Tiger and Mark IV tanks advanced on their positions, they found themselves in the same situation as us, with nothing to stop the tanks with except a few 6-pounder anti-tank guns, whose shells bounced off the Tiger tank like peas off a brick wall.

The widespread Italian hatred of the war ensures that Allied troops are welcome

Lieutenant-Colonel Ted Hillersden was wounded in the chest. A shell dressing was applied and he was given a jab of morphia. A letter M was marked on his forehead and he was left there in the hope that he would be rescued. Major John Van Gelder and Major Sandford and their Fusiliers had to surrender. They were marched off by the German Infantry into captivity. I am sorry to say that the morale of the Grenadiers and the Fusiliers had been so shattered, they started to panic under the intense bombardment by the Germans. They tried to go back to the beach, just like the Yanks."

KURSK

Beginning of the End

As the Germans retreated, pursued by the Red Army, they attempted a last-ditch attempt to encircle the Soviets. In the heart of the Russian steppes, ideal for armoured divisions, the forces met around the town of Kursk in July 1943. Some 1,500 vehicles closed in one of the largest tank battles ever fought – victory went with the tide of the war, to the Russians

Sergeant Grigorii Sgibnev had started his career in 1941 with the Pacific Fleet, but in July 1943 was a platoon commander in the Russian 44th Guards Infantry Division. He recalls the fighting at Izyum, an action for which he received the Hero of the Soviet Union award.

"At first everything went well. After an hour's artillery preparation when, it seemed, not a single survivable place remained of the fascist positions, we dashed into the attack. So long as we were running among the trees and bushes, the Hitlerites remained quiet, but as soon as we appeared in the open in front of the of the fascist positions, their trenches became alive. Machine guns and automatics rattled out. Grenades also flew to meet us – one of them spun around beneath my feet.

Everyone who has been in battle knows the feeling, when it seems that one is in the space between life and death, a space, so the saying goes, that would be too narrow for a mouse to jump. One acts automatically, half consciously. I also, quite instinctively, seized this grenade without thinking and hurled it back towards the enemy trenches. It exploded as it reached them. 'Smash them with their own grenades!' I shouted.

All this happened about 20 metres from the enemy defence line.

It was too close for us to get artillery or mortar support, but the fascists could not use that kind of support either, without risking being caught up in it. A grenade battle flared up. Moving towards their trench, we bombarded it with the same grenades that the fascists hurled at us.

Having overcome the first defence line, we moved on to the second trench on the village outskirts. We had to take this by storm also – and once again we threw back the enemy's own grenades.

I can remember that I had managed to pull off the firing ring of one of my own grenades and was preparing to throw it, when a German grenade fell at my feet. I seized it with my left hand, and it exploded ... From hospital I went home. My father met me and said, 'You've come back alive, that's the main thing.'"

Georg Berg was First Ordinance Officer from the SS General Command with the division Das Reich. Almost surrounded at Kharkov, they were ordered to hold the town, but commanding general Paul Hausser decided to withdraw – an initiative which proved successful.

"The decision to disobey an order from the *Führer* was a rare occurence and in this case testifies to the civil courage of one of the most important commanders of the Waffen-SS.

The SS Panzer Corps with the Divisions *Leibstandarte* and *Das Reich* was virtually encircled in Kharkov. Awaiting it was the same fate as befell the Sixth Army in Stalingrad – unless, at the eleventh hour, an order to withdraw and evacuate the town was issued.

On 13 February Russian tank units broke through to the outskirts of Kharkov – only the arterial road to the south west, direction Poltava, could be kept clear. As First Ordinance Officer of the SS General Command, I experienced those fateful hours before the break-out from Kharkov, and witnessed first-hand how Hausser was thrown into a terrible crisis of conscience by a senseless order from the *Führer*.

The order from the *Führer* of 13 February was curt and simple, 'Kharkov is to be held'. In a situation report to the Army Section Lanz, Hausser requested permission to evacuate the town, which was rejected, citing the order from the *Führer*. Following a number of telephone conversations with the High Commander of the Army, General Lanz, Hausser was permitted to speak personally.

I passed this conversation on in the evening of 13 February. Hausser, unfortunately, had been unable to get Manstein's consent, on the grounds that we were dealing with an explicit order from the *Führer*. However, Field Marshal von Manstein empowered Hausser to seek direct contact with the *Führer's* HQ, in order to give his own explanation of how precarious the situation was. I succeeded in relaying this conversation to the *Wolfsschanze* (*Führer* HQ near Rastenburg), and the Chief of General Staff of the Army, General Zeitzler, promised Hausser that he would persuade the *Führer* to change the order during the *Lagebesprechung* (situation meeting) at 0200 the next morning.

In the meantime, on 14 February, the orders to the Divisions *Liebstandarte* and *Das Reich*, instructing them to withdraw from Kharkov, had long since been written up, and the Ordinance Officers of the Divisions were waiting impatiently for the orders to be distributed.

In the late afternoon of 14 February, Paul Hausser came out of the cramped farmhouse into the shivering cold and paced up and down in silence. Turning, he said calmly, 'Give out the orders to the divisions to withdraw'. I held my breath then said, '*Obergruppenführer*, the order from the *Führer* states quite clearly ...' Paul Hausser interrupted me, 'An old man like me is no loss, but I can't do this to the young boys out there. Give out the Corps order.'"

Olga Rybakov was a housewife in Leningrad as, under German siege, the city ran inexorably out of food and necessary supplies. With nothing to sell, shops disappeared – the blockade left the city to face a winter of terrible hunger, cold and, eventually, starvation and death.

"The most terrible time was in December, because before, I think till August, we had commercial shops, so we could buy something. We could even buy caviar, but then the commercial shops were closed. The blockade began. And in September/October it was passable, although already in October a great friend of my mother's died. It was the first death that we heard of and in November it began to be cold and the rations were short – and were shortened.

In time there got to be less and less food. November, December and January were most tragic times. Firstly it was cold – minus 40 degrees – then the famine and hunger began to be felt and people began to starve and die from the cold. Undernourishment and cold had their effects but the most deaths came at the end of February and March. Then, always when I went to find food, or when I went to the shops to receive the rations for my family and some friends living in our house I found I had to pass dead bodies – and then, on my way back, some more.

We would manage to live on these small rations only because we were rather organised people. We got them in, we put the bread in three little slices for morning, dinner and evening. Then we had something to make our rations a little more abundant – we had some gruel and preserves that were stored before the war. We had wood enough and we were warm so we could cook our meals. For the child I had milk and gruel from the district milk kitchen. Instead of white bread, which my child would not eat, I received biscuits. I think the most effective thing was that we were rather optimistic people. My mother and I met four people that were in a dreadful state and these people couldn't survive. And as I was very occupied and busy with all my duties in the house and in the family, I had no time to be ill. My mother was ill and all the time I was dealing with a family of five.

The force that kept us alive was our wish to live and to see the happy end – to see the victory and to see the punishment of the fascist regime. Another force that kept us alive was mutual help. We helped each other – and did for the old and disabled all that we could, bringing them water and rations."

Herbert Brunnegger, with the SS-Totenkopf (Death's Head) Division, moved from France to fight on the Eastern Front. In the summer of 1942, having suffered heavy losses in the Demyansk pocket, they were now being topped up with raw recruits from all over the Reich who had little hope of survival.

"During May and June 1942 our units were being topped up with young ethnic Germans and reservists from the *Reich*. Training in the rejuvenated units took place in areas close to the battlefields and under very realistic conditions.

Up until the end of July we had light security duties and in the following months we were thrust straight back into heavy fighting. I was given one of the young recruits as a dispatch rider to assist me with my duties. He was called Hugo Schrock and came from

Timosoara (Romania). What he told me sounded almost criminal. One of his stories went like this: 'With many of the young lads from the village I was invited to a sports event in the neighbouring town. After this finished we were given a lecture about the brave struggle of the German *Wehrmacht*. We were told that we should all think deeply about this and that it was our duty to protect the German homeland from the *Untermenschen* (subhumans) from the East. Without more ado, we were then declared volunteers for the war effort, and without even being able to go home first, were transported off and assigned to the Waffen-SS or the *Werhrmacht*.' I thought I'd misheard him at first and asked him to repeat the story.

So these were our 'volunteers'. But in spite of all this, they were magnificent lads, very determined to do their duty. But, they would soon find out that they had the raw deal, the 'lucky ones' who had been put into the *Wehrmacht*.

On 13 July we went into battle again south of Demyansk, before being deployed a few days later as a 'fire-brigade' in a nearby area, where the Russians were trying to break through the pocket. On 17 July we came under a colossal barrage from heavy enemy guns.

Under the hurricane of fire from the Russian rockets and artillery, most of our battlestations bedded in the swamp were blasted to pieces. Our young lads' baptism of fire was horrific. Their limbs were crushed and they suffocated under the splattered bunker covers. The branches of the birch and alder trees, which had recently sprouted new leaves, were hung with human insides. We could hear the cries of the dying young soldiers all over the battlefield, and this drove even many of the 'veterans' to lose their wits. For days on end, the Russians pounded us with shells, pummelling us literally into the foul, stinking swamp.

After this terrible waste of human life on both sides, there was a brief respite. We then got down to building new bunkers."

TARAWA

Island Graveyard

Since the attack on Pearl Harbor, Japanese control in the Pacific had widened considerably, challenging the United States to reclaim lost territories. By late 1943, the Allies were on a dual drive across the ocean, their ultimate aim Japan itself. But the tiny islands of the Pacific would witness remarkable carnage as their Japanese defenders fought to the end, under the blistering sun.

Carl J Moore, later to become Rear Admiral, was Chief of Staff to Admiral Raymond Spruance during the campaign in the Gilbert, Marshall and Mariana islands. His view of the Tarawa assault was from aboard the cruiser Indianapolis. From this vantage point he observed the bombardment – but later landed on Tarawa.

"The particular job of the *Indianapolis* was to bombard suspected gun emplacements and ammunition dumps on the east side of Tarawa Atoll, while the rest of Harry Hill's outfit bombarded Betio, at the south end of the atoll, and while the troops disembarked from the transports. We made a run the length of Tarawa's west side and along the south coast, firing at lookout towers in the beautiful palm groves and at Japanese barges. We started a few fires, one of which burned for a couple of days.

By the time we reached Betio it looked like a shambles. It had been bombarded and bombed for two hours. Fires were burning everywhere. The coconut trees were all blasted. It seemed that no living soul could be on the island. Then we joined with Hill's ships in the bombardment of Tarawa and the troops approached the beach. It looked like the whole affair would be a walkover.

We saw the first wave reach the beach. Then we saw the next two or three waves get stuck on the edge of the reef that fringed the island. We saw the troops disembark and advance for about 400 yards in water that was waist-deep. It was in this phase that we had our greatest losses, for with all our bombardment, the Japs had not been routed out of their beach pillboxes. For the next 24 hours they made it hell for our Marines.

The destroyers remained in close support and the big ships continued to bombard all the next day. Finally, by ingenuity and by taking advantage of the breaks, the Marines managed to beat down the opposition on the main beaches and to land on a couple of others. By the night of the second day we felt pretty secure. The fighting continued hard, however, for a few days longer. It must have been awful tough on the men ashore and those in the boats waiting to get ashore. We couldn't see much from the flagship except the raging fires, the shells and bombs falling, and the destroyers and small boats manoeuvring about the harbour. We had to keep moving because of the threat of submarines. But the destroyers did a fine job and good luck kept us all safe from the enemy subs. Through it all we on the flagship kept in pretty close touch with what was going on and had a general picture of the situation.

One week after the first assault, our flagship entered the lagoon at Tarawa. Raymond went ashore to meet Nimitz and his party, who had come out from Pearl Harbor. Raymond got separated from them and didn't find out the things I had hoped he would. I went ashore for an hour that afternoon but had to hurry back because Raymond and I couldn't both be away for long.

The place was swarming with Marines. I had never known that men could look like they did – dirty, burned, ragged, hot, a week's growth of beard, tired, hungry, thirsty. They were about as fine a lot of men as I ever have seen. What they had been through that week! I have never seen such a shambles – coconut logs everywhere, sheet iron, guns, ammunition, smashed tanks, equipment, shot-up cars, bicycles, carts. In fact, everything that goes with war was scattered all over – pillboxes, tanks, traps, slit trenches dug up through concrete strongpoints in such numbers they couldn't be counted. Some were smashed to smithereens. Others, still good, had contained live Japs the day before.

When I was ashore that day, all the dead Marines had been properly buried and most of the dead Japs had been thrown into bomb craters and bulldozed over. There were many Japs lying about in an advanced stage of decomposition. I contented myself with smelling them and avoided any closer examination. Some of the strongpoints were still full of hundreds of them. No-one knew it was so thoroughly defended."

Lieutenant-Commander Donald J Ramsey, Captain of the destroyer Hughes, was at hand with his ship when US 'jeep' carrier Liscombe Bay was sunk by torpedoes from the Japanese submarine I-175 off Makin Island at 5.13 am on 24 November 1943. He rescued some survivors – but 712 men perished.

"Apparently bombs, torpedoes, gasoline and ammunition all went up together. The whole ship was enveloped in flames so rapidly that damage control and fire fighting appeared to be out of the question. The personnel who did manage to escape were all very badly shaken up and some of them had suffered bad burns, broken limbs and shock.

Nearly every man aboard had some bruises and cuts. One man died while the medical officer was administering blood plasma – another died in the water before being picked up by the motor whaleboat. This ship has rescued survivors from the old *Lexington*, the old *Yorktown* and the old *Hornet*, but it was unanimously agreed that the sinking of the *Liscombe Bay* and the condition of the comparatively few survivors constituted the most heart-rending disaster yet.

Inspiring is no word for the conduct displayed by the men picked up in the water, and the absolute courage of these men was electrifying. One man, who had been operated on for appendicitis just two days before not only scrambled up the life net without assistance, but on arriving on deck, asked if there was not a rubber boat handy for him to take out and assist others whom he knew needed help.

It was a common comment on this ship that though the personnel losses were horrible enough as it was, it was a miracle that anyone managed to escape the inferno."

The same scene of destruction seen from the comparative safety of the battleship New Mexico, which lay 1,500 yards off the carrier's starboard quarter, was described by a young lieutenant as follows in his combat report.

Marines advance on Red Beach to Burns Phillips Pier, Tarawa, November 1943

"A few seconds after the first explosion, a second explosion which appeared to come from inside the *Liscombe Bay* burst upwards, burning fragments and clearly discernible planes, 200 feet or more in the air. The entire ship seemed to explode, and almost at the same instant, her interior, except the extreme bow and stern sections, glowed with flames like a furnace.

The ship was showered from forecastle to quarter-deck with oil particles and burning and extinguished fragments. The whole central section of her starboard hull seemed to be blown out and she immediately took on a heavy list to starboard. About a one-hundred-foot section of her flight-deck had blown clear of of the ship. One of her Helldiver aircraft, already ablaze, was also blown clear of the ship and in turn set on fire the floating oil fuel that had leaked from her shattered hull. The floating flames spread over a wide area, making rescue attempts of the survivors in the water a difficult business."

Lieutenant-Commander Ed Owen, senior officer of VF5 (known as Fighting Five) from the US carrier Yorktown II, and his team took off in Hellcats as they were jumped by 18 Japanese Zeros, 4 December 1943.

"This was a first-line team, and they knew what they were doing. Six Zeros positioned themselves on each of our two-plane sections, with two of their planes always firing on each section. When we headed for them, they would make a violent pull-out and climb at a 60 degree angle. Then the next two would come at us.

We pulled into the standard protective 'thatch weave' formation, with each of our sections swinging back and forth to protect the other. It was a case of hit them with all you had, reverse, and do the same again. We were giving them everything we had with no quarter asked on either side. There wasn't time to see what happened to the Japs we hit. I would have given ten years of my life for another gun (I had only one operating and my sight was out of commission), and for 5,000 more feet of altitude.

This continued for several minutes until one of the Jap bastards set Si Satterfield's plane on fire, shooting him on the outside of his weave. Both his wing tanks were burning, with flames reaching half way down the fuselage, apparently out of control. Why they didn't get us all down is more than I can figure out. Maybe they would have if they had been better gunners."

FLYING FORTRESSES

Watching the Bombs Fall

The USAAF braved the flak from February 1942 to bomb Germany's industrial cities and exact revenge for the Blitz on Britain, convinced of the effectiveness of precision daylight raids. American losses were massive, particularly over Schweinfurt, where nearly half of the country's output of ball-bearings, crucial to all rotating machinery, are produced. And civilians suffered utter chaos

Pilot Officer Tony Bird DFC, of 61 Squadron, had survived several narrow squeaks when, on 2 December 1943, after he and his crew had completed their sixth operation to Berlin, British Movietone News visited the squadron and provided his mother with a glimpse of her son at war.

"Close friends were made and lost in so short a time – and by the end of the war, over 2,000 aircrew were to die in operations over Germany from the two squadrons based together at the airfield.

As was the custom, as a newly arrived pilot, I was sent on an operation with an experienced pilot and crew, so that on this occasion there were eight of us in the aircraft instead of the usual seven. The target was Berlin, which I was soon to get to know rather well, if only from the air.

The thing to worry about was from shells about to burst in the vicinity – but there was no way of knowing of them until too late. We were fortunate, however, and were able to avoid the dreaded searchlight fingers probing the sky, our only damage being slight peppering from the shrapnel of shells that had burst some distance from us. We arrived back at base for debriefing and the usual breakfast, having been in the air for almost eight hours. Conversation rarely strayed from details of our flight. In common with other returning crews, we had witnessed several of our aircraft going down in flames – a sad and frightening sight, visible for several miles on a clear night. We did not see any escapes by parachute, but it was no easy matter to exit a diving burning bomber.

I remember in my pilot's log book 23 August 1943 as the date of my first operation to Berlin, and on 27 August, I was ready to carry out my first operation over Germany as Captain with my own crew. The target was Nuremberg and the bomb-load 9,100 lb or about 4,116 kg. On a short flight, the Lancaster could carry well over 5,000 kgs of bombs, but the longer the journey, the more fuel was needed, and consequently less bomb-load to avoid exceeding the safe permitted level. Our operation to Nuremberg was completed safely.

On 3 September, a groan went up from the assembled aircrew at operational briefing. The target was Berlin – known to us as 'the Big City'. Not only was the Berlin trip a long and arduous eight hours' flight, but we were over the most heavily defended area of Germany for longer than on almost any other target. The worst part of the operation was the need to fly the aircraft straight and level on the bombing run to enable the bomb-aimer to take accurate aim at the target, and then to continue on until the automatic camera had recorded the bombs exploding on target. During all this time it was not possible to change heading or to weave so as to avoid attack from any enemy fighters or flak.

B-17 planes on their way to Stuttgart for what will be a seven hour raid, 1943

The Germans had started to use barely visible ultraviolet master searchlights, which were used in conjunction with a number of 'slave' normal white searchlights. Within a second or two of an ultraviolet beam shining on one of our bombers, all the white lights in the area would converge on to the unfortunate aircraft, forming a dazzling searchlight cone, several hundred yards wide from which it would be impossible to escape. The bomber pilot and crew would be dazzled and quite unable to see attacking German fighters coming in from the surrounding darkness.

Just as we released our bombs over the target, we found ourselves caught in a searchlight cone but in spite of that we still had to continue flying straight and level until the camera had taken the vital photograph of our bombs exploding on the target. There was great rivalry amongst bomber crews to bring back a clear picture proving that they had hit the target accurately. The photographs were enlarged and posted up for all to see, and any crew whose picture was off target was the subject of some derision.

It seemed like hours instead of seconds during which I had to maintain a straight and level heading while flak shells were bursting all around us in a proximity much too close for comfort. Suddenly the flak in our immediate area ceased, and almost as the camera shutter opened to take the picture, the fighters attacked. I was now able to take avoiding action and put the Lancaster into a steep dive on full throttle. With the four Rolls Royce Merlin engines on maximum power and with the help of gravity, the airspeed quickly exceeded 300 mph – twice our normal cruising speed – but still far less than the fighters were capable of.

We felt and heard the thud of the fighters' cannon shells hitting our aircraft as I twisted and turned, first one way then another, to make it difficult for the fixed-gun fighters to aim accurately. We knew, then, why the flak had stopped so suddenly. It was a signal for the fighters to attack. The searchlight fingers were, by now, pointing almost horizontally in their effort to keep us illuminated – and suddenly we were in blessed darkness.

The port outer engine, which had been hit by the fighters' cannon shells, was now useless, and we had dived over 5,000 feet below our normal operational height. Our navigator hurriedly worked out a revised flight plan for the return journey while I trimmed the aircraft to fly on three engines due to the damage. There were no further sightings of the fighters, who had probably returned to the main bomber stream above. Due to the limited time that they could stay airborne, the single-engine fighters were reluctant to lose too much height for fear that they would not have sufficient fuel to climb back up again.

We were an hour late in arriving back, limping along at 115 mph on three engines, and had been given up for lost by our ground crew. They were still waiting up as usual to welcome us back. 'We thought we would wait up in case you made it,' one of them said laconically – but the joy of relief on their faces needed no words. We had made it back. The air battle over Berlin was starting in earnest and we were destined to complete six bombing missions to 'the Big City'.

In December 1943, we completed our sixth operation to Berlin and British Movietone News visited the squadron to interview us and make a short movie film. This was shown throughout the country and was seen by my mother at a Croydon cinema. In her amazement and excitement, she jumped up and cried, 'That's my Tony,' no doubt to the surprise of the surrounding audience."

Lt.-Colonel Jim Goodson was on board the Athenia on the first night of the war when she was sunk by a German attack. Outraged, he resolved to join the RAF and flew during the Battle of Britain. Leading 133 Eagle Squadron which transferred to the 4th Fighter Group of the USAAF, based at Debden, it was as fighter escort to the daylight bombers that Goodson acquired a unique insight into the bombing of Germany.

"When you talk to people like Albert Speer and Göring, both of whom I've talked to, there was no question in their mind but that the bombing, RAF at night and US Air Force in the daytime, really won the war for us. There was no question in their mind – and Speer gave all the production statistics – that they were particularly impressed by the US Air Force in the first place because it expanded so fast – you had 1,500 bombers going over there in a raid, and of course they were impressed by its accuracy in the daytime, which the RAF didn't have. The RAF targets were really the city itself – the US Air Force could pinpoint specific targets like factories and so on.

I think it was very important, and of course it very nearly didn't get started at all, because the RAF told the Americans that you can't possibly go over in the daylight, you'll be massacred. And indeed they were, because the fighters at that time couldn't go all the way with the bombers, and it was very, very dramatic. But when we transferred from the RAF, from our Spitfires to our P-47 Thunderbolts, we could at least go into Germany – not into Berlin or anything, we couldn't quite make Schweinfurt. Schweinfurt was where the ball-bearing factories were, and was very important, because if we could take out the ball-bearing factories, we would really give them a knock-out blow. I can remember the Schweinfurt raids. We could go about half of the distance and we could see a hundred or so Me-109s and 190s waiting for us to turn back, they then attacked. It was terrible because they were just massacred. We lost an enormous number – about 50 per cent on the two Schweinfurt raids. Then of course we got the P-51, and it could go all the way to Berlin – I led the first Berlin mission with them – and it even went to Russia. It could go anywhere the bombers could go, and Göring said in Nuremberg, when they asked him when he knew the war was lost for Germany, he said it was when he saw the red-nosed mustangs over Berlin, escorting the bombers.

The most unforgettable raid for me would have to be the Berlin raids. They were the long raids – we were sitting in that little cockpit for eight and a half hours, and of course, one of the things that impressed me most about escorting the US Air Force bombers was the tremendous affinity which grew up between the bomber crews and the fighter crews. They needed us so badly, that when they got back they would look us up and just thank us for doing what we did.

And we, in turn, were so impressed by the bravery of these fellows, because they just ploughed right on – they had to stay on course – and once they were on their bomb-run, which was where the German fighters hit them, they couldn't deviate at all. Sometimes when they were hit, they just blew right up, their whole bomb-load went right up, and where an aeroplane had been, there was just a smoke-ring. We of course were doing what we could do to at least keep the fighters off them, but for us it was easy – we were so manoeuvrable. Over the target, when the flak came up, we'd just move off to the side, but they had to go on through it. We had tremendous respect for these fellows. I've seen B-17s diving into the ground, the rear gunner still shooting out his tracers right up to the moment when the bomber hit the ground. There was tremendous mutual respect on both sides."

CASSINO

Mountain Inferno

The Allies had taken Naples and broken out of the Salerno beachhead in October 1944. They now sought to advance on the capital. But the key to the road to Rome was the small town of Cassino, dominated by the hilltop monastery. German troops had formidable mountain defences there and the Allies faced a long and bitter fight, during which the monastery itself would be bombed

Guido Varese, now a lawyer in Cassino, was 19 years old when the bombardment of his home town began. He was evacuated after Italy had signed the armistice with the Allies

'The first bombs fell at 9.00 am. We were not expecting this at all, due to the fact that the armistice was already in effect. For us, we thought that the war was over. I was in the piazza with a friend when we saw Flying Fortresses, going towards Rome from Naples, which unloaded their bombs on the outskirts of the town. We were all amazed at these marvellous flying machines, when we realised what was happening.

This first bombardment caused enormous damage and killed many, many people. I took refuge in the shop where I usually had my hair cut. While in there, in came a German soldier with his ear shot to pieces by shrapnel. I put a towel, the first thing I could see, around his head to stop the blood pouring from his ear. He certainly would have died otherwise.

There were two more bombardments that day, the first was down by the station, the other was on the outskirts of the town, destroying mostly the road to Rome from Naples. They had spotted retreating German columns and decided to attack these. After this, my sister and my sister-in-law decided to retreat to the mountains, just under Monte Cairo. Here we thought we would be safe, as the road came to an abrupt end.

We were wrong. We found ourselves near the front lines of the German army. This was the position of the German Alpini troops who had been fighting around this location during the winter months when several attacks were centred on Cassino. Due to the bad weather, the terrain was very muddy and the attack in December by the Allies was staged off. Tanks just got stuck in the mud and were unable to cross the fast-flowing river. The Germans had blown up all the bridges.

15 March was the total bombardment of Cassino, which I watched from a nearby village. The abbey was destroyed on 15 February. The day before the bombardment, the Allies dropped leaflets telling everybody to leave the church and that they would be bombing the area. The Germans at this time were not inside the church – they were outside, around it. Freyburg, the Allied commander on the spot, was worried about the Germans using the abbey as a stronghold, at which point the Allies would be confronted with a huge task to get past that point.

A German lieutenant decided to tell everybody that they would not be able to leave the abbey until the evening after. The bombers came and 300 to 400 people, still waiting to leave, were killed or buried alive.

When we were transferred from Terelle to Montforte by the SS, who wanted all civilians well away from the front lines, we witnessed a dog-fight between an English and a German aircraft. Due to the sun it was very difficult to tell which was which, but all of a sudden, one caught fire and started to plummet to the ground. We saw the pilots jump out with their parachutes. Then we noticed that the remaining aircraft did not go away, but turned steeply and shot the two flyers in the air. This has to be the most horrific thing I have ever seen. We were under the misapprehension that there was a certain camaraderie among even opposing pilots. The flyers fell from the skies to crash against the rocks below – I will never forget the sound of these poor flyers as they screamed and shouted."

Corporal Cadet Officer Zbigniew Fleszar with 3 Company, 1st Battalion, 1st Brigade, 3rd Carpathian Division, 'deserted' from a temporary post in a rear echelon to join his company at the front line to see some action.

"We knew Cassino would be a very significant battle. We simply didn't want to miss it. After breaking relations with the Polish Government, Stalin accused us Poles of not wanting to fight the Germans, so, however small our contribution, we had to be there. The victory at Monte Cassino was to be our gift to Poland.

We were assigned the task to take the Gorge. My company was to reach the slope over it and protect the march and attack of the following company. We were loaded with equipment and already hot. I don't think we were scared – just apprehensive.

The company left the Big Bowl immediately after dark and slowly progressed over the rocks and bushes. Then a whistling shell flew low overhead – and another, and another. I felt as if a bridge of iron was being erected overhead, and wondered how it was that shells did not collide. Over a thousand guns were firing. The noise reverberated over the mountains. One could pick out whistles, crying and sobbing and roaring of shells. Then it all changed. The Phantom Hill in front of us was suddenly on fire. There was an explosion every split second. The mountain trembled.

Sweat running down our eyes, battledress wet, chests like smithies' bellows, we pushed forward on the slope. Then all hell broke loose. The heavy shells started breaking among us. At first we thought it was our own artillery firing short. The code for this was 'Oranges'. This went out over the wireless – but the explosions were not oranges. This was German artillery. The explosions sounded like an enormous giant clearing his throat. I had an extraordinary wish – to be one of the smallest pebbles under one of the biggest rocks.

Douglas Lyne, age 20, was a gunner in the Royal Artillery, acting as Observation Post Assistant in the 57th Field Regiment, part of X Corps. To him the destruction of the Cassino Monastery had a special significance, his ancestor Father Ignatius of Llanthony having founded a Benedictine monastery in Wales based on this very edifice.

"Suffice it to say that by the end of January, no real progress had been made towards the capture of Cassino Monastery, without which it was impossible to proceed along the road to Rome. It was about this time that my own regiment of artillery was posted into the line there. From an observation post at about 2,500 feet we could see across the valley, whenever weather permitted, this shining monument of Cassino monastery, which, I must say, did look in a way menacing and odd,

Cassino Monastery, founded in 529 by St Benedict, fell victim to Allied bombs in 1944

in so far as it was the only undestroyed object in a vast waste of destruction. It was rather like seeing Buckingham Palace in the middle of Passchendaele.

On 15 February we'd been up there about a week and were absolutely miserable – it was terrible weather. In the occasional breaks in the clouds we saw this monastery all the time, and it got on our nerves, to be quite frank. It became, from being a thing of beauty, a thing of monstrosity – and somehow it was the thing which was holding up all our lives and keeping us from home. It became identified in an obsessional way with all the things we detested. Remember, I had been about two years in almost continuous action, and action is barbarising and our sensibilities were blunted.

Suddenly out of the mist of the south, on this really rather nice morning, just after breakfast, appeared this vast armada – a huge bomber force – mainly Flying Fortresses. We were wondering where on earth this vast armada was going, when all of a sudden, the bombs started dropping out of these things, and came bashing down on the jolly old mother of monasteries of St Benedict, about ten miles away over the valley. I must confess it was a gigantically stimulating sight, to suddenly see this – it must have been comparable to seeing the early Christians being eaten by lions in the Colosseum, I suppose. We all started cheering wildly and hugging each other.

But there was, with me, a remarkable Welshman called Tom Roberts, who'd been my constant guide, philosopher and friend since the early days. He was a man of great spiritual merit who knew about my connection with Father Ignatius of Llanthony. After I'd stopped trembling and the laughter and hysterical gaiety faded, he sat me down and said, 'Steady on Doug – I mean, are we really in this war for the business of bombing monasteries? What would old Father Ignatius think of that?' Suddenly, I had a sort of complete bloody double-take. I thought, 'What the hell are we doing, up on this hill and surrounded by destruction and mayhem, and everything gone to pot? What are we fighting for or against? Here we are, cheering the destruction of one of the great monuments of Christendom.' One's mood changed from exultation to a peculiar sort of horror and self-questioning, which was very disturbing..."

The Allies finally leave Cassino and advance on the road to Rome

OPERATION OVERLORD

Falling into France

For three years, the Allies had been planning a return to the shores of occupied France. While the German army strengthened their coastal defences, Allied troops trained for the eventual landing. But when they landed on French soil in the small hours of 6 June 1945 – D-Day – they found themselves surrounded by confusion and chaos

Lt-Colonel Michael Forrester DSO, MC, was serving with his Regiment in Palestine when war broke out. Joining the 7th Armoured Div., he fought through Greece, Crete, the Western Desert Italy before returning with the 'Desert Rats' to train for the European invasion.

"We didn't know, of course, when D-Day was going to be – in fact we knew very little about anything. We were given training directives and facilities in Norfolk at that time were quite good. But there were things other than training to be dealt with. Everyone had been abroad for a very long time. Leave was the first thing. I remember we got as many people as we possibly could away on leave. This was the first time they had seen their families for a long time.

We were back in England again for the first time after a considerable number of years, and this meant being at home as opposed to being in the desert where there were virtually no inhabitants, so all needed reminding of the importance of local public relations. We were trying to weld ourselves into the community and become part of it, although we knew we weren't going to be there for very long. The people of that part of England were open-hearted and kindness itself and they gave us a marvellous welcome – they could not have made us more at home.

Training directives indicated that we were going to be fighting in fairly close country, and in the event, when we got to Normandy, we found the so-called *bocage* country there even more restricting and close than even we had anticipated. It was, because of its nature, almost as great a change from Italy as the desert had been to Italy, because the fields were so very, very small, with high banks with hedges on top of them dividing up the fields, making fields of view and tank movement very difficult indeed. Of course, the Germans had the advantage over us there – they were familiar with it.

Of course we were aware from the start that we were going to take part in the invasion of Europe, but we didn't know where we were going. It was as closely kept a secret as that, right up to the end, and when our time came to get ready finally, we moved out of our areas in Norfolk down to camps – very sparse, primitive tented camps – but perfectly adequate for the purpose, in Essex. There our camps were sealed, and we were briefed properly, and allowed to brief right down to soldier level – but up until then, no-one had known.

It's very relevant to talk about fear. The unknown, which we were going into, meant uncertainty. You don't know, and uncertainty very naturally leads to apprehension, and so the adrenalin is flowing. I don't think fear actually comes into one's thoughts until one is confronted with something dangerous, but the apprehension is there all the time. I would say I felt really frightened on several occasions. I think too, that the definition of war (which is anonymous, though someone may lay claim to it) that 'War consists of long periods of intense boredom, punctuated by short periods of intense fright', is a good one. I think it was coined for the First War, but it was very relevant for the Second War too.

Once confronted with a situation, there are certain sorts of fear. I think the predominant sort of fear, in the case of some, is 'Am I going to be up to this myself?' I think it's awfully important to recognise that – it takes a certain amount of personal drive to overcome it, and to say, 'Yes, I am'. Certainly, while people were very frightened, they went on because they felt they couldn't possibly not go on. *Esprit de corps* is very important for morale because you drive yourself to meet the challenge, and you know other people are meeting it too, and you are going to be in it with them."

Lieutenant Sumpter Blackmon was leader of 1st Platoon, Company A, 1st Battalion, 502nd Parachute Infantry Regiment. He recalls his part in the 101st Airborne's D-Day drop into France. Their aim was to seize bridges and main road junctions to prevent the Germans from flooding the estuary area behind the beaches and to nip any counterattack in the bud.

"The officers and men of our First Platoon joined hands and prayed that God guide us. We took off just after 10.30 that night and all the planes circled above the airfield and waited, then began forming up in Vs. It took us an hour to get into formation. Then our formation turned inland and the sky erupted in fireworks – flak. All around my plane the others were jinking and diving, but my pilot flew the course without a tremor. He flew directly into a fogbank, and all the other planes disappeared. When we came out of the fog, we found that we were all alone.

I stood at the cargo door with the equipment bundle of machine gun and ammunition, ready to kick it out when the jump light came on. I saw the proper landmarks come up. Then I saw the ground disappear and then whitecaps – we were back over the sea. The pilot looked worried. 'Lieutenant', he said, 'we missed the drop zone and are over the Channel, headed back to England.' I told him to take us to land and we'd get out.

The pilot dived, came around and headed for the French shore again. He took us down just above the waves to evade the flak, and as the plane reached the shoreline, he put it into a climb so steep that it threw several men off their feet. I decided it was now or never. I pushed out the equipment bundle, hooked up my chute ring and followed. I was jerked by the ring and my parachute opened automatically just before I hit the ground.

After I landed hard, I cut myself loose from the parachute. I found the equipment chute in a low tree, a part of one of the Normandy hedgerows – thick, nearly impenetrable lines of trees and bushes. I crawled into a hedgerow and waited and listened. Finally Private Day came up. We had no idea where we were. I pulled out my flashlight and map. I studied the map but could not find any points of terrain that matched – we'd obviously jumped off the map.

Finally we met up with some other troopers and I really felt as if I had an army, with the 34 men I collected. Just then, a German soldier stood up in the ditch and raised his hands. I could not understand what he was saying. Private Nick Denovchik came up and said the German was speaking Polish, which he understood. The Polish German told Denovchik that he and his buddy were manning an aircraft listening station. He shouted and his buddy stood up about 50 yards away. After some more talk, they led us to a pillbox buried underground in a grove of trees, in which was a big radio set and enough ammo to withstand a minor siege.

The two prisoners helped us destroy the listening device, four large instruments perfectly camouflaged in the trees. We blew up the ammo dump and wrecked the radio. We accepted these two soldiers as our allies, and they showed us the way to the causeway. We were still a long way from our assigned objective, the locks of the Douves. It was nearly time for the troops to be landing on Utah Beach; I could only hope and pray that someone else had taken the locks at La Barquette.

They had, and a vast armada of ships were in the English Channel – the invasion of Normandy was on."

Flight Lieutenant David Warner, a navigator with 296 Squadron, had returned from North Africa late in 1943, and started to train in towing gliders, dropping paratroops and supplies in accurate zones, and using Gee radar. All this was in preparation for the D-Day assault.

"In between training and the invasion we were sent out to France to drop supplies to the Maquis. That also gave us training for map-reading at night. A typical exercise was to go to somewhere where the mountains start, in the middle of France, where the Resistance were.

All the searchlights would be out looking for something, but at 500 feet they couldn't get you, because as they came down, they would go out, and you could duck underneath the lot. Usually we would be over the top of the flak before they could get organised, but there would be quite a lot of things shooting behind. Then you would come to the rendezvous and the dropping zone, where there would be the reception party.

We would go round and then we would lower the flaps and the wheels, reduce speed and go 600-800 feet above the line of torches to drop the goods.

When it came to D-Day we were given lots of pictures of the French coastline. I had to look at this panorama all day long. I had it in my room, when I woke up in the morning with my cup of tea – I tried to memorise it.

I have to say the operation didn't worry me at all – you get used to it, don't you? It's like driving a new car you've never driven before but after you've had it for about six months it becomes second nature. The only thing that would have been frightening would have been if we had lost an engine – then we'd have problems. There again, I planned for all exigencies. I used to take with me all sorts of things. Just before I left the mess, I used to tear the front page off the Daily Mail and stuff it in my back pocket. This was because if I had to land in France, the Germans were setting up decoys, pretending they were British airmen trying to escape, to try to find out the French families who were helping them, then rounding them up and shooting them. So to let anybody know I am a British airman, I would have that day's date on a newspaper.

I thought of everything for survival – I carried yards of string and had razor blades stitched into my trousers. They gave us one or two pieces of survival equipment – a handkerchief with a map of France on it, some French money. I had a pipe which had a compass built into the bowl, and that sort of thing. Most of this was my idea. But on D-Day I didn't do anything at all. I felt it was a mass organisation and we'd all be back in five minutes. It didn't worry me one little bit."

The harbours of southern England are solid with the men and ships for the invasion

D-DAY

Struggling Ashore

After years of painstaking planning, the Allies launched one of the history's largest invasions. While the Germans knew that an attack would come, the date – 6 June 1944 – and the targets were a well-kept secret until Allied troops arrived in Normandy by air and sea. Despite the advantage of surprise, they met stiff resistance from the very edge of the sea as they carved out their beachhead

Richard Todd, possibly better known for his acting role in The Longest Day than for his real-life action on D-Day, went through officer training at Sandhurst and after a varied career in the Army joined the 6th Airborne Division. His battalion was to be the first in on D-Day.

"I was to be in aircraft 33. We had very carefully worked out our load tables for the aircraft in terms of who should be in there first, who would have such and such weapons and who would have other things with them. First of all we were in a *laager* on Salisbury Plain, wired in for about a week, even our supplies and food were just dumped outside the wire gates, because we weren't allowed to talk to anybody. We were being briefed, a week or so before D-Day, we knew where, when, how and everything about it. We had no communication at all with the outside world except me one day, because I was Assistant Adjutant, and I was sent to Southern Command Headquarters. I was terrified. I thought, 'Oh, my God, I hope I don't open my mouth'.

We knew the whole thing, all the planning. We knew our own particular thing – we had sand-table models of the area we were dropping in and we knew every tree and every house intimately. We had maps galore and every day we had a fresh batch of aerial photographs for our intelligence officer to interpret.

We were getting worried because we saw a lot of little holes being dug and we found out that it was posts being put in with wire between them as anti-glider defences. We also saw large areas flooded – we wondered if the whole thing had been blown.

That night of D-Day, or the night before, at about 11 o'clock, we drove round the airfield perimeter, each stick of paratroopers in a three-ton truck, and each truck stopped by its numbered aircraft. Mine stopped at aircraft number 33 – and I was going out first from the aircraft. The pilot and crew were lined up beside the aircraft – they shook hands and wished us luck and all the rest of it. The pilot said to me, quite blithely, 'As I'm the senior officer going in tonight, I'm going in first, because we've got the gem crew'.

I thought, 'Oh Christ – I'm going to be the first out of the first aircraft,' but I couldn't argue with them because he was senior to me, and I couldn't say, 'Look, this will upset our load tables.' So I got in – and that actually saved my life. I'll tell you why in a minute. I think people thought I was very cool because I fell asleep on the way – but that's a thing of mine. If I'm very worried or really down about something, my tendency is to be like an ostrich, and put my head in the sand and go to sleep – and I was very worried that night.

I was wakened up – we lined up and hooked up. The old green light came on and out we went, with me in the lead. It was a very big hole in the bottom of the Stirling, with enough room for two men to straddle it, and on the word 'go' pull their legs together and drop out through the hole. The man behind me had to hold on to me because the aircraft was jinking a bit. I could easily have fallen out – in fact a few people did fall out over the sea – because I hadn't a hand to hold on with as I had kit bags on each of my legs.

Out I went. We dropped from 400 feet, which didn't give you much time in the air – about seven seconds. I let the bloody kitbag on my right side slip instead of letting it out hand over hand. That gave me a nasty burn down my right hand. Then I thumped down.

We had got in with the element of a surprise. A certain amount of light flak came up and we could see tracer, floating by us. But nothing hit us – the big stuff hadn't really started, and as I was getting out of my 'chute on the ground, looking up at the other aircraft, they started getting shot down. By that time, the ground defences had wakened up to what was happening and the ack-ack guns had gone into action. The aircraft round about the numbers 30 were the ones that all got shot down, and it was just my luck that I went in first."

Friedrich August Freiherr von der Heydte was CO of parachute Regiment 6, part of the 2nd Parachute Division under Commanding General Ramcke, which fought at the French coast from 6 June onwards.

"I was in the north of Périers, just in the middle of the peninsula, the most westward part of Normandy, covering Utah Beach. The funny thing was that the Germans were expecting a landing north of where the landing actually occurred, west of Ste Mére-Eglise. On the first day I received no orders. I was my own boss. Most of the divisional commanders had been called to Rennes for an operational exercise. I tried to get through to the corps commander General Marcks.

The only contact was by the normal French phone network. The Germans were forbidden to use this because of the spies. But I couldn't get through on our own network – the French Resistance had prepared for the invasion, sabotaging the phone lines.

I first saw what was happening when I arrived in St Come du Mont. I had come across an old church tower and went up there to take a look out over the coast. I knew that I had to tell General Marcks what I had seen. I wanted to tell him that in my opinion the forces we had were not in a position to offer vigorous resistance to the invading forces. At every mile along the coastline was a German bunker and, of the three that I could see, only one was actually firing. In my opinion, they feared for their lives, considering that they would be easily wiped out by the invading Americans. Only one bunker did its duty, forcing the Americans to spread out.

I felt that my troops were very vulnerable with no artillery assistance. We had our heavy company with 12 cm mortars. I gave the order for them to get forward quickly and fire. When I saw the invading troops, I made a detour, and came across a German battery which had been totally deserted. This was the second line of defence, the artillery line, about six guns in the battery, totally unmanned, but all ready to fire. I don't know what had happened to the gunners, but it was my opinion that they had deserted. But all the Americans had to do was turn the guns round and fire them at our men. I had no artillery men with me, so I could do nothing with the guns. When I finally contacted Marcks I reported what I had seen.

At Carentan I had parts of the 2nd and parts of the 3rd Battalion with me, and some regimental units, intelligence troops etc. Then I was given a reinforcement battalion of Russians, Georgians, in fact.

These were anti-Communist Russians fighting on the German side. They fought very well, but they couldn't stand the bombing from the air. The American bombers attacked my regiment near Carentan the whole day, and after the attack the Russians deserted.

The heaviest fighting was at the north-west part of the town. The Americans had managed to get over the flooded area by the railway

British soldiers assemble 30 minutes after the landing on Sword Beach, 6 June 1944

bridge, which my 2nd battalion had used. The only way of destroying the bridge would have been by bombing it from the air, but the Luftwaffe was held back by the superiority of the American airforce. I did not see one German fighter plane. As we said then: 'We have the ground but the sky belongs to the Americans'. So, in my opinion, the crucial factor was American air superiority – and second, the lack of unity among the German forces."

At the age of only 19, Bill Williams joined the RASC, seconded to the 3rd Division for supplies. Having led, by his own admission, a sheltered life until then, his first foray abroad on D-Day was a voyage of discovery.

"It was around midnight on 5 June when we became aware that we were moving. One could sense tension rising. At last the order came for us to don our equipment and prepare to move down to the vehicle deck. Nothing could be heard except the drone of the ship's engines, and it was 6.00 am when we sensed that we had stopped. Once outside, we found we were at least two miles out from the coast, which we could just see from our low position. The sea was full of ships of all shapes and sizes. Naval destroyers were firing over our heads towards the coast.

I suppose one could describe the scene on the beach as organised chaos. A boat had been sent out to guide us in and the engineers had done a fantastic job in clearing areas of the beach enforcements, which were all piled in huge heaps. I can't say how many landing craft were on the beach at that time – a number of them were burning and had obviously been struck by shells. But apart from the spasmodic shell coming over on to the beach, there didn't appear at that time to be very much danger. We understood that the Canadians had moved inland some half, three quarters of a mile. One was still conscious of a lot of gunfire – in other words, ships were still firing inland to various points, but basically we were very tensed up about it. The beach itself was cluttered with debris.

My first shock was spotting the first dead body. I'd never seen a dead body in my life before. This particular chap was so immaculate – just as though he had been stood to attention, with all his small pack and his webbing all beautifully blancoed. There he was, and we had to stop for a moment right beside him. It was as if he had been standing then just gone flat down on his face. It absolutely shattered me – I couldn't take my eyes off him.

We passed into the centre of this small town then we turned into an open field. Looking over the fence, the best part of a herd of cows had been slaughtered by the shell fire and were lying around with their feet in the air – which rather upset me, coming as I did from the country.

After that we dismounted and unloaded the ammunition into heaps and were escorted back down through Courseulles to the outskirts of Bernieres-sur-Mer. We turned into a fantastic driveway of a chateau which had hardly been damaged at all. We were very delighted to have got there in one piece. We got together and dug one hell of a big trench and covered the top with apple branches. We had a hot meal of stew and did nothing else but smoke and talk about the events of the day."

CAEN

Hard Fought Prize

The Allied Armies fought their way into Normandy hindered by bad weather and a landscape crossed by thick hedgerows. The inital shock of the landing had faded, allowing the Germans to organise their defences, and Allied troops faced a fierce battle at the town of Ceaen, which blocked the road out of Normandy. They finally captured it on 9 July 1944

Walter Heritage, a Regimental Sergeant Major with the 20th Anti-Tank Regiment during the battle for Caen, had to witness the effects of continual attrition and heavy casualties on his men.

"Having landed at Sword Beach on D-Day, we pressed on inland. The object was that we would be in support of the 6th Airborne Division, some of whom had landed the previous night. There were a lot of minefields and we suffered very heavy casualties en route.

We made our headquarters about four or five hours' march inland. We made contact with the 6th Airborne Division who were established at the bridgehead at the now famous Pegasus Café. In those days it was called Maison Vendre. It was owned by Georges Vendre, his wife and his three daughters. They were delightful and very kind to us.

I was responsible for discipline and behaviour, as well as for ammunition for the guns and the general administration of the regiment. We had very good equipment and there was no shortage of ammunition. There were four batteries, so it was rather a spread out job as they were all in different places.

Whether you are fighting or not, there is the daily routine to be done, such as the maintenance of guns and vehicles and the supply of ammunition, and it was my job to ensure that the daily tasks were done. We were there for six or seven weeks, and it was out and out warfare. Morale among the men was very good – very high. There were casualties, of course – people got wounded, some killed – but morale did not waver.

The Germans had their headquarters in a factory on the outskirts of Caen and their observation posts were in the tall chimneys. They were shelling and bombing us. Our bombing of the line which the Germans held was colossal, and a lot of them were killed in their tanks. When we got through we saw that the German equipment was good, but there is a limit to how much saturation bombing any equipment can stand up to, however good it is.

Everything in Caen was dead – dead horses, dead cattle – everything. We were told that the people of Caen were in the church. They had been suffering wartime conditions for a long, long time. Caen had been a beautiful old city, but now every building was destroyed. It was so obliterated that you couldn't go through it. It was in ruins, but fortunately we did not have to stay there because our avenue of approach into Europe was open and we were all anxious to get on."

Adolf Mertens, age 24, was commander of the regimental intelligence unit of the German 6 Parachute Regiment, as German forces struggled to break out of the area of Coutances, where US troops encircled them.

"We were constantly on the march, initially in vehicles and on motorbikes until the petrol ran out, and we had to leave the cars and bikes and continue on foot. I would say that the combat readiness of the troops was more or less unbroken, although the demands on the troops were very high and we had no chance to sleep or rest and there was absolutely nothing to eat. But none of this affected our will to do all we could to get out of the pocket.

We had been moving throughout the whole of the night. Sleep you could forget – we did not get a wink. We had to be alert at every moment, as the area was under constant fire from the naval artillery off the coast, and we had to take very opportunity to find room between the falling shells to push forward. It was impossible to get any kind of overview of the area, it was total chaos, and so the troops were dispersed into groups.

You couldn't really talk of specific orders on this day. The regimental commander succeeded merely in gathering together as many of the units as possible and instructing them to wait in a specific place until he came back to take them away. Of course, we discovered that it was impossible to wait very long and so we decided to break up into groups and break out on our own.

Now in a situation like this you live totally on hope that you will get out in a reasonable state. You'd had no sleep. You thought very little about it, and if you did, these thoughts were very quickly washed away by the sight of dead comrades, destroyed tanks, corpses lying all around, men hanging dead out of blown-up trucks, and your only thought was, 'how am I going to get out of this?'. I'm not saying that you were not affected by the sight of all this horror, of your dead comrades lying around. You were cut to the bone by this, but this did not change the bald fact that you had to carry out your duty to the men and get them out of this encirclement.

The day had no beginning and no end. It was simply a continuation of the day and the night before. Pushing forward constantly, trying to find cover where you could get it, and where possible trying to find something to eat. We had no provisions with us but we would sometimes come upon destroyed trucks, which had some provisions in them. In a situation like this it is difficult to say what actually drives a man forward – you run on adrenalin. You have to imagine that we had been involved in uninterrupted heavy fighting since 6 June. We were used to such extreme situations by now. Comradeship is a major factor here. It is very important to you not to bring your comrades into dangerous situations.

I remember particular experiences. There were about 12 of us together, 12 paratroopers, under the command of a lieutenant, and we were trying to get through a path. We could hardly see anything, and had not a clue where the path would take us. We were just trying to make our way north out of the pocket. There were shots ahead of us, and then we heard English voices shouting out: 'Hands up!' We were taken prisoner by the large group of American soldiers standing before us. We were told to stand against a wood at about 20 or 30 metres from our captors, and just at that moment, a fighter plane dived down and fired a salvo directly at us as we stood with hands over our eyes. Fortunately, the shots went over our heads. Then we were taken away on American jeeps. We were treated reasonably well, I have to say, and we were taken off to an open camp where all the prisoners who had been taken in the pocket were assembled. Quite a high number. We were then taken to the church at Sainte Mére-Eglise, and we spent the night on church pews.

We were then taken to England, to an interrogation camp in Manchester, and after about ten days there we were shipped to America. The paratroopers were volunteers. It was clear to us now what sort of scrupulous brutality the enemy would stoop to against us, the bombing of our cities etc., and in this sense, we were fighting the war not for ideological purposes, but to protect our fatherland."

Sergeant Bernard Griffith was a Driver Operator with the Royal Horse Artillery when he landed in Normandy on D-Day. As his regiment saw the total destruction of the city of Caen, he recalls the pitiful sight of shell-shocked civilians fleeing the town.

"We had got quite far inland by the first night. After we got into position, it was decided that we would need the four vehicles that had been lost in the actual landings. I went back to the beaches, which were only about 2 km away, on my motor bike. It was pitch dark and the British had scattered smoke canisters all over the beaches as camouflage for movement because they were under such heavy air attack. It was very hard to breathe in the smoke.

We found two of the vehicles, and we got them going. When you don't have proper facilities, you learn to make do, using tricks of the trade. I wasn't in the best of moods on the way back. Suddenly my motor cycle and I parted company. I was sent head first into a hedge, and as I landed, my dispatch-rider's helmet got jammed on to my head, right down to my eyebrows. I couldn't get the bloody thing off. We used everything to try and lever it off. I ended up with black eyes and a broken nose. It was funny afterwards, but not at the time.

We pressed on with the two new vehicles. We were stopped outside Caen for about ten days. It was difficult with heavy fighting – the Germans were very keen to keep it.

The town had already been attacked when we got there. We were bombarding it heavily and the Typhoon bombers did terrible damage. Most of the civilians that had survived had gone underground, but we saw some that had managed to escape. They came through our lines on horses and carts or on foot. It was terrible – their suffering was often worse than that of the soldiers.

After we captured the town, it was a clearing-up operation. The

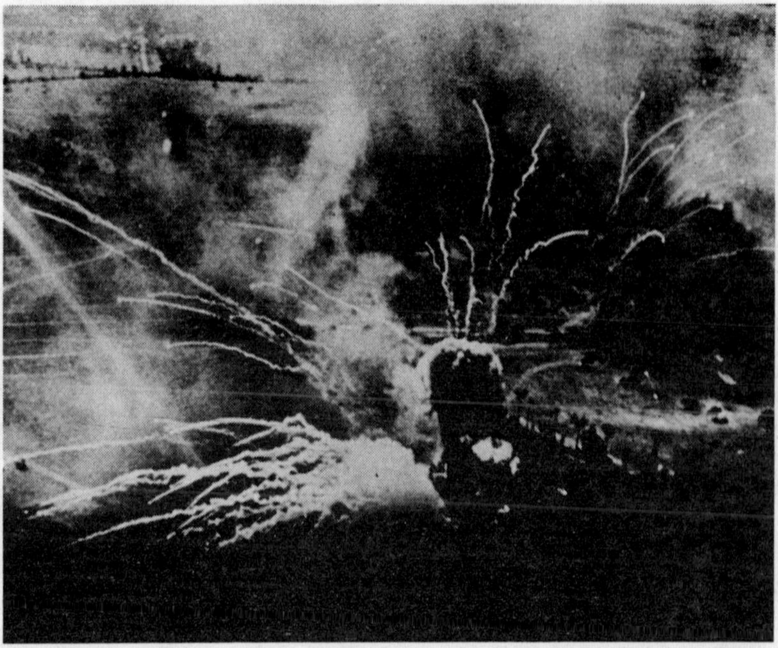

The French countryside has to bear the brunt of massive air bombardment by the Allies

infantry went in to get rid of the rubbish and to winkle out any snipers. Bayeux had been taken and our next objective was Falaise. The Germans had two armoured divisions in a pocket there and we bombarded them for four or five days amid very heavy fighting.

Most of the Germans who had been killed in the Falaise pocket had been buried by their own people. They buried the British too, if they were in their sector, and we did likewise. If we came across a German who hadn't been buried, we used to dig a six foot hole, wrap the body in a blanket which we would sew up with a big needle, and lower it into the grave. Then more often than not you stuck a rifle into the ground and put his tin hat on top of it, with his name written on the hat.

I have never seen so many dead horses. Although the Germans had very modern panzers and equipment superior to ours in many ways, their artillery and some of their supply vehicles were horse drawn. I have never seen anything like those horses. They were bloated up lying there. It was an horrific sight. When everything was over, the horses were burned by the French farmers."

THE ROAD TO PARIS

Liberation of a Capital

It had taken the Allies two months to push out of Normandy, trapping 100,000 retreating enemy troops in the so-called Falaise pocket to the west. Spurred on by their approach, Resistance groups in the French capital rose up against their Nazi occupiers in August 1944. Supported by massive air power, Allied troops surged into Paris to an ecstatic welcome

William Spray had served in a Friends' Ambulance Unit in Morocco until the invasion of France, when his unit became attached to a tank column of the USA Third Army.

"We had no idea of the shape of the war. The Falaise Gap got closed and we stopped fighting, then the buzz got round that it was Paris. This was terrific. On 25 August we went, a mixture of fêting and fighting on the way, into Paris.

It was unbelievable. I don't think I'd ever attached any particular meaning to the word 'liberation' until now. Certainly I can't ever now see or use the word 'liberation' without thinking of the experience of that day, rolling into Paris.

We were bang behind the tanks. People were out on the streets, throwing flowers, hugging every soldier they could see, and suddenly discovering we were English, and transferring their affections to us, quite as much as to the French. There was this enormous outpouring of joy and relief and everything else fell into what seemed the right perspective – that is, as unimportant. I suppose on that day, it was.

So we drove in slowly. I remember going across the Pont du Sèvres, rolling across the Pont du Sèvres, rolling down into the Place

Victor Hugo, down into the Avenue Raymond Point Calais, and there we stopped and a lovely lady handed out vin rouge from her sitting room window.

Snipers opened up. We had wounded in the Church of the Place Victor Hugo, and we had to evacuate them to the nearest hospital. We slept, that night, in the street, in our ambulances, with the local Parisians absolutely marvellous in their welcome and hospitality.

We were the first lot in, apart from the British Secret Service. I'm sure there were lots of British in Paris before, but we were the first – and only – ones to make a public entry. So it was the French and these 30 conscientious objectors, rolling into Paris. There was not a lot of resistance going through. What had happened was, I think, that the hardened Nazis were clearly going to die fighting and they were some of the snipers, I've no doubt....

Paris looked just like any other town. Certain bits of it were obviously damaged, but it was difficult to know when. My memory is mainly of people – great crowds of people cheering. Where the French ladies got their lovely dresses from on this sunny morning, I don't know, but there they were, looking simply magnificent – the young ones. Then there were the old ones and widows in their black, being motherly. It was a great occasion for the human spirit. It was astonishing, really, that it required a war to produce it."

Herbert Eckelmann was an official in the Reich Ministry of Economic Affairs when he was suddenly drafted into the army as Germany built up her military power before the war. August 1944 found him living in Paris's Hotel Raphael, the Stadtkommissar, responsible for the economic running of occupied Paris.

"My new – and last – commanding officer, von Choltitz, received his scorched earth orders that Paris was to be destroyed – gas, electricity, Métro, the lot. Choltitz summoned me to hear my opinion, and I answered that on military grounds such destruction was pointless.

On 17 August, Abetz came to Choltitz to explain that he was removing the Vichy regime. On the 20th, we agreed it was too late in the day for any destruction. Had we simply marched out of Paris along with the rest, however, we would certainly have been condemned to death by a military tribunal. So we remained at our post in the Meurice. Jay asked Choltitz what orders he had to give, for the soldiers could not be expected to continue fighting after their senior officers had been captured. Choltitz replied that he had no new orders to give.

Choltitz's bedroom and sitting room were on the fourth floor, and he and Colonel von Unger and Jay and I and a few orderlies had retired up there. Then in came an older man in a German uniform with the insignia of the Resistance on it, and a hammer and sickle on his helmet. He manipulated the bolt of his Sten gun, and that was too much for Choltitz, who told him to rip off his badges. At this point there came a French lieutenant who saluted and asked whether he had the honour to be speaking to General von Choltitz. The Frenchman said, 'Will you give the order for a cease-fire?' Choltitz answered, 'Since you are in my bedroom, it's a little late for it.'

We were led off to Leclerc. Out in the street a huge mob had already assembled, and they screamed and spat at us, which was

Jubilant Parisians pose defiantly in front of Hitler's portrait

none too good. A French Red Cross van then drove us through Paris to the Préfecture of Police, where I was preparing myself to be sentenced to death. Instead, the behaviour was perfectly correct. About ten of us German officers were driven to the Gare Montparnasse, and on the way the Resistance men were polite. De Gaulle had arrived, and was with other officers, when Leclerc and Choltitz turned up.

We drove out toward Vincennes, which was where I knew there were German troops. I told the Frenchman that he might be shot at and should therefore wave a white handkerchief. We crossed into the German lines and there my French officer was held prisoner, though really he had come under a flag of truce. My conscience still bothers me a little about this. But I was free. I had been in the hands of the French only one day. And I'd lived through the occupation of Paris from the first day to the last."

Flying Officer Philip Murton was with 183 Squadron of the RAF, based at a makeshift airfield just outside Caen. Flying rocket-armed Typhoons, it was his job to clear obstructions from the Allies' way and hunt down the retreating Germans.

"On any operations there would be, say, a section of four going out looking for anything – anything German. We had the bomb-line marked on our maps that we flew with, so anything beyond that which was moving – guns, artillery, dispatch riders – was fair game. Depending on what it was, the leader decided whether to use cannon or rockets, or whether it warranted a second attack.

This was simply freelance stuff – anything you found, you just attacked it. The leader tried to make a note of where it was so he could report the exact position when he got back. But sometimes we'd go to do a rocket attack on a gun somewhere, and that was probably the army that had called us up, given us a map reference and said, 'There are guns here which are holding up the advance in one part on the front' – then you would go and knock them out. Very often the army would fire red smoke on to the target which gave us an extra guide – until the Germans learned this and of course, they would fire red smoke in the hope that they would confuse us.

A lot of the time it was cheating in a way because there was nothing firing back at us. It was almost like a practice, though obviously the tanks and troops on the ground would fire back. Later on, when the Germans increased their flak everywhere, you could be attacking something and there would be no flak at all. Then, as soon as you got in a dive, they would open up and you would have to go through the lot.

We had complete air superiority, so we never had to bother about looking for German aeroplanes. In fact, apart from chasing two *Focke-Wulfs* over the Channel after they had bombed Brighton, I never saw a German 'plane in the air through the whole of my tour.

The Falaise Gap was an absolute shambles. There was a pocket of hundreds of tanks, vehicles and goodness knows what, and there was this gap which wasn't closed. Montgomery didn't make the right decision and thousands of troops got away through it. They reckon that if the gap had been closed three or four days earlier, we would never have had the Ardennes offensive or Bastogne, because all those German troops went back and reformed.

Falaise was horrible because it was absolute carnage. There were dead bodies and horses and cows all over the place, and after three or four days, you could actually smell rotting bodies at 2,000 feet. The smell actually came into your cockpit. An awful lot of the local French people (because of the ground battle going on) were down in cellars but at one stage we piled into an army three-toner to go and look around. There were still bodies lying around and the cows and horses all tended to lie, goodness knows why, with their legs up in the air, and they were all bloated and swollen. There were vehicles everywhere too – everything left behind by a retreating army.

When we went in on an attack I honestly don't think we had any feelings about it. We were young, and you intended to enjoy things. Over the years you tended to forget the horrible things, and shooting up a whole lot of troops on the road was a lot of fun. It was very impersonal. I know you were killing people, but it wasn't like the army who went in hand-to-hand fighting. You were just letting loose at a whole lot of people on the ground and you would see them fall over like nine-pins and not think an awful lot about it.

We were doing it because it was a job to do. We didn't hate the Germans – possibly not as much as I hated them after the war after Belsen and all the atrocities came out. We were fighting to knock out Nazism really, and I think a lot of the army boys who were involved in hand-to-hand fighting and the tank boys who were literally blowing up people 100 yards away, were revolted by it. But eventually you got very hard. You go hard too because you saw one of your chums shot down or crash – and it was no good getting all soppy and sentimental about it, so you built a shell. About five or so years ago, I started having the most God-awful nightmares about being shot down, shooting up troops, planes, and goodness knows what. I mentioned it to my doctor and he said that it was a natural reaction. All the nasty stuff is stored away in the back of your mind and now it is starting to come out. We all had the feeling it wasn't going to happen to us."

SOUTH OF FRANCE

From All Sides

In August 1944, Allied troops from Italy landed on the French Riviera in an operation aimed at the underbelly of the Reich. In the face of overwhelming odds, the hard-pressed German defenders pulled back after only limited resistance in the towns of Toulon and Marseille, leaving the way clear for the Allies to advance north and for De Gaulle to establish a new provisional French government

Aimé Fallère, age 26, was one of the first inhabitants of Cannes La Bocca to see US troops arriving. After being captured by the Germans in 1940, while fighting in the French Army, he escaped to work as a member of the Comité de Liberation.

"We all knew that the Americans were on their way, but it always seemed a dream because we had no way of knowing when. We had no means of communication and everything we heard was based on rumour, though a few people sometimes managed to listen to the English radio. We all knew about the Allied landing in June in Normandy, and we were all waiting and praying for our freedom to come.

Cannes wasn't a heavily occupied town in comparison with the North – it was a bit like a holiday resort for the Germans. But the *Gestapo* headquarters was based in the Montfleury Hotel and the small islands opposite the town were crawling with German troops. A huge wooden wall was built along the seafront and no civilians were allowed on the sea road. We knew from 14 August that our liberation would soon come. On that day, two French warships, the *Emil Bertin* and the *Georges Leygues*, appeared in the Bay of Cannes.

The next day we heard that American bombers were destroying

German troops surrendering

the major bridges and viaducts in the Alpes Maritime and the Var – the main rail line for German convoys. The Germans knew the Americans were coming before we did. It was all so unreal. They just packed up and left on the evening of 23 August. They were in flight, but it was all very ordered. There was no panic – but before going, the Germans blew up Cannes Harbour.

It was on 24 August at about 11 o'clock in the morning, when I saw two American soldiers standing in the street in Cannes La Bocca. When I saw them I started shivering all over and I still shiver when I think about it now. It was a feeling of unforgettable joy – but fear at the same time. Deliverance had come in the shape of these two Americans. There weren't many people about at the time and nobody spoke any English. The soldiers gave out some chewing gum and then walked away. A couple of hours later, a force of about 100 Americans walked through the town, giving out chewing gum, chocolate and cigarettes. The women kissed them and we all danced and sang. It was complete euphoria. The joy and the look on people's faces was unforgettable.

After that the main army came through with the tanks and we knew our liberation had finally come. The look on the face of every man, woman and child was the same – an explosion of joy. It's a day I shall never forget."

Colonel William Quinn in the Office of the Assistant Chief of Staff at the Headquarters of the US Seventh Army, documented the action between the liberating American forces and the occupying Germans.

"By the time the German Nineteenth Army recovered from the surprise of the Allied landings on 15 August, it was too late. Although the German High Command had every reason to expect such an Allied operation, and knew in advance, from aerial reconnaissance, that the invasion fleet was under way, it failed to deduce the target area of attack.

There are conflicting versions of just what the enemy did expect. Some prisoners, including General-Major Pieringer, *Feldkommandant* of the Var Department, stated that the Germans were alert for an attack in the Genoa area – others say the landings were expected west of Toulon, although this area was unsuitable. In any case, the enemy was not prepared in the right area.

The shock and surprise of the assault, and the resulting speed of the advance in land, so disorganised the Nineteenth Army that its commander, General Friedrich Wiese, never succeeded in assembling the bulk of his forces to attempt to contain the beachhead. By the end of August, he had lost four of the nine divisions that had been available to him, in whole or in part, on the 15th; all of the rest had suffered heavy losses in both men and equipment; he had lost Toulon and Marseille; he had given up nearly 60,000 prisoners, and, faced with the threat of being outflanked and cut off by the simultaneous successes of the United States Seventh and Third Armies, he was withdrawing northward and had abandoned all of France south and south-west of Lyon.

It would not be correct to say that surprise was the only factor entering into the Nineteenth Army's failure to put up appreciable resistance to the Seventh Army's northward drive. The weakness of the Riviera garrison, which made possible the accomplishment of a decisive breakthough as early as D plus Two, was a result of two factors: the enemy's conviction that that attack would come somewhere else, and the fact that his overall strength in southern France was on the deadline.

In summary, after the operation, prisoners taken on the last day of the month brought the total to 57,068 since D-Day. The enemy had also lost an unestimated number of dead and wounded and large quantities of equipment; he had abandoned two divisions to their fate in Toulon and Marseille, and had lost two others to guard duty on the Italian border.

But by deciding on evacuation early in the battle (the disengagement order had been issued on D plus Four), then carrying it out boldly despite our efforts to block the route, the Nineteenth Army had salvaged a considerable portion of its strength for renewal of the fight on the approaches to the Fatherland. In particular the 11th Panzer Division had escaped and was to be met again in subsequent weeks."

Monique Acerbo was just six years old when the Allies arrived in her home town of Marseille, but she clearly recalls the dramatic events that occurred in the weeks leading up to the German surrender.

"During the war my family lived in the Quartier St Gabrielle to the north of Marseille. When the bombing started in May we were evacuated for safety with some friends and relations to a small hamlet further in land called Le Grande Prètre, a short way from the village of Destrousse. At that time my mother was pregnant with my sister Danielle. Destrousse was occupied by German soldiers, and by August the Americans had reached the neighbouring village of Peypin. The Germans installed their cannons in readiness, and when the fighting began we were in the middle of it all. On 15 August, my mother gave birth to my sister, while the fighting was going on all around. The adults were terrified, but being so young I thought nothing of it.

Then we were evacuated to Destrousse. My parents thought it was the Germans coming for us, but it was a group of American soldiers. They took us to an old château, owned by three sisters, all spinsters. We stayed there about three hours. Then the Americans came back for us and took us to my grandmother's house in Destrousse. They were very kind. They gave us tins of condensed milk, biscuits, corned beef and chewing gum, and made us shelter from the fire in the cellar. We stayed there, about 20 of us, for 21 days. The rest of the village had been evacuated and there was no way for us to get out. The house was next to the main road running through the village, and there was a small peephole through which the adults could see what was going on. We had taken the food that the Americans had given us down into the cellar, along with some fruit and whatever we could find, but it didn't last long.

We had no radio and no cooking facilities. I was with some cousins of my own age, and to us it was an adventure. We weren't scared, but the adults wouldn't let us look out the peep-hole. I remember there was a German soldier who one day stole a ring from a dead woman by cutting off her finger. The Americans caught him and rounded up 15 young Germans to kill as a reprisal. I saw them marched at gunpoint into the cemetery. Then I heard gunfire as they shot each one.

My mother had no milk to give my sister. Her own had dried up and we didn't understand how to use tins of condensed milk, so she was fed for weeks just on herbal tea.

Both the Germans and Americans had loudhailers, which kept us informed of what was going on. But I remember the real celebrations when it was all over. We adored the Americans – they gave us chocolate and chewing gum. When we finally returned to Marseille, it was quite a shock. Half the town had been demolished."

Elated French civilians line the streets as US Seventh Army troops enter Aix

EASTERN FRONT

Soviet Revenge

After more than three years of vicious fighting, both Russians and German troops were shattered and weakened. In the aftermath of Kursk, July 1943, the Red Army began to push back the aggressors from their homeland, their massive resources and dogged determination stacked against the demoralised Germans who, without supplies or equipment, were now in retreat

Léon Degrelle was Commander of the Belgian Legion Wallonie fighting with the SS-Division Wiking and witnessed the human suffering from the cold and hunger in the Cherkassy pocket in the middle of February 1944.

"From our makeshift position in Nowo-Buda we had been expecting the breakthrough to come on Monday. By Tuesday it had still not come. When would it happen? What were we to live on in the meantime – that is if we managed to escape the bullets?

Wherever we found ourselves, we soon came under enemy fire. Sanderowka was under fire day and night from 'Stalin's organs'. Wherever we went we came upon dead horses, smashed-up vehicles and corpses which we no longer had time to bury. We had turned the kolkhoz (Russian collective farm) into a field hospital, which was open on all sides, but at least provided a roof for our wounded soldiers. We had completely run out of medicaments, and there was no more material for bandages to be found in the whole of the pocket. To get hold of bandaging our medical orderlies had to wrestle the peasant girls to the floor and pull down their long military underpants – presents from German Don Juans. They screamed and ran off, holding on tight to their skirts. We just let them scream.

The Stalin's organs bombarded the *kolkhoz*. The roof caved in. Dozens of wounded men were killed in the bloody confusion. Others went crazy, letting out terrifying screams. The barracks had to be evacuated. Even our wounded men now had to stay out in the open. For several days and nights more than 1,200 wounded men from other units lay out in the open on hundreds of farm carts on a bed of straw. The rain had soaked them to the skin and now they were at the mercy of the biting frost.

Since Tuesday morning it had been 20 degrees below freezing, and lying outside in their hundreds were wounded men whose faces were nothing more than a hideous violet mass, men with amputated arms and legs, dying men, their eyes rolling convulsively.

Snow fell endlessly in the evening. It was soon a foot high. Twenty or thirty thousand people waited in our village for some kind of military end to the drama, with no sort of accommodation. Oblivious to the danger, the people stood out in the open in groups around fires they had lit in the snow. Sleep was impossible. Lying out in this biting cold would have meant certain death. The flames from burning the *isbas* could be seen from far away. In the valley hundreds of little fires burned, around which disconsolate shadows huddled, soldiers with reddened eyes and ten-day-old beards, warming their yellow fingers. They waited. Nothing happened.

They were still there in the morning – they didn't even bother trying to get some food. Their eyes looked to the south-west. Wild rumours were flying around. Hardly anyone listened to them any more. The silence was suddenly broken by the Stalin's organs. Everyone threw themselves down into the snow and then got to their feet again wearily. Wounded men screamed out. The doctors saw to them, to salve their consciences...

Twelve hundred wounded men still lay on the carts. Many of them had given up asking for help. They lay crushed together under a miserable cover, all their efforts geared to the task of staying alive. Hundreds of vehicles stood in a confused huddle. Horses reduced to skeletons chewed on the wooden slats of the carts in front of them. Here and there you could hear isolated groans and cries of wounded men. Crazed men raised themselves up, bleeding and with snow in their hair. What was the point of driving yourself crazy thinking of how you might feed these unfortunate men? They hid their heads under the covers. Every now and then the drivers would brush off the snow from these lifeless bodies with their hands. Many had been lying on these carts for ten days. They could feel themselves rotting alive. No injection could ease their most unbearable pains. There was nothing to be had. Nothing! Nothing! All they could do was wait – wait for death or a miracle. The number of yellowing bodies beside the carts kept increasing. Nothing could surprise us any more, nothing could stir our feelings. When you've witnessed such horrors, your senses are dumb."

Ivan Varzalov was a technician with the rank of Junior Lieutenant, serving in the vehicle platoon of a Russian signals battalion. He recalls the ferocious Ukraine offensive in 1944 to reclaim their lost territory.

"Before the start of the Carpathian campaign, the offensive of our 11th Rifle Corps was so powerful and victorious in the Chernovtsy and Kolomy areas that the fascist warriors got confused. Some of their detachments, left behind by other troops fleeing in disorder, hid in the woods, hoping to make their way through to their own side across the front. Those left lay in wait for our detachments.

As it turned out, their plan was to beat off our fighting vehicles to enable them to catch up with their retreating units. A fierce exchange of fire developed, but the soldiers of my detachment kept calm. Orientating themselves perfectly in the complex night situation, they took up defensive positions and then closed with the enemy and destroyed him.

I can remember another incident. There was a big battle, so hard-fought on both sides that a small settlement changed hands several times. It became apparent that one of my detachment's radio vehicles had been left in the area between the two sides. The Germans kept it under constant bombardment, trying to drag it over to their side. In the depth of the night, illuminated by the flaring of enemy rockets, under a hail of bullets and exploding mortar bombs, we pulled the vehicle back from under the noses of the enemy."

Untersturmführer Heinz Landau, a Transylvanian Saxon, returned to his SS unit after leave in Vienna in 1944. They had been sent to the Debrecen region of eastern Hungary, near the Romanian border. As he joined them, they were expecting an attack by the Soviet Army and were ready in their foxholes.

"Our positions had been under constant aerial attack, alternating with devastating artillery and rocket barrages. All of us were absolutely terrified by the Russian rocket-launchers. The devilish shrieking, thundering noise in itself was paralysing. The accuracy of the Soviet artillery was, I have to admit, incredibly good.

I very clearly remember one particular case on the Donetz, when heavy shells and rockets, fired simultaneously from about 1,000 guns, straddled our front lines. About 15 metres from my somewhat elevated position, the surface of the earth began to open in huge endless cracks, as in an earthquake, then the soil, including our trenches, men, weapons, everything, started to lift, in slow motion, into the air. Terrified shrieks rent the air. It all lifted to a height of about 20 metres, hung there for a second, then started to break up into small pieces, turning somersaults, crashing back into the huge empty, black gap thus created, burying a whole line of our defences, a minimum of 300 men. The Russians, unaware of this unbelievable bit of shooting, did not take advantage of the situation – it should have been a walk-over

Well, here at Debrecen, this sort of magnificent target-practice had just come to an end, and on raising our heads, we could just discern the enemy approaching through the smoke and fumes. No tanks this time, just huge numbers of infantry. Suddenly, up went the cry, 'Romanians! The treacherous bastards!' The blood-pressure nearly lifted the helmet from my head. One could easily believe every man on our side used a machine gun. The Romanians were withering under the murderous fire pouring into them, and their attack was faltering. Our lads, without any orders, jumped up and clubbed, stabbed or shot the Romanians in a veritable orgy of frenzied, long-pent-up hatred and fury. I could not see more than a dozen of them reaching the safety of their own lines. Even the Russian commanders must have been stunned at the complete rout – nay, annihilation – of such a large force.

We then had several days of relative peace and quiet. Inevitably the steamroller, in the form of huge numbers of tanks, followed by endless numbers of infantry, started rolling again. We steadily retreated, destroying Russian tanks by the dozen, every now and then assisted by our Stukas, which somehow still managed to fly and cause havoc amongst the Ivans. Russian casualties were astronomical and we never encountered Romanians again. Every square foot of ground was fought over desperately.

Just outside Tisza-Füred, having knocked out a large number of T34s, we got involved in hand-to-hand fighting. This was by now tantamount to suicide, as the odds were against us. Here we were outnumbered by ten or 15 to one. Russian morale was now at its highest, while ours was at its lowest. The Russians were now a well-fed, healthy lot, while we were a sorry-looking lot of flea-bitten, skeletal scarecrows. My weight was down to under nine stone, from 10 stone 5lb, and we were wheezing and tottering on our feet. Nevertheless, the spirit was still there and we still considered ourselves far superior to the Ivans.

The Russians retreated, but we had no strength left to follow up. Just outside our trenches, something hit me on the back of my helmet, and I toppled forward into the trench. The pain in my head was excruciating, and I was trying to remove my helmet, but found it literally nailed to the back of my head. A grenade splinter had penetrated my headgear like a dart, and was stuck in my skull. I was carried into Tisza-Füred to a first-aid station but lost consciousness. How they got my helmet off, I shall never know, but they did, and I was back in action within 48 hours, the damage being negligible."

A group of Russian guerillas discuss tactics for a raid against the Germans

THE MARIANAS

Turkeys & Shooters

In June 1944, the Americans pressed towards the strategic Marianas islands, which lie in the Philippine sea within bombing range of Japan. In the massive sea battle that ensued, the Japanese were overwhelmed by American skill and numbers in the air. On one day, US fighters destroyed 300 enemy planes in the 'Turkey Shoot', tipping the balance of air power in the Allies' favour

Commander David McCampbell was Commander of Air Group 15, the three fighting squadrons of the US carrier Essex which took part in the battle against the Japanese Combined Fleet. He later became the most celebrated US naval airman and was awarded the Medal of Honour.

"On 12 June 1944, Admiral Raymond Spruance had led the 5th US Fleet to the Philippine Sea, preparing to invade Saipan and the other major islands of the Marianas chain, which were needed as air bases for the B-29 bomber to strike Japan. My carrier, the USS *Essex*, was part of the fleet's Task Group 58.4, which comprised three carriers, three cruisers and twelve destroyers. The other carriers were the *Langley* and the *Cowpen*. Altogether there were 15 carriers now with the 5th Fleet.

Our first task was to soften up the air defences of Saipan and the smaller island of Pagan which was important because it housed an airfield with one small runway, and a number of barracks and shops. Saipan was the first objective. The job – destroy enemy aircraft.

Just before 1.00 pm on 11 June, we had the order to launch the planes. I led the air strike, which consisted of 15 fighters from the *Essex* and two dive-bombers along with a dozen fighters from the *Cowpens* and a dozen from the *Langley*. The two dive-bombers were rescue planes, equipped with extra life-rafts and other survival gear to drop to downed pilots.

Seven of our F6F fighters dived from 12,000 feet and bombed at 2,300 feet, and then formed a strafing line and strafed the island from east to west. The other eight fighters stayed above flying cover until the bombing runs ended, and then they went down to strafe. For an hour and a half they concentrated on strafing runs on Saipan's airfields and seaplane bases.

The Japanese drew first blood. On the way in over Tanapag Harbour, Lieutenant Kenney's fighter was hit by flak. He was diving but he just continued to dive straight down to the water and splashed. Lieutenant-Commander Brewer led the fighter attack on the harbour seaplane ramp. I saw his bomb strike in the middle of three seaplanes parked nearly on the ramp, and destroy all three.

Brewer then strafed, came around and headed out to sea. Five miles out at sea, northwest of Marpi Point, Brewer and Ensign Fowler spotted a dark green Kawanishi flying boat called an Emily, with the dull red circles. They attacked. As they came, several other fighters were shooting at the Emily. Brewer attacked from above on the side of the plane – he said he saw his bullets hit the Emily's number two engine and the port wing. Fowler reported that he attacked the cockpit and noticed that the plane was smoking. Twenty seconds later the flying boat turned over on one wing, dropped with engine aflame and smoke coming from the fuselage, and struck the water. It exploded in a geyser of smoke, water and flame.

This was our first encounter as an air group with enemy aircraft. We had heard a great deal about the Zero fighter. I was pleased to note that the F6F could stay with the Zero in turns, climbs and dives – particularly at altitudes above 12,000 feet, where most of the air action took place. I noted two deficiencies of the Zero – its lack of armour and its unprotected gas tanks. All but one of the Zeros I saw shot down that day went down in flames.

On 19 June Admiral Ozawa launched his first strike against the American fleet, beginning from Guam. At 10 o'clock our radar picked up a large force of 'bogies' approaching, distance 150 miles. At that point Commander Brewer was already in the air, in command of the combat air patrol, and he was ordered to take his planes up to 24,000 feet. We heard Brewer shout 'Tallyho! 24 rats, 16 hawks, no fish at 18,000' (24 fighters, 16 dive-bombers and no torpedo planes at 18,000 feet). He then spotted 15 Judys (Aichi dive-bombers) at 18,000 in tight formation with four Zeros on each flank

– and, 1,000 feet above and behind, 16 more Zeros.

Brewer selected the leading dive-bomber and came up to 800 feet from the plane. The Judy exploded so quickly it was unbelievable. He flew through the debris and attacked another. This one blew up too, half the wing fell off and the plane cartwheeled into the sea. Two minutes after Brewer's 'Tallyho', my fighter was launched, and I led 12 fighters to join in fighting off the attackers – but by the time my fighters were organised, the fighter controller announced that another raid was coming in – 50 planes travelling at 150 knots, 45 miles to the east. I was to intercept and stop them.

My first target was a Judy (dive-bomber) on the left flank and approximately halfway back in the formation. It was my intention after completing the run on the plane, to pass under it, retire across the formation and take under fire a plane on the right flank with a low side attack. The plans became upset when the first plane I fired at blew up practically in my face, and caused a pullout above the entire formation. I remember being unable to get to the other side fast enough, feeling as though every rear gunner had his fire directed at me.

After my first pass on the leader with no visible damage observed, pullout was made below and to the left. Deciding that it would be easier to concentrate on the port wingman than on the leader, my next pass was an above-rear from seven o'clock, causing the wingman to explode in an envelope of flames. Breaking away down and to the left placed me in a position for a below rear run on the leader from six o'clock, after which I worked on his tail and continued to fire until he burned furiously and spiralled down out of control. During the last bursts on the leader, gun stoppages occurred. I decided I must be out of ammunition and started back for the carrier."

Yoshida Katsuyoshi was a naval warrant officer in the Japanese 202 Air Group when the Americans showed signs of moving against Biak Island. The Group transferred to the Island of Yap and then to the Solong base to make preliminary arrangements for operations.

"On 17 June I was transferred from Kau to Peleliu. It was the night before what was called afterward 'The Battle of the Marianas' (the Battle of the Philippine Sea). In discussions, it was decided that 202 Air Group was to fill up the bomber gap. All our planes were to be

A F6F Hellcat comes in to land on the carrier USS Lexington

fitted out with 60 kg bombs. We would become a fighter-bomber unit, and attack enemy forces landing on Saipan.

The next day reveille was at 3.30 am, and we set off, breathing in great lungfuls of the bracing air of Peleliu. After one and a half hours, we landed at the airfield on Yap. The ground crews bustled to and fro, filling us up with ammunition, bombs and fuel. At the control station, the Z-flag flew, as it had traditionally since the Battle of the Japan Sea, as if to stress the crucial importance of this battle for our country. We set out at 12 noon, a large formation of about 200 aircraft, and made a big detour east of Guam. The plan was to attack enemy ships at sea south-east of Saipan. When you fly for three hours with a load of two 60 kg bombs, the hand grasping the joystick gets tired. I felt tense just after setting off, but after two hours had gone by, I felt pains in my legs and bottom in the narrow seat, and dull-spirited.

We were flying in a bomber role, so other fighter units were in formation in front of us and behind, and below and above us acting as escort. Soon the southern shore of Guam came up on our left, and we came out over the eastern sea. About 30 minutes later, we were in enemy skies. High overhead, our escort unit and the enemy fighters were already engaged in dog-fights. Today, whatever happened, we were going to introduce the enemy to our 60 kg bombs, but below the clouds our field of vision was not too good, and apart from ten transport ships up ahead, no warships could be seen.

Suddenly a bunch of fighters, ours and the enemy's, came falling down through the sky ahead, to my right. At the same time there was an uproar on all sides, and little time to take aim at a target. Even for objectives close to, the distance was too great for the height. The instant I became aware of this, the ack-ack fire from below became more intense than anything I'd experienced so far. A pillar of flame, as if from a dozen heavy ack-ack machine guns, roared past.

I felt a long time had elapsed up to the time I burst through, and I took a quick glance above and below, but whether or not our bombing unit had spread out, what entered my field of vision was about 20 or 30 aircraft, apparently suspended over a 5,000-ton transport, but the angle was too narrow for horizontal bombing. Partly from impatience to return to my true role as a fighter, I dropped my bombs from both wings.

An enemy fighter came in to attack me from the right as I tried to confirm what had happened below me, and I switched to the right to dodge him. The joystick had stiffened, and I put some force into it and finally came out on top of the clouds, where both sides were engaged in dog-fights. Some distance off, a number of aircraft were locked in combat and tracer shells flew to and fro. My wing plane was no longer behind me. I must have come out in the opposite direction of the cloud after dropping my bombs.

I could see what looked like a military position and an enormous number of landing-craft. I decided to dive straight down and strafe them. Aiming at a spot on the shoreline, I put her nose down. Once again, intense ack-ack fire came up at me. After glancing behind and above, I took aim at the enemy position which had come into my sights and squeezed the trigger. I felt terrific and let out a roar as if my 20 mm and 7.7 mm guns were bursting through at the landing craft which were touching down on the sandy strip of shore. The aircraft's nose juddered as I aimed and fired.

No flames burst out, so it wasn't very satisfactory, and I thought, let's put the finishing touches to it, but then I realised all my 20 mm ammunition had gone, so I climbed out through the middle of the dogfight and turned the plane's nose towards Guam. As I looked around, I could see streamers of black smoke on the surface of the sea, and in the sky, far off, distant aircraft looking like rubber balls..."

BURMA

Jungle Nightmare

In only two months early in 1942, Japanese forces overran the British colony of Burma. To the Allied troops, the ease of the invaders' victories in the inhospitable jungle conditions made them seem like supermen. The perception was only challenged by Orde Wingate's Chindits, specially trained troops who operated deep in the heart of enemy territory

Private Ernest Faulkner was 23 when he was drafted out to the Far East. Although in the same regiment as Jim Howard (page 181), his reminiscences are from the men's, not the officers', point of view.

"We went through all the proper training for jungle warfare – marching and walking, sleeping out in the wild. We used to go on tea and rubber plantations, and of a night you could hear the beaters keeping the animals away. There were quite a lot of wild animals around – elephants and leopards.

We had scorpions and centipedes too. The chaps used to dig a pit and take a scorpion and a centipede and let them fight it out, taking a bet on it. Then they'd get a little snake and put it in too. The centipedes were five or six inches long.

We relied a lot on air drops of food and we used to look forward to them. A couple of times we ran out of rations. Once, our officer said to a chap, after we'd left one area, 'Go back and get the potato peelings.' We'd buried them in paper (we used to bury things like that). This chap had a tin of jam, so we dipped the peelings in it. We were on half rations sometimes in Burma.

We were mainly on the defensive. In Burma they were building these roads right down to the Chindwin and as the roads progressed, we moved down to the Chindwin itself. Whilst they were building these roads, the army was preparing all these defences on the hills – trenches, so that when we did withdraw, it was all already dug and all we had to do was wait for the Japs.

It was good thinking. It must have been about 50 miles we withdrew, from the Chindwin up into these hills. We went into prepared positions all the time, so we had an advantage on the hills. You only dug trenches when you were advancing. We would just lie in wait for them in these trenches and they'd arrive – swarms of them. We were really outnumbered and on each hill we had a small number of men. Sometimes on a hill you'd just have a section of chaps – another one might have a platoon, another one a company. The Japanese would capture one hill, then bypass the next one.

The Japs' main attacks were by night – daytimes there was just shelling with mortars. They had these 105s and 75s, and you could tell what they were by the noise. The worst ones were these whizzbangs – little things on wheels – cannons deadly at about 500 yards. You never heard them – it was just SHOOSH.

The Japs were really vicious – they'd fight to the end. They were so good at camouflage and getting underground, they couldn't be seen by aircraft. The artillery would bombard them, but they were still there. We, on the other hand, would attack during the day. We never got any peace or sleep at night. Half the night they'd shell you, then half an hour would go by – and then another attack. They'd do the same thing again, the Japs. On Nippon Hill they had barbed wire and left a gap, and you could see them there – they'd be shot down and a little while later another mob would come in. In the morning they had 60 to 70 bodies lying by the wire. They had no brains to alter their tactics. They seemed doped!

It was a job to get hold of any prisoners, but we started getting more on the Ukhrul road. They all had their hair shaved off. They were only kids, a lot of them. Maybe it was just shock – or it could be that they were brain-washed. They knew their officers would mow them down with their swords if they failed them. On several occasions we found these Japs, not a mark on them, with skin like a new-born baby. They must have been killed by the blast. We found bodies stone dead without a mark on them.

On another hill at Tamu there was an outbreak of scrub typhus – we lost a lot of blokes through that. Everyone was going down with typhus. We had to scrape all the green vegetation off the hill and burn it. They reckoned these ticks were living on it.

Native craft on Burma's numerous rivers prove useful for evacuating wounded

We did this patrol for six or seven weeks and no-one was allowed to shave – in fact, our CSM did shave, and they busted him down to a sergeant. It was in case they cut themselves and got an infection. We ended up like a load of tramps. Fleas – don't talk to me of fleas. We went up this hill and there were head-hunters' huts. When you came out of them, you were running alive – scratching.

In the monsoons you were never dry. You got used to it and plonked down where you were in the mud. The gas cape was your only protection. We were on the move and it would take all day to get up one hill, slipping and sliding in the mud with these mules – they went through hell. We had elephants too, on some hills. We fed them on special rations which came on the air drop and they ate grass and bamboo too. Boys would give them biscuits – mouldy stuff from their rations. The corned beef was really corned mutton and when it was hot you'd open the tin and it would come out liquid. Horrible. It was rotten, but we'd boil it up as a stew. I think it was First World War rations – some of them had 1918 on the bottom. We had some Canadian rations too – Quaker Oats – and they were full of weevils. You just put them in the pot too.

Eventually we knew the Japs were taking a hell of a beating. The men were pushing the Japs back on to us. It was a nightmare for them. You should have seen the graves. Bones and arms sticking out – they couldn't bury them. We knew we were winning."

Jim Howard was Second Lieutenant with the 1st Battalion of the Devonshire Regiment – otherwise known as 'the 11th of Foot' or 'the Bloody 11th'. The name was coined by the Duke of Wellington in 1811 due to the frequency of their getting decimated ...

"One thing that was a great comfort – and was always true – is that the Japs are a lousy shot. If he gets a machine gun, he'll tear hell out of the trees above your head, and with luck he'll get nowhere near you at all. But he's absolutely deadly with a mortar – and the first thing you know about a mortar is that you've got a bomb among you.

We developed an attitude of crawling about the jungle – we stalking them and them stalking us. We had a Gurkha battalion with us and a Sikh battalion and we all learned from each other. We got acclimatised to the jungle. You'd get people in high command saying, 'It's only seven miles – ought to be able to do that in a couple of hours'. Seven miles in thorn jungle in Ceylon takes you *five days*. You learned that sort of thing. More important, the officers and commanders learned too.

In Ceylon we picked up about seven to ten casualties a week with malaria. It was recognised that you couldn't expect to operate in that sort of country without doing something about it – so they got top scientists from the UK and they brought out malarial suppressants. It took a month to get anywhere, and by that time 40 per cent were down with malaria. In action, if someone came down with malaria, they'd be taken off. Later in 1944, the Americans were there with these tiny light aircraft and they'd take you away.

We would wander around in the jungle singing – in the most unmelodious sense – *You are my Sunshine* – in the pitch dark. Wherever the Devons went you'd hear this converging through the jungle. We always had scouts out in front making a single track through the jungle. If you've got mules with you you've got to cut it twice as wide and it takes you twice as long. Something happens – and you can hear it. Everybody just scatters – the whole column disappears, because you're all mobile. You've got nothing – everything is with you, on your mule or on your back.

It was a very relaxed war for the Devons. I said to my sergeant one day, 'Look, somebody reckons there are some Japs down there'. He replied, 'Ooh ar. I should leave them alone, sir. They ain't doing you no harm'. That's what we did.

In battle you knew what would happen if you were captured – so you didn't surrender. *They* didn't surrender. There was no heroism involved – it just wasn't one of the options open to you. We lost one officer as a prisoner – we were pretty sure he was killed, and I'm sure we didn't lose anybody as prisoners. Surrender wasn't an easy option, which makes it a lot easier for a young officer. When you fought a reasonably civilised enemy like the Germans (not including Buchenwald) you've got a chance of being treated decently as a prisoner – but not with the Japs. A young officer was never under pressure to surrender to save unnecessary casualties. It takes a load off your mind. The troops never wanted that either – it was a different fighting ethic from any other circumstances. You just fight on to the logical conclusion. It was win or die, and that was it."

Toshio Hamachi was a section commander in No. 3 Platoon, Sakazawa Company of Takemura Battalion. After months in Burma, the battalion commander, Takemura, assembled all his companies to plan an attack on the Chindits towards Katha.

"Two days before Sakazawa Unit arrived at Katha, a British airborne unit tried to cross the Irrawaddy in broad daylight. The enemy was crowded on to wooden rafts, the weapons and ammunition piled up, with mules to complete the load. It looked to be only 80 metres across at this point, as the raft left the river bank.

The LMG chattered and spat flame, breaking the peace and calm of the river. The enemy troops, crowded and bunched together on the raft, were mown down with no chance of returning our fire. In the smoke, the screams of British troops in the agony were drowned by the din of rifles. You could hear the mules whinnying as the bullets found their mark. It was as if the enemy were so many blood-sacrifices. The bullets sang in the midst of the scattering spray of water. 'Got you! Die, you hairy bastards!' our men shouted.

Those British troops who were still alive dived into the water, only to sink into the weeds at the river bottom. In the eddies you could see the profuse bright blood of the British troops. It was the work of a moment, and we had knocked the heart out of the astounded air-borne troops."

IMPHAL & KOHIMA

Green Hill

The Italian town of Imphal, guarding the British supply line into Burma, was an obvious target for the Japanese, and General Slim was ready for the attack that came in March 1944. The town was well defended, but to the north the settlement of Kohima was far more exposed. The Japanese turned their attention to the hills around the village, but determined resistance by a handful of troops lifted the siege and drove the attackers back into Burma

Lieutenant-General Nobuo Tanaka succeeded Yanagida as commander of Japanese 33rd Division. This excerpt comes from his diary at the point where he and his men reached Three-Pimple Hill, west of Bishenpur.

"Both officers and men look dreadful. They've let their hair and beards grow until they look exactly like wild men of the mountains. Over a hundred days have passed since this two-month operation began. In that time the men have had almost nothing to eat – they're undernourished and pale.

The weather's been clear for two or three days, but last night it began to pour, which adds to the men's hardships. Last night some comforts and a few rations came up from the rear. Up to now we've been short of candles and have had no light except when absolutely necessary.

I was particularly pleased to get some pickled plums. Jungle greens have a bitter taste and a grassy smell, but we eat them because there's no alternative. But even one plum each makes the food taste better.

Since 15 June I've not used a watch. Watches aren't much use on the battlefield. The rain pours down endlessly, but enemy aircraft are still flying. They're at it twenty-four hours a day, almost as if the skies were clear."

Jim Howard, Second Lieutenant with the 1st Battalion of the Devonshire Regiment, was only 20 years old when he sailed from Britain in 1942. After rigorous training in Ceylon his men are put into the fight in the jungles of Burma.

"Sometimes when we really achieved something, we'd just tear right through a Japanese position – and we didn't stop but went straight on and disappeared. This was rather fun – guerrilla warfare. That's what we were trained for.

In 1944 they set us on top of a hill and said that no Jap must pass. This was in March. By July we'd lost about 500 yards and about 2,000 men – but we were still there.

Infantry battle must necessarily always be the same – someone throwing shells at you or throwing mortar bombs at you; someone shoots at you with a machine gun; if you were unlucky, the air force joins in and gives you a clobbering. It depends very largely on what you've got and what he's got, and the good position you've chosen, who succeeds. With the Jap, of course, it was a great advantage that he wanted to die – and it was our job to see that he did. So we and he had the same object. There were two schools of thought among the Japanese Army – there were the militarists who were completely stupid – and there were those who were just good soldiers, who valued their soldiers' lives and military principles above all the suicidal nonsense.

One of the things that makes me smile was that the Japs used to come up – and we'd sit there in amazement in the same place, night after night – and get clobbered. They'd never get to the top of this hill where we were sitting. It sounds daft, doesn't it? Their general would be told to go take a hill – he'd get there, plant his flag and in doing so get all his men killed – and that's seeing the Japanese fighting from the other side. It's no pleasure having to kill people.

We were lucky in another way too. As we went in, we moved ever so cautiously from Imphal, and did patrols as we'd learned in Ceylon. One of our patrols hit some Japs. You were expecting something knee-high to a grasshopper with ruddy great pebble glasses – not on your Nellie. They were six foot three – it was a lie about these small chaps!

Even though they were a lousy shot, they were lethal with mortars – and nobody likes mortars. They don't make a noise as they come, then suddenly BANG! I never personally had any individual thoughts about them at all. As far as I was concerned, we always had a task to perform, and we did it. As far as I'm concerned, in infantry battle it's the survivor who wins. If there's only one man left, he's the winner. But you're there to perform a task, so individuals trying to stop you don't matter. It's all terrifying – then that's what you expect it to be. It's just as bad, but infinitely worse than anything you'd ever dreamed of – and yet it is something set totally apart. You can't have experiences like that and not be affected by it.

It's odd, sometimes a unit runs out of steam. They deliberately put us through that, to see how far they could go and to see how the troops would put up with it. In the defence of that hill after March, April, May, they reckoned we'd had enough. We'd been knocked about something rotten, and they were honest, our generals. They didn't relieve us – they said we were due for a change of air, so instead of sitting on a hill and being shot at by the Japs, we went in right behind the Jap and attacked him! It was literally trackless jungle – and we only had mules at this time. Much of the time we were carrying the loads and pulling the mules through the mud with ropes – it was that bad. Down in the valleys it was warm and steamy and wet – it was on top that the Nagas and Manapuris used to build their villages. One of our patrols found a deserted village and said they'd have a nice rest there. They went into the hut and the whole floor was alive with fleas and bugs – bed bugs. They were crawling!

It was raining, raining, raining. And the first thing that happens is that all your blankets get wet. Ever tried carrying a wet blanket? You just have to throw them away. We all expected to get arthritis, but we don't seem to have done too badly really. Wet for six weeks on end – literally never dry. The medical authorities were more worried about us than we were. We were winning, we were happy to go on – but we found we couldn't digest food. They never understood why, but it just passed straight through, undigested. We weren't getting enough food anyway, but we just lost the ability to digest it. Some were all right – the army found it odd, though, that morale was high. We were tickled to death that we were winning and clobbering the Japs something terrible.

In those days, you buried a bloke and didn't give a twopenny damn whether he was a Roman Catholic, a Presbyterian or what. You'd say some prayers over your mate, and that was it. They were all people who believed in God somehow – and that would do. We had a Roman Catholic padre for a long time, and he was just a padre as far as we were concerned – he did his best to please all denominations.

There was one chap, late in the campaign, who got a bullet which entered the top of his head on one side and came out at the front. Well, we didn't waste too much time making deep holes for burial, you understand, but they wanted to cover him up decently. So they did a couple of dog scratches around him and, as is the way (some people may take it badly), if anybody had a good pair of boots and you didn't, you had them. Someone said, 'That's a good pair of boots there'. So they took his boots off – they weren't even buried, and as they took them off, his toes twitched. 'He isn't dead! Dig him up again!' He became consciously aware a year and a half later – became himself again – if they hadn't pinched his boots he'd probably still be there. He had a sort of free leucotomy – but he doesn't want to talk about it, though...."

Lance Corporal Miragishi, serving with II/60 Battalion, Japanese 15th Division, was involved as two sections of his company were under British artillery barrage on a steep hill on the Imphal front. To his disbelief, four British tanks climbed the hill.

"Four tanks came towards us, but the Kagawa platoon hadn't a single anti-tank gun to confront them with. Not only Kagawa platoon – there wasn't a single anti-tank gun in the whole of II Battalion.

The men held their breath and went rigid with fear as the tank caterpillars grated towards them – ready to trample down the trench sides. At that moment, one of our men heaved himself up out of the trench and seemed to prance in front of us. It was Lance Corporal Uehara of 6 Company. Just before leaping out of the trench, he said in a low urgent voice, 'I'm going to get that tank. Just watch me!'

He dashed forward, just as the men in the trench understood what he said. He was clutching in his right hand a globe the size of a fist. He closed up to the tank and, from about ten yards, hurled the globe.

Immediately, for some reason, the British tank was enveloped in white smoke, like steam. It wasn't a hand-grenade nor an armour-piercing mine, nor a mine of any sort. When the ball struck against the tank and splintered, the white smoke poured straightaway inside the tank, which was covered in it.

A few seconds later, the lid of the tank's gun-turret was thrust open and the tank crew, giving queer screams, jumped out and down from the tank. Down the slope they tumbled, rolling over and over as if to escape something. From the turret of the now empty tank a terrific amount of black smoke gushed. Uehara had climbed up the side of the tank, slipped the pin of a hand-grenade and flung it inside.

In no time at all, the black smoke turned into a red pillar of flame, while the echo of explosions reverberated among the hills. The tank began to blaze. The bursting grenade had induced an explosion of the ammunition inside."

A British 3-inch mortar team supports the defence by firing bombs over the jungle

ARNHEM

No Garden Party

In September 1944, Field Marshal Montgomery launched a daring plan – history's largest airborne operation – in which paratroops would seize the bridges of the Lower Rhine in Holland and hold them until met by a land-based thrust. But relief failed to reach the besieged paras at the furthest bridge, in Arnhem, and the operation left some 7,500 Allies dead, wounded or missing

Willi Renner was a sergeant in the 2nd Battalion of the German 6th Parachute Regiment and was involved in fierce house-to-house fighting in the town of Reusel as Operation Market Garden began.

"Hand-grenades were thrown up or down, and our raiding group, which consisted of about 15 men, was given the task of fighting clear one street's worth of houses. That meant clearing the enemy out using whatever means possible. On the way back, while clearing the houses, we came upon an Englishman who had been shot in the stomach. I assumed that the man had been hit by someone from the street or something like that, and that his own men had left him lying there in the house – they couldn't take him with them.

I came towards the house and, while we ran, shots came out of the cellar window. A few metres to the left of me, one of our men was hit in the throat. Blood came pouring from his throat – it was terrible. Another comrade of mine was hit in the chest. In his wallet he had a picture of his girlfriend, and the bullet went straight through the photo. We took cover to the right and ran round to the other side of the house. We moved so that we couldn't be seen by the English soldiers in the house, and kicked in one of the cellar windows. We threw in a hand-grenade – whether it was one or a few, I can't remember exactly. There was a terrible explosion. It's a terrible thing when a grenade explodes in such a small space – I had experienced this myself. The English emerged – a few of them were wounded and some inside must have been dead. Four of them came out and I took them back with me.

So, the direct fighting was now over, and we searched the house – and now we had to take care of the wounded and dead men. We took from the dead men all their papers, all their valuables, their watch and identity tag. Then the dead were buried and the wounded taken to the main field hospital. I was given the job of taking the four prisoners back. Everything was going smoothly until at one point I could see that the prisoners had become afraid. The first thing that came to mind was that these men were afraid that they were going to be shot. Then things relaxed a little. We exchanged cigarettes. These were only young men and they were suffering from the psychological effects of the house fighting – the guilt that they might have killed someone; the shock from the exploding grenades."

Brigadier J W Hackett DSO, MBE, MC (now General Sir John, GCB) was commander of the 4th Parachute Brigade. Injured after six days' furious fighting, he discovered the extraordinary compassion and determination of the Dutch Resistance workers as he made his recovery.

"It was really a major error not to open the port of Antwerp before this operation. I'd add to this, that it was really very important to get the 1st British Airborne Division into action.

This Division was really the cream of the British Army at the time. These were very highly motivated, highly trained men, who had been much mucked about. They had something like 15 abortive operations, on three of which we were already in aeroplanes with our parachutes on ready for take-off, all our letters to our loved ones posted. Then somebody would come round, open the aircraft door and say, 'It's all cancelled, everybody gets three days' leave.' You can't go on doing that without irreparably damaging the morale of a first-rate, highly strung, wonderfully trained, admirably chosen and officer-manned division – without its going very badly downhill. Even though the omens were not good, it was important to go.

What they did to us was put us down six to eight miles from the objective. They feared the flak defences of Deelen Airfield, which,

Soldiers of the 1st Para Battalion take cover in a shell hole

when we got up to them, proved to be far less formidable than expected. There is the added complication that airborne operations depend very largely on surprise. The 17 September was the day on which Market Garden opened, and when the first lift of the 1st Airborne Division went in. I commanded the second lift the next day, when surprise had gone, and instead of brandy and bonhomie, we met a whole lot of angry Germans.

People who hadn't fought the Germans enough thought it was a piece of cake, but the thing about the Germans was that they were the finest professional army fighting in World War II, and whatever there was on the ground that was weak, as soon as you threatened something vital, the German response would be swift and violent. We were told, on the intelligence available, that there were only a few Mark I tanks on the Corps front, and units of trainee cadets with a battalion of broken-down old men were all we would find.

I was asked, 30 years after the war, 'When did you first realise that this operation was, if not doomed to failure, at least, not very likely to succeed?' I said, 'Before it began', and recounted my own experience.

I had a final briefing with all the officers of the Brigade and key personnel – about 100 people. I went through, in meticulous detail, what we were to do, down to platoons, in the occupation of the northern defences of Arnhem town, to form the bridgehead around 1st Brigade's seizure of the bridge. When it was all over, I dismissed everyone but the three Battalion Commanders and key personnel and said, 'Now, you can forget all that. Your hardest fighting and worst casualties will not be in the defence of the northern perimeter of Arnhem town, but in trying to get there.' We never did.

Brian Urquhart was G2 Intelligence in Boy Browning's Corps HQ, 1st British Airborne Corps, and had some inkling that there might be German armour in the area. He had tacked on to a fighter sweep going over the area two days before some oblique reconnaissance photography. There was clearly some armour there, and it wasn't old Mark Is at all – in fact, as we knew later, and as the outcome says, they were the 9th and 10th SS Panzer Divisions, going to refit in Germany. They were not fit to go into battle as armoured divisions, but they did have a few tanks and some SP guns, and it wasn't difficult to rustle up some more along the railway line within 24 hours.

On the 18th they were too much for us. I did what I was intended to – I tried to move in, but it was quite impossible because of the tanks. What can lightly armed airbornes do against even a trace of heavy armour? The tragic thing – and this relates to the whole battle – was that General Urquhart, who was a splendid battlefield commander – went forward to see for himself what was happening at the bridge, owing to the fact that signals communication was not of the best and, indeed, failed on the very first day. He got pinned by the enemy there and couldn't get out. There he was, incommunicado, for about 36 hours at a really crucial stage of the battle. Had he been back in command and in touch, he would have called off the 4th Parachute Brigade from this abortive attempt against hopeless opposition to reach the northern end of the town, and put it into the reinforcement of Frost and the perimeter the Division had established around Oosterbeek.

Why did the Guards Armoured Division never arrive to relieve the 2nd Para Battalion? There were some good reasons for this. One was, I believe, XXX Corps planning. There was a euphoria that hovered over everyone after this dash from Normandy to Holland – a wonderful, thunderous advance of a victorious army against an enemy defeated, but not destroyed and still formidable. They were so cockahoop they thought it was all a bit easy. Then there was the choice of the single road from Nijmegen to Arnhem – that really was a great mistake. This road is about 60 km long, and built on an embankment running across low-level fields. You couldn't everywhere get tanks off the road because very often the fields on either side were too wet and boggy – and it was very easily interrupted by well-placed anti-tank guns.

Urquhart withdrew into the perimeter around Oosterbeek about the 20th, and I was brought in, my brigade very ragged, but splendid – this lot were absolutely first-class. They'd had a terrible time, and suffered a reduction from about 1,000 to 300, and that didn't do their morale any good, but they were absolutely on top of the world.

I was wounded on the 23rd and was carted off to St Elisabeth's Hospital in Arnhem. I got a splinter in the stomach and spent four and a half months in Holland, hiding. My dear wife knew that I was alive, but in poor shape – this thing inside had carved ten perforations and two sections in the lower intestine – and one perforation is lethal! A miraculous operation was done on me by a British airborne surgeon.

I was helped out of the hospital by the Dutch underground and spent the next four months, hidden, nursed, cherished, fed, loved, by a Dutch family – four elderly ladies and the son and daughter of one of them. In the house where I was hidden, I was put up in the loft or down in the cellar when the house was searched. I read – one of the aunts had trained as an English teacher and she had a bunch of books in the house – the authorised version of *The Bible* (I must be one of few people who has read the whole of *The Bible*, straight through). That was how I occupied myself – I read the *Complete Works of Shakespeare* too.

I learned some Dutch and I was our military correspondent for a Dutch underground paper. We used to have a little wireless under the floor and we'd listen to the odd broadcast. Then I would write a column called *Notes on the War in the West* by our military correspondent. It only went to three editions because the *Gestapo* got on to it, and they had to move me somewhere else less dangerous.

It is remarkable, the degree of adaptability in the human constitution. You live a life which you consider to be normal, and suddenly you are thrust into something quite different. It's astonishing how soon that becomes the norm, and you live that life as if you had always lived it. It is when you come back that it's difficult to adjust."

BATTLE OF THE BULGE

Cold Christmas

The Allied advance had come up against a major German counteroffensive in the wintry Ardennes. Ill-equipped against the cold, with supplies running dangerously low, troops were weary. Hitler ordered a last-ditch offensive to drive the Allies back to the sea. But by the end of January 1945 German losses were around 120,000 – and the Allies were approaching the Rhine

Private Alfred Jenkins of A Company of the 2nd Battalion of the Argyll and Sutherland Highlanders, was training in Holland for the forthcoming Reichswald offensive, when the Germans launched their all-out attack in the Ardennes.

"When the Germans broke through, all the available troops were rushed south and as I remember it for the first few days, we seemed to be going all over the place in Belgium. We finally wound up at a place near Maastricht, near the German border, and that was just before Christmas. It looked as if we were going to be there for a few days, so they had a sit-down Christmas dinner planned for us. Well, what happened was, on Christmas morning we were put on a half hour stand-by which meant we had to be ready to move at a moment's notice. That meant we had our Christmas dinner out of mess tins and standing up in the open. We finally moved at eight o'clock that night.

From there we went to a suburb of Liège. When we went into the house where we were billeted, the owners of the house were a middle-aged couple with a young daughter, and it was obvious that the daughter had been suffering from the food shortages, but they had this banner across the living room 'Welcome to our liberators –

welcome to brave British soldiers'. We were there a few days then we moved over to the other side of Liège, where we actually did guard a bridge at Amay. It was while we were there that we captured what we thought was a German spy. One of our section came in one day with a chap he had met, dressed in American uniform. He shook hands all round – which made us a bit suspicious, because this is a continental, not a British or American habit. So we had difficulty understanding him and asked him if he spoke English. He said no, but he said he spoke American. We noticed that he was only wearing the liner of his steel helmet, which we knew had been forbidden by the US command. Then when he told us he had come from Paris that day, we thought 'Aha, what have we got here?', because we knew that all movement between Paris and the front had stopped, because it was at that time they had the scare that there was an assassination team out looking for Eisenhower. We handed him over to the American Military Police. Whether he was a spy or not, I don't know.

We were there over the New Year, and it was about this time that it really started snowing. Up until then it had been fairly cold, but not the sort of snow you usually associate with the Ardennes.

On 7 January we spent the night travelling in an absolute blizzard and arrived the next day at Bertogne and then they decided the roads were unfit for vehicles and we had to take to our feet. We went on to a place where the East Lancs had had a battle – we found several of their bodies lying around there. We got a warning that there were some German tanks and infantry approaching, so we stood to, but all that happened was we captured one prisoner, who said he was a Polish deserter. It was funny, you usually found in the German army that there were no Germans – they were all Poles and Russians. When we got into Germany, we never found anybody who supported Hitler. They were all members of the 20th July bomb plot! You had to wonder where he got all his troops from!

We had to march back to Bastogne. I remember that march as though it were yesterday. It wasn't exactly cross-country, but the roads were fairly indistinguishable, and the shelling had brought down a lot of branches of trees – and they are nearly all fir trees down there. There must have been a slight thaw, then it had refrozen, and each individual needle on these trees was coated in ice, so trying to march over that in hob-nailed boots was rather like walking over ball bearings.

We had as many layers of clothes as we could, balaclava helmets, greatcoats, leather jerkins – at that point we didn't have snow suits.

They didn't think of issuing them until it was all over. It was so cold there that we had to wipe all the oil off our weapons. Usually you had to keep the moving parts of your weapon slightly oiled, but we had to wipe it off because it was freezing.

Each section had a Bren gun – I had the Bren gun in our section. The rest were armed with rifles, apart from the corporal who had either a Sten gun, or, if he was lucky, he looted a *Schmeisser* machine pistol – this was preferable to a Sten gun because they were notedly very unreliable weapons. At one point earlier in the year after a couple of accidents, anyone who had Sten guns in their battalion was told to remove the magazines from them when travelling in transport, because more than one had been dropped and gone off. Bren guns were different – they were using them in the British Army up until the 1960s, because they said it was so accurate that you could shoot through its bullet-holes.

En route from Lavaux we stopped at a sort of barn at a crossroads. We could see the road ahead of us went down into a valley and up again – and just at the bottom of this valley was some sort of small hut. There was this burst of machine-gun and shell fire from the ridge ahead of us. It caught there, and it took several hours for them to get back.

There was one chap in that section, he had his younger brother with him, and he saw him killed right in front of his eyes. They told

The crew of a King Tiger gloat over a dejected column of American POWs

us afterwards that they had to hold him back because he wanted to take off after these Germans by himself. Then another section had a go. The same thing happened. They would just get down to this hut, and the Germans were waiting for them. Then it was our turn to go. As you can imagine, everyone was trying to be last out of this barn where we were sheltering.

It was at this point that Major Samwell, the Company Commander, decided that he'd come down with us. He called up a troop of Sherman tanks we had there, and we started off down. He walked behind one of the tanks to use the phone on the back of it – it was for communications with the infantry. He just walked behind this, and the tank was hit by either an armour-piercing shell or a shell – but my main memory of that was a cloud of shrapnel and dust flying everywhere. I saw Major Samwell fall there. We beat it back to the barn.

They decided, after all this, that it really was a waste of time trying to get round that road. According to the records, there were something like 28 casualties. Fighting there had come to a stop and the Americans were just sweeping up. What happened was that we were at the top of our movement forward, and we were pinched out by the Americans coming in from each side of us."

Lieutenant Virgil Lary was with Battery B of the US 7th Armoured Division's 285th Field Artillery Observation Battalion. On 17 December, he was ordered to help reinforce the slender American line at St Vith.

"The battery was on the road that morning, and by noon had reached a point three miles south of Malmédy on the St Vith road. Some 300 yards behind the crossroads of the cutoff for St Vith, the column was suddenly stopped by German machine-gun and mortar fire. We jumped down from our vehicles and took cover in the ditches on the sides of the road.

The German unit was an element of Colonel Peiper's 1st SS Panzer Division. They had stopped at the crossroad, surprised the MP who was directing traffic there (and who had escaped behind a house), turned the signs around to confuse us and then opened fire on the convoy.

I jumped down from my truck and crawled to a small stream 40 feet from the road. I covered myself with grass and mud and headed for that house. By this time, three more tanks had come up the road. They were all Tiger tanks of the newest German design. They moved along the road, spewing fire at the ditches. One German tank shot up an American ambulance. Other German tanks knocked out 24 American vehicles of the convoy.

The German infantrymen came down the road, examining the ditches. I surrendered again and soon found myself in a field with about 150 other POWs, guarded by paratroops. The Germans searched the Americans and took wallets, gloves, rings, cigarettes – and all weapons. They ordered us into a field south of the crossroads, and I noticed that they had set up machine guns surrounding the field. We were told to raise our hands above our heads. Tanks at the two ends of the field along the road covered them.

A German command car drew up and an officer spoke: 'You will go across the Siegfried Line, will you, you dirty swine?' The officer took aim at an American doctor and fired his pistol. The medical officer fell. The German fired again, and another American dropped. Then the two tanks and the machine guns in the field began firing.

I dropped. I was hit in the arm and the foot. I lay, bleeding – as if dead. German soldiers came along the line of bodies and shot some of the wounded and bayonetted some and bashed the heads of others with rifle butts. (When the bodies were found later, the eyes of some of the soldiers had been gouged out.) The Germans came up to me. 'Is he dead?' asked one. Something diverted his attention and he moved away. I lay perfectly still, my eyes closed, but I could hear the sound of pistols firing and the noise of rifle butts against skulls.

After about an hour, the German column moved off, leaving the field silent. Several survivors decided to make a break for it and got up and ran for the house on the road – including me. The Germans opened fire. Several men dropped, but I made it to the house and lay doggo. The German armoured column began to pass and for two hours, tanks and half-tracks ran down the road to St Vith. When they seemed to be gone, two of us ran down the road toward Malmédy. From the crossroads the Germans began to fire at us, but they didn't hit us and we ran on for two miles. Then a jeep came along and picked us up, and took us into Malmédy and safety. A few days later, I learned that of the 150 Americans in the field, only 43 survived, and three quarters of *them* were wounded."

ATLANTIC VICTORY

Masters of the Atlantic

At the end of 1942, German U-boats posed a serious threat to the lifeline of Britain – supplies from across the Atlantic. But the tide was beginning to turn – by the beginning of 1944, as the marine forces of Germany and the Allies battled for control of the icy seas, the U-boats were suffering increasing losses. With more air cover, the Allies soon managed to subdue the 'wolf-packs' for good

Chief Officer Robert Leonard, on the Merchant Navy's heavy-lift ship, Fort Halkett, had seen action in the icy North Atlantic. Then his ship was 'rewarded' with an easy trip to South America, to pick up troops.

"It was August Bank Holiday, 1943, that we caught a torpedo in number two hold, that sunk us 680 miles off the coast of Brazil. One of the lifeboats was destroyed, so I took one of the 18-foot bridge boats and my crew – of which I was the second oldest, and I wasn't yet 21.

At that time, when you were moving independently, you had an envelope with a number of letters in it – ABCD – these were points, at random, in the ocean, and in order to keep the ships apart, so it would be more difficult to sink a number of them, you set off for a point and just before you got there, you would get a radio message in code, telling you where the next point was. We were knocked off on one of these tuning points. We changed course at 4.10 am, and at 4.40, BANG. A submarine was sitting waiting at our turning point. It was clear that the code books had been acquired.

She was an excellent ship with a tremendous captain. For a merchant ship, she was very much a fighting ship – and even with the loss of one boat, we got everybody off in an orderly fashion – and the U-boat came alongside us. They asked if we knew where we were, which we did – and was anybody injured, which they weren't.

He was sunk that night by two American Hudson bombers who had heard our SOS from naval control in Brazil. There was something about other mariners being done for by aircraft – it doesn't matter what side you are on. With the German submariners there wasn't that ferocious antipathy that there was with the Japanese submariners, who were hated and loathed and feared because of the horrendous things they did. Not just killing people – but taking the water, food and sails out of the life boats and leaving the men there.

By the end of 1940, with the desperate shortage of shipping, they lifted the load-line a foot – which might mean getting on for between 700 and 1,000 tons extra per ship. This is great fun if you are sitting in an office, but if you are running a ship in a North Atlantic hurricane, it's a joke in doubtful taste, I may tell you. The ship's like a half-tied rock, and we lost, killed and injured and drowned, a significant number of men washed off these grievously overloaded ships. The more overloaded the ship, the more difficult she is to handle in heavy weather. I developed quite a cynicism about 'experts'. People aren't quite what they think they are, and what they know is sometimes only what they think they know.

When you get an enormous stretch of bad weather in the North Atlantic, even the most experienced have a constant air of disquiet. You don't sleep properly and you get bumped about and you physically get knocked about. You are covered in bruises and you can't eat properly because the galley can't operate. You are turning the watch out two or three times a night. It was very corroding to morale to listen to ships broadcasting that they can't launch their boats and that they were sinking. You could lose a man in the length of this room, then he would be gone. You'd have 40 men watching for him – then you'd spot him again – and then you'd lose him.

One of the big advances in how we improved the survival rate was with the lifeboats – how the water was stored and the food. Before, there used to be hard biscuits which men with false teeth couldn't eat – instead there were proper pemmicans. There were survival suits like wet suits, which kept the wet, and more importantly, the wind, off you. That used to cause havoc – the older men and the younger ones used to die tremendously quickly. If you were not picked up that night, your chances of survival, if you were under 22 or over 50, faded very fast."

Hans Lemke from Potsdam was just 20 when he set out on his first U-boat, U-1229, in August 1944. Its sinking off Newfoundland sent him as a POW to America, then England. He finally married an English girl and settled in Yorkshire where he lives today.

"The journey across the Atlantic was two or three weeks – I can't remember exactly – constantly underwater, because of the *schnorkel*. This wasn't the best of experiences, because when there were heavy seas, the float valve would shut off the *schnorkel* to stop water coming in. So every time that happened, the diesel still needed the air, which it sucked out from the inside of the boat.

It was very boring down there in the torpedo room. I was in charge of the stern section of the torpedoes, so I was on my own. All I had to do was make sure that the pressure and all that other stuff was kept up. I had no other job – I had to be at the ready all the time, in case we had to fire. We had to sleep down there as well – on bunks fixed between two rails. You would spend your time polishing or checking something – waiting, reading, sleeping, talking.

There were about ten of us down there, in a space measuring about 10 feet by 30 feet. Some of them, the ordinary seamen, would go up to the bridge to do their watch, and when they came back they would sleep. I never remember us quarrelling, really – and what did we talk about? Well, the usual sort of thing. Wouldn't it be nice to have a woman and that sort of stuff... philosophy, crosswords. We talked about what each thought of the universe, God and all that. We were still pretty optimistic then, and nobody was anti-Nazi.

We had a ration of about 15 cigarettes a day – no alcohol on a mission like this. I suppose we had to keep a clear head. Except for the captain who, I believe, did have some spirits with him. The food was very basic – all tinned stuff – but it wasn't too bad.

So, on 20 August, we were off Newfoundland, and for some reason, the captain decided he would bring the submarine up to the surface. I don't know why he ordered us up. Nobody could find out, because he was killed. We had absolutely no idea that there were ships in the area and that aircraft were engaged against us. But as soon as we went up, we had to dive down very fast again. Alarm!

I don't think we had dived down ten feet when a bomb hit us. A lot of damage – some of the men overboard. After about 20 minutes to half an hour, we couldn't hold ourselves any longer – we had to surface. Before we even got to the top, they started to shoot. So we had to go up, and the captain shouted, 'Everyone aboard! Save yourselves!' I was the furthest back, so I was the last one to the conning tower. When I came out I saw them all dead there on the deck. Nine aircraft were strafing us.

I dived straight into the water, and didn't come up until I was yards away. I was in the water for about four hours. I didn't even have a life-jacket on – in fact, we had stripped off completely to make us as light as possible. The aircraft kept firing and quite a few of us got shot in the water. There was no need for that, because it was quite obvious that we had abandoned ship. I've never forgiven them for that.

After five or ten minutes, the sub suddenly reared up and the propellers came out of the water, still turning slowly. Then she just slowly went down. As she went down, we gave her a big cheer – strange – why were we cheering? After a few minutes, she blew up – I think because of the pressure – and this nearly ripped our insides out. It was then four hours until we were picked up by a destroyer. We were absolutely shattered – frozen stiff – and we had to climb up rope ladders to get on to the destroyer. We were numb at that stage and one of us, the wireless operator, dropped dead from exhaustion after climbing up on to the destroyer."

Signalman Trained Operator Albert John Newcombe was aboard the American-built sloop HMS Kilbride on her maiden voyage. Her task was to escort a convoy of 32 ships from Halifax to Greenock in Scotland, a dangerous voyage across the Atlantic for a small craft.

"We joined the 5th Escort Group, which was led by a destroyer called HMS *Hotspur*, at Halifax. We left with about 30-odd ships and did a steady old run across the Atlantic at about 8 knots. The weather was atrocious most of the way. When we started off, it was calm but misty, with a lot of floating small icebergs about. Then it really got up to blow. I have never seen anything like it. I had seen 40 foot waves – well, these must have been about 80 on average! When I was standing on the bridge, I just hung on for dear life. I was terrified. When you were on top of a wave, you could see a couple of miles away, and then you went down into a big, deep trough. It calmed down after a few days – we never lost a ship.

Then we had another scare. There was a ship at the end of the line and somebody had hoisted a flag. As soon as I got a look at the flag, it said, in international code, 'Your attention is drawn to bearing 270'. We looked around and couldn't see anything, because we were much lower than this ship. So, we steamed back, flat out at 17 knots and after ten minutes we spotted some masts. We went to

The armament of two destroyers is silhouetted against the sky

action stations and I called them to identify themselves. They acknowledged the code of the day. It turned out that they were three 'bird' class frigates which had been going like the clappers to catch up! They were put into position in the screen and we carried on.

When we got just north of Ireland, we ran straight into another convoy. I don't know how it happened, because we all had radar. You know how soldiers countermarch? Well, it was just like that. Everybody put their steaming lights on and they went through each other, just like that – and there wasn't one accident. There were about 100 ships involved. I remember one huge French ship passed us about 50 yards away! We got into port and I was that tired. It had been four hours on, four hours off, and I was wet. I used to crawl underneath the chart table and sleep on deck. I slept for 48 hours after that trip."

WARSAW UPRISING

Underground Army

In 1944, the Soviets began to turn the invaders from their soil – and beyond. Almost five years after the German invasion of Poland, the bubbling lava of the Polish underground was ready to erupt. The Polish Home Army were determined that they would free their capital. But on 2 October the leader of the Army surrendered to the Germans after fighting that devastated the city

Lucjan Kinlein was 21 when he left his law studies to train with the military, so when called upon to fight with the Polish Home Army, he was already part-trained – part of a great national movement who would use all their resources to reclaim their homeland and re-assert their independence against Russia too.

"To a certain extent, we all enjoyed it, because it was the first time that we could really stop running from the Germans – and make them run. We had a very limited amount of arms and ammunition. My unit was lucky – we had quite a lot of automatic weapons and ammunition. Therefore we were used on many occasions where there was a bit of trouble. We were very busy in the first few days of the uprising. We had a few losses of course, but after a few days, we adjusted ourselves to this different way of fighting.

Street fighting is something you have to be specially trained for. We found that we could even cope with the German tanks – and we didn't have to be afraid of them. In the town they were very vulnerable, and we threw grenades and burned them with petrol. We learned as we went along.

On many occasions we were asked to attack particular objectives and we had to suffer some losses, but we had a number of wins, and one of these was the police headquarters. At night we dug holes through the buildings to get nearer to the German positions. This was supposed to be a surprise attack during the night, but to a certain extent it wasn't, because they were waiting for us. We met with heavy fire and were stopped, so we had to find some way to go round. That cost us some lives, but we had our ways to do this – mainly by burning them out. We had flame throwers and we managed to penetrate their line, and after about 12 hours, we succeeded. They had to surrender. We managed to capture quite a lot of arms there, and it was a great victory.

I remember on the telephone exchange, the second big attack, there were a number of units involved. We were facing quite a lot of heavy machine-gun fire and grenades from the building coming down on us, because it was occupied by the SS. They knew that eventually we would attack them because the telephone exchange was very important. This operation cost us quite a number of lives, but somehow I survived and got only one bit of metal in my forehead – I'm still carrying it somewhere here – but again, we managed to get in only by burning the heavy front door. Once we got in, it was all in darkness, and we could hear only the bells ringing – they had an alarm system and it had been switched on by the short circuit at the door. There was a lot of noise and you didn't know which your friends or enemies were. Some Germans shouted, in German, *'Kamarad, Kamarad! Nicht schiesen!'* and we took it that they had had enough, but unfortunately we were not very experienced – they just wanted to find out where we were. When one of our boys called, *'Komm her. Waffen abwerfen!'* that was what they were waiting for – they threw a couple of grenades on us and that was the end of our operation. We knew then, that in the darkness, when they shouted, it was better not to reply to them.

We were fighting for 63 days – it went on and on, and the suffering of the civilian population was even greater. Where we were, we only had the army against us. Sometimes they were drunk; sometimes they were not German really – they were just Ukrainians and people they had employed.

We didn't have their heavy artillery or the Stukas against us, because they were afraid of bombing their own positions. Sometimes we would be facing each other over the other side of the same building! So we were better off to a certain extent than the civilian population because the civilians suffered from the bombardment of artillery and the Stukas, and shortages of water, food and medicines.

We got quite a lot of our ammunition from the Germans, and a bit of food, too – and German uniforms. In the end we were all dressed differently. Some of the units in the old town were dressed as German parachutists, but with the Polish emblem on their helmets.

With the town so much under German control, we had our headquarters in strong buildings, in the basements. We had to have

Civilians emerge from the sewers where they have been forced to take shelter

some rest and food, and in the first month, the arrangements were quite reasonable. In the second month, we were hungry and short of water – but we were still better off than civilians. Each unit had their own ladies who tried to find food for us. In the last weeks of the uprising there was no water and practically no food.

There are some people who find it too upsetting to talk about it, but I myself find it was the most interesting 60 days of my life. I have no doubt about that. There was great comradeship – great elation. We found we were doing something that had to be done, and we were taking part in, as we found out later, one of the biggest battles in the last war. It looked, in the beginning, just to be a skirmish, but in the end it was a very important battle.

You must remember this was after nearly five years of occupation. We had to do something. We had had enough of this treatment from the Germans. Enough is enough. We were preparing ourselves for this during the four years of the occupation. We were building, training, collecting arms. Life was near normal before the uprising. You could buy anything you could think of because Warsaw was on the way to Russia, and there was very heavy movement of troops and supplies from the German war apparatus – and some of it got 'lost' in Warsaw on the black market.

The Germans terrorised the people. They were trying to find out about our Home Army and the underground organisation. They were killing people without any proper trial – taking in the intelligentsia, arresting them for no reason but reprisals.

At the beginning, some elderly people who wanted to have peace, were apprehensive about the violence the uprising would bring. But most of we young people were not afraid – so it was the sacrifice and the effort of young people. Even kids were fighting.

The Polish Home Army was part of the overall operation of Polish forces. It was all geared to that final act – we wanted to show the Germans that we were in power in our country, and were taking revenge for what they were doing to us. It was also to protect our young people from being taken to labour camps.

But the third and most important reason was that Warsaw, as a city, in the centre of Poland, had to be taken – not by Russians, but by the Polish Home Army. That was why we had to do it."

Herbert Brunnegger was a platoon leader in the SS Totenkopf Division when, in autumn 1943, he was posted to Warsaw – into the tense atmosphere which prevailed as the Polish resistance built up their ultimate counterstrike.

"Warsaw was a dangerous place. Poland's capital was like a pot of bubbling lava whose lid was about to blow. My orders were to report to the Replacement Battalion III at the Marbuta Barracks. On the way from the station to my new unit, I witnessed a shoot-out as men from the Polish Resistance were chased through the streets.

I soon discovered that scenes like this had become routine. It was strictly forbidden to go out alone or even in twos. If you wanted to go into the city, you had to be armed. We were told quite clearly which bars we were allowed to visit, and were told to stay clear of the others. Nevertheless, soldiers kept disappearing without trace. Their uniforms and weapons would turn up again on men from the Polish underground.

One *SS Unterscharführer*, awarded the Iron Cross I Class, was suddenly arrested because the Security Service had found out that he had been seeing a very pretty Polish girl, and through her had latched on to the Polish underground. He jumped from the first floor of a house on the street and was gunned down by a sentry. Yesterday he was a brave soldier in Russia – today a traitor to his people. Yesterday a comrade – today an enemy. Was it only the Polish girl who changed his mind?

In Warsaw I couldn't find any volunteers from the 'class of 1938'. The place was swarming with foreigners in SS uniform. What had happened to our once so-proud elite troop? Croatians, Galicians, Lithuanians, Estonians, Hungarians, Russians and French were now members of the SS. We'd soon be having Tartars, Turks, Serbs, Romanians, Bulgarians, Indians and Italians with us! Alongside the volunteers from Holland, the men from Denmark and Norway in the *Wiking* and *Norland* divisions had already proved their worth. The *Freikorps Denmark*, who had fought with us in the Demyansk pocket, had shown fantastic bravery.

The continuing deployment of new SS divisions could not disguise the fact that the original fighting strength had been whittled away. One day I was awarded the Iron Cross II Class. My company commander had sent on the decoration certificate. As platoon leader, I would have been delighted and very proud, but now, having been through three field hospitals, where I'd seen medals dished out like they were going out of fashion, I saw this differently."

Polish soldiers fiercely defend their city

LEYTE GULF

Last-ditch Attack

In support of a landing in the Philippines, the US Navy engaged the Japanese fleet in one of the world's greatest sea battles in the straits and channels of the archipelago during September and October 1944. Although both sides suffered losses, the 28 Japanese vessels sunk, along with the destruction of many of their remaining aircraft, left them virtually impotent as a sea power

Lieutenant L Odum, the Aerology Officer of the 'baby flattop' carrier, Gambier Bay, was on the starboard catwalk as, his devastated ship's decks covered with dead and wounded, the order came to abandon the stricken ship.

"I didn't relish the idea of going off the high side, so I started walking to the passageway in the centre of the ship, down the stairs by my room, heading for the port side. Near my room there was an explosion and I was thrown against the bulkhead. Shell fragments were ricocheting around me but I wasn't hit. I reached my stateroom and found my bunkmate collecting survival gear. I picked up a palm-sized mirror and stuffed it and an unopened pack of cigarettes in my shirt pocket.

I got to the port side, unlaced my shoes, dropped my helmet and sidearm and holster and slid down a heavy rope. First I was dragged under by the weight of my shoes but I kicked them off and started swimming away from the ship. I spotted a raft and swam to it. About 30 men were aboard. Suddenly I found I was in charge. The leader of the group had sunk into a stupor. I got the uninjured men off the raft and had them cling to the ropes on the sides. We were so close still that we could see the American fighters and bombers attacking the Japanese cruisers and destroyers as they were heading north. We could only wait until someone came to find us.

That night in the water we all had one biscuit the size of a Ritz cracker with a piece of Spam. There was no fresh water. One by one some of the men just drifted away from the raft and were not seen again. Somehow we got through the night. In the morning we had another bite of biscuit and a malted milk tablet. Sharks began to appear round the raft. Some of the men began drinking sea water and they became delirious.

The second day the sun was hot and the men were dispirited as they saw planes flying overhead which didn't see us. I swam over to the raft next to ours. The men here were in as bad shape as we were, without food and water. The night was full of terrors. Men who had drunk sea water began hallucinating. Some of them thought they could swim to Samar, and went into the water and had to be dragged back. Some did not come back.

Most of the men had given up hope. I was sure that we would be rescued if we waited. Flares were sent up every hour in hope. At one o'clock the next morning, hope arrived. A crew member on PC 623 called out to us, 'What ship are you from?' None of us would answer. What if these were Japanese rescuers? Then the patrol boat snapped on its searchlights and began probing us. Suddenly, as with one voice we all yelled, 'Yes, yes, we are all Americans. *Gambier Bay*.' By now we could see the big number 623 on the patrol craft. It slowed down and sailors began lowering nets over the side for our men to climb. I started swimming over and was nearly drowned by some men as the boat pulled in towards the rafts. Men were crawling over me to get to the boat. I shook myself free and climbed to the deck, lay down on that cold steel and wept and thanked God for his deliverance."

Torao Suematsu had climbed through the ranks of the Japanese Imperial Army since 1939 and, by late 1944 was Staff Officer, No. 1 Special Attack Forces. He recalls the events in the Sibuyan Sea, 24 October.

"At about 2.00 pm, *Musashi*, battered on all sides, and already the victim of at least ten torpedoes and countless bombs, was ordered to make for Manila, and we sailed on leaving her behind. She had her escort vessels, of course – however, air attacks by enemy ship-borne aircraft increased in ferocity as time went on, and as the damage we had sustained was not insignificant, we needed to turn back and take stock. At about 3.30 pm, Commander in Chief Kurita changed fleet course westward.

He judged that if we continued to advance as we were, we would sustain far greater damage (besides, *Musashi*, and the flagship of No 5 squadron, *Myoko*, had been torpedoed and had fallen out of line, and both *Yamato* and *Nagato* had been damaged by bombing), since the enemy assault planes had increased in number. He decided to wait for the results of the attack on the enemy's mobile force by our aircraft, avoiding for a while bearing the brunt of the attack – also, I think there was the chance that he would mislead the enemy.

So there's not the slightest justification for thinking he was going to abandon the breakthrough into Leyte. I think this was sufficiently clarified by the second reverse course after 5.00 pm, because of the receipt of the signal from Combined Fleet C-in-C Toyota, 'Heaven is on our side. Attack with all forces', was made about 7.00 pm.

Kurita realised that the breakthrough into Leyte Gulf would be delayed – he wouldn't reach it until dawn on the 25th. I remember we were anxious about adjusting with Nishimura Force how we should go about it. But there was a more urgent problem – the passage through San Bernardino Strait. I mean, we were worried that we might be ambushed at the exit from the strait.

At any rate, because we'd taken a fair hiding from the submarines the day before, we would be in a real fix if we became a target at the exit from the strait, when we would have no freedom of manoeuvre. However, the enemy seems to have judged our previous reverse course to be a withdrawal, and made no provision.

At any rate, that night we were able to pass uneventfully through San Bernadino Strait. Even if there were no submarines, we expected to find the enemy fleet lying in wait for us. We had to pass through the strait in a single column. At the exit, if it had come to a gunnery engagement, with the enemy formed up in line abreast, we wouldn't have stood a chance.

The loss due to the reverse course alone was about three hours, but besides that there was considerable delay due to the air attacks by enemy aircraft, so that when we came out of the strait, it was already just past midnight – deep night. And at exactly that same time, Nishimura Force was approaching Surigao Strait. They came down on the 25th, and when our force reformed into a ring for night sailing, enemy aircraft carrier units suddenly came into view. I was standing on the bridge at the time, and I was astounded – it was something we had not considered.

For an instant we had a bit of a scene on the bridge – of shock, surprise, quite unheard of. Ordinarily you'd never consider such an encounter. Clearly the enemy had not properly interpreted our movements. I said, 'Commander, we must move towards the enemy'. 'Yes', he answered, and then gave the order, 'Column unit turn, let's go!' looking at the compass. We raised the flag, 'column unit turn', on a bearing to contain the enemy – it must have been 110. (The order means the fleet changes direction completely as one unit, not just as individual ships.)

Because the enemy were a force of aircraft carriers and destroyers, they could not open fire on us at once with their guns. So as soon as we had complete 'column unit turn', *Yamato* began to fire. However, when she'd fired four or five rounds, enemy destroyers advanced at speed and spread a smoke screen.

This was the first time *Yamato* had opened fire with her main guns on an enemy fleet. She had only fired her AA guns before that. So everybody shouted, 'We've sunk her!' – but in fact it wasn't possible to confirm whether we'd sunk a ship or not, because of the smoke screen. Passing close by later, we saw an enemy aircraft carrier up to the deck in water, so we can have only sunk one ship for certain. Nearby, half-naked crew members were drifting on rafts.

As far as the sunk aircraft carrier is concerned, it's anyone's guess whether she was hit by a torpedo or by gunfire. She was an escort carrier, so the enemy was not a large force. At the time we thought they were standard carriers. At any rate, we made an all-out attack. Then, unluckily, when we were getting a thorough pasting from enemy bombers, a squall came up between us and the enemy. How can I describe it? When we were going into the attack, a squall comes up – how about that?

We spent about two hours searching for them, but we too had been the victims of torpedo attacks from the enemy's destroyers. In order to dodge these torpedoes, *t*had to run in the opposite direction from the enemy. We ran for about ten minutes, but that was a lot of time to lose. But because visibility was poor due to the squall, it was impossible to estimate what our situation was in relation to one another. Fleet high command was possibly no better off.

Estimating was out of the question, so we had to consider our fuel situation. To control the battle line, we ordered the fleet to concentrate. The basic course in this case was north and that was a problem. On that course, we were increasing our distance from

Medics administer blood plasma to an American casualty

Leyte. Moreover, the units were pretty scattered – it took a fair amount of time to concentrate them, but then we made course once more for Leyte and ran for about two hours.

The enemy bombed us the entire time. They bombed us for three days during this sea battle, without a break, and it felt as if your head was being pressed down into your shoulders – but when we ourselves went into the attack, it was exhilarating.

What kind of psychology is that, eh? The air might have been hot and humid, but we felt as if we were under blue skies. When we pursued the enemy, even when they were bombing us, we weren't worried. There's a big difference between defence and attack.

Kurita Force ended up not charging into Leyte Gulf – in fact, we withdrew northwards – and I bear some responsibility for it. I've had misgivings about it, even in post-war days. Was I the cause of an appalling failure? That's been my worry. Because I brought about the occasion by which Jurita Force reversed course. I was on the bridge, but I had no idea what was happening in Leyte Gulf."

RETURN TO THE PHILIPPINES

The Tables Turn

In October 1944, after their naval success, US troops landed on the Philippine island of Leyte, which they won in two months' fighting. They then travelled to the main island, Luzon, landing in January 1945. Even though the US rapidly captured the capital, Manila, the occupying Japanese withdrew to the island's countryside and maintained the struggle for months to come

James Fahey enlisted in the US Navy in October 1942 and was assigned as a seaman to the light cruiser USS Montpelier. After leave late in 1944, after the US invasion of Leyte, his ship left to join and give support to the Seventh Fleet.

"On Saturday 5 November 1944 we pulled into Leyte Gulf in the Philippines at noon. This is a very big place, they say it is 60 miles long and 30 miles wide. We also passed the spot where our navy and the Jap navy slugged it out at 3.00 am.

We will now be under the Supreme Command of General MacArthur. Our job is to patrol near the spot of the sea battle and destroy any Jap warships that try to attack our merchant ships and our troops on Leyte.

27 November. At 10.50 this morning, General Quarters sounded. All hands went to their battle stations. At the same time, a battleship and a destroyer were alongside the tanker getting fuel. Out of the clouds I saw a big Jap bomber come crashing down into the water. It was not smoking and looked in good condition. I felt like I was in it as it hit the water not too far from the tanker, and the two ships that were refuelling.

One of our P-38 fighters hit it. He must have got the pilot. At first

I thought it was one of our bombers that had engine trouble. It was not long after that when a force of about 30 Jap planes attacked us – dive-bombers and torpedo planes. Out two ships were busy getting away from the tanker because one bomb-hit on the tanker and it would be all over for the three ships.

Jap planes were coming at us from all directions. Before the attack started we did not know that they were suicide planes, with no intention of returning to their base. They had one thing in mind – and that was to crash into our ships, bombs and all. You have to blow them up – to damage them doesn't mean much. Right off the bat a Jap plane made a suicide dive at the cruiser *St Louis*. There was a big explosion and flames were seen shortly from the stern. Another one tried to do the same thing but he was shot away. A Jap plane came in on a battleship with his guns blazing away. Other Jap planes came in strafing one ship, dropping their bombs on another, and crashing into another. Jap planes were falling all around us – the air was full of Jap machine-gun bullets.

We knocked our share of Jap planes down, but we also got hit by three suicide planes – but lucky for us they dropped their bombs before they crashed into us. It looked like it was raining plane parts. Quite a few of the men were hit by pieces of planes. We were supposed to have air coverage, but all we had was four P-38 fighters, and when we opened up on the Japanese they got out of the way of our exploding shells.

The men on my mount were also showered with parts from Japanese planes. One suicide bomber was headed right for us while we were firing at another attacking plane, and if the 40 mm mount behind us on the port side hadn't blown the Jap wing off, it would have killed all of us. When the wing was blown off, the plane turned some and it bounced off into the water. The bombs blew part of the plane on to our ship.

Another suicide plane crashed into one of the five-inch mounts, pushing the side of the mount in and injuring some of the men inside. A lot of five-inch shells were damaged – it was a miracle that they did not explode. If that happened, the powder and the shells would have blown up the ship.

A Jap dive-bomber crashed into one of the 40 mm mounts, but lucky for them it dropped its bombs on another ship before crashing. Part of the motor hit Tomlinson. He had chunks of it all over him – his stomach, back, legs and so on. The rest of the crew were sprayed with gasoline from great distance and at first they thought he was

Troops of the 37th Infantry Division pour ashore during the landing in Lingayen Gulf

knocked over the side. They finally found him on a corner in bad shape. The explosions were terrific as the suicide planes entered the water not far from our ship. The water was covered with black smoke that rose high in the air. The water looked like it was on fire."

Chester W Driest was with the 1st Control Squadron of the US Fifth Army Air Force, operating from Australia. His squadron was sent to Leyte to control air traffic then, after a few weeks, was ordered to take part in the landing in Mindoro, set up a base to cover later landings on Luzon and go in with the landing forces.

"We loaded in LST 1036 and 1025 and sat off Leyte. D-Day was postponed for twelve days.

Twelve days aboard an LST can be a very long time. Since few men had prepared for more than a few days aboard ship and the facilities of an LST are not designed to accommodate a large number of men comfortably, baths and changes of clothing were few during this period. Beards often remained unshaven, clothes became very dirty and grease-streaked, and a miasma of body-odour came up from down below through the open doorways and vents of the landing craft.

Bunks were assigned to the enlisted men on a ratio of eight beds to 32 men, so most of the men slept above the deck. The sleeping quarters in the hold were, for the most part, unventilated, and after a few days the air became foul and foetid. Water faucets were turned on for only a few minutes each morning to permit hasty ablutions.

The convoy set sail on 12 December. On the voyage to Mindoro the convoy was attacked by Japanese aircraft a number of times. The anti-aircraft guns boomed and the Allied fighters overhead moved in to hit the enemy planes. Planes of the Marine Air Group 12, Fifth Air Force fighters, and Navy aircraft from Admiral Felix Stump's escort carriers protected the invasion force.

But on the second day out of Leyte, a Japanese reconnaissance plane discovered our invasion convoy at about nine in the morning. That afternoon the kamikazes came. They arrived at 3.00 pm as the convoy was about to turn around the southern cape of Negros island, into the Sulu Sea. An Aichi dive-bomber zoomed down to crash into the cruiser *Nashville*, near the cabin of Rear Admiral Struble. The flag bridge was wrecked and 133 men were killed, including Struble's chief of staff and several high-ranking officers. Colonel John T. Mutha, commander of the 310th Bombardment Wing, was one of them. Another 190 men were wounded, and the *Nashville* was out of the battle.

Two hours later, we aboard the LSTs watched another kamikaze attack. Three fighters escorted seven kamikazes. The combat air patrol intercepted the Japanese a dozen miles out, but three kamikazes were broken down by a destroyer, another was shot down by a cruiser, but the third ploughed into the destroyer *Harden*, doing great damage and killing 14 men and wounding 24, putting that destroyer out of action.

On 13 December the Japanese planned to destroy the convoy and sent 186 planes to find it – but they missed the convoy and their attacks were diluted elsewhere. The convoy steamed on to Mindoro.

The landing began early on the morning of 15 December. First the destroyers and landing craft equipped with rockets hit the beaches. The mission was to establish a perimeter around the village of San Jose and begin airstrip construction at the four Japanese airstrips in the area.

I was in LST 1025, under Captain M Bonfoey, and this was the forward detachment of the 1st Fighter Control Squadron. We landed at Blue Beach near Agustin, virtually on the bank of the Bugsanga river. The LST pulled right up to the sandy beach and the men landed with dry feet. We began unloading – it was very quiet and there was no enemy opposition."

Members of the 1st Battalion on the route to Luzon, March 1945

THE RHINE

Operation Varsity

Germany's historic border, the mighty Rhine, represented a formidable barrier as Allied troops gathered at the beginning of 1945 to pour into Germany's heart and end the war in Europe. One of the biggest airborne invasions of the war brought Allied troops to support ground forces confronting a stunned enemy, who, although they were staring defeat in the face, did not give up easily

Sergeant Derek Glaister with the 7th Battalion was dropped into the Wesel area on 24 March as part of the force intended to strengthen 21st Army Group's bridgehead to the east of the Rhine. The overall operation was a success – but individuals often paid dearly.

"When we got the Rhine it was murder, because Jerry knew we were coming. Every farmhouse was occupied by Germans. They put a lot of smoke down, so instead of coming down to 400 feet, which is the lowest height you can drop from, we had to go up to 1,000 feet. We were also travelling quite fast. I was No. 20 – last man out – so you can imagine how far off target I was. Miles out. I and ten others came down near a farmhouse which had an 88 mm gun just outside it. Just before my feet touched the ground, a bullet smashed through my left elbow, so I lay on my stomach and pretended to be dead. I saw nine of the others come down, some into trees. The Germans shot them as they hung there helpless – it was a sickening sight.

I tried to give myself some cover by throwing a smoke bomb, but just as I was making for the nearest ditch, a German SS officer came up and shot me in the back from ten yards away with a Luger pistol. I shall never forget him – he was about six foot four and covered in boils. I spun round and fell down, and this officer grabbed my left arm and shoved it through the straps of my webbing. Then he took my water bottle, flung it in a ditch and looted whatever he could. I was worried that he'd finish me off with my knife, but I had the presence of mind to lie on it, and when he had gone, I got hold of it and threw it into the ditch.

I lay there feeling pretty rough and watched those poor fellows swinging in the trees. One of our gliders came over, but the 80 mm cracked it open like an egg and the jeep, gun, blokes – all fell out.

Towards evening I was still lying there, in one hell of a bloody mess. I was finding it difficult to breathe because the second bullet had touched my lungs. Then a couple of captured airborne soldiers came by – a glider pilot and Lance Corporal Butler from my own battalion. They asked their German escort if they could pick me up. So they gave me a shot of morphine, which helped, and put me in this wheelbarrow. They carted me along in this along a bumpy old road until the Germans took them away for interrogation and I was wheeled to a big mansion near the town of Hamminkeln.

At dusk a German lorry came along and two Jerries picked me up and dumped me in the back of the truck on top of some dead blokes sewn in sacks. They must have thought I was dead. That was the first time I fainted – my wounds had opened up and were bleeding again. I came to in a German toilet with my head near the pan. That was where all my troubles started. Two orderlies took me into an operating theatre and pulled my clothes off – which was very painful. They must have been operating on some chap and they slithered me straight on to the aluminium table which was still covered in his blood. Then they put an ether mask over my face and out I went.

I woke up five days later, my arm in a Nazi salute in plaster and paper bandages all around my back. No medicines or antibiotics. My back had opened up again as the stitches had come apart, so I was carried off to be restitched. When we got to the top of some massive stairs, I was tipped off. I landed on my head, breaking my nose and smashing the plaster.

There was a hell of a row about it and those orderlies didn't appear again. They stitched me all up again and put another plaster on, still in a Nazi salute. Then they had a go at my nose with no anaesthetic. They probed about, pulling bits of bone out but they went too close to my eye and damaged it, so I've still got permanent pain and double vision from that.

I lay in that hospital until the British arrived. They flew me over to the RAF hospital at Wroughton and sent for my wife and parents

German prisoners are marched across the Rhine as the Ninth Army moves into Germany

as they didn't expect me to live, My father was also in hospital at the time, having his leg amputated as a result of World War I. When my mother and wife came into the ward, they went straight past my bed – they didn't recognise me.

When at last they got around to taking the German plaster off, one of the nurses fainted. The stench was bad enough, but the plaster was full of maggots, put in by the German doctor to eat the dead flesh. No wonder it itched. A surgeon took one look at my arm and said, 'Off', just like that. But there was a lady doctor, Miss Wagstaff, who said she'd like to have a go at saving it, since I was left handed. It took three years in hospital and 55 operations to get me where I am now, which is 80 per cent disabled.".

John Leopard, formerly Staff Captain with the artillery of 6th Airborne Division, was transferred to the 10th City of Glasgow Field Regiment, Royal Artillery, and witnessed what was, reportedly, the heaviest artillery bombardment in military history, covering the Rhine crossing.

"The plan was to so damage the opposing forces that our assault troops could gain the enemy shore with the minimum casualties. The main crossings were to be made by the 15th and 51st Divisions, just north of Xanten. We in the 52nd were in close support.

For days before the attack, shells and masses of equipment for the crossing were brought well forward under the cloak of continuous smoke screens. On the night before the action, all the field guns were deployed in positions as close to the river as possible. Artificial moonlight to provide reasonable visibility was produced by a long line of searchlights, with their beams reflected from the clouds into the area of activity. The reason for bringing the guns so far forward was that they would still be in range of more distant targets without the need for time-wasting redeployment during the early stages of the advance beyond the Rhine. I had a map showing the scores of target areas and the artillery units responsible for each of them. It was my unenviable task to assess the accuracy of the fall of shot and to signal back such corrections as I deemed proper. How I was supposed to accomplish this during the night, lit only by the light of thousands of exploding shells, I had not the least idea. In the event, the light of the many fires started helped a bit.

Our guns in their vulnerable positions remained silent all day. There was quite a lot of random fire from the Germans, no doubt in the hope of an informative response. At night, there was a cautious movement of men and equipment between my dam and the river. Came the hour, and the world exploded. The noise was ear-splitting and got worse as the German guns hit our side of the river. Terrified stampeding cattle, some of whom thundered along the top of my dam, presented a far greater danger to us in our slit trench than to enemy shells.

Some of our shells just fell in the river – this I knew was incorrect, so I went through the motions of making adjustments. To be honest, it would have been pure, blind chance had any of them been accurate, but at least it kept us busy.

Eventually the devastating shelling ended and our advance troops made a triumphant crossing and established a bridgehead from which the advance proceeded. The dawn came up and everything was relatively peaceful. Our questionable night's work was concluded.

I looked with admiration at the long tank-carrying Bailey bridge the Royal Engineers had built. At a forward aid post, I saw a well-bandaged German officer inside. At the same time, the 6th Airborne Division, with its scores of aircraft and gliders, was passing overhead to stiffen our forward troops. I pointed upwards. The German looked pretty glum, but said in passable English, 'Zee var ees ofer'."

Heinz Deutsch (24) was a lieutenant with the 12th Paratrooper Storm Gun battalions. He recounts the events of 9/10 March 1945 in the vicinity of Wesel, when his unit was attempting to cross the Rhine.

"German troops had withdrawn, and we were on the left side of the Rhine about to cross by a railway bridge leading to Wesel. The German engineers, however, had blown this up earlier to prevent the Allies crossing there. So there we were with all our heavy weaponry. I had been given the order to oversee the crossing of the bridge, so I had to wait until last. The bridge had been blown so that it was still possible for infantry to cross, but no vehicles. The engineers put this together on the night of 8/9 March, with steel supports and wooden planks laid over these. It floated by means of empty air canisters. On 9 March, then, this ferry managed to carry across most of the guns.

When we reached Wesel, it had been completely destroyed. We were then told to withdraw to the north-east with our guns. But we had no other reason to use them. The enemy troops were staying back. We didn't know exactly why. Perhaps they thought it was a trap.

Later there was an enemy landing from the air, partly with the gliders. I shot down two of these gliders with the storm gun. The other two I could see had already landed, and it wasn't usual to fire at them when they were on the ground. We would point the storm guns at them and the infantry would take them prisoner.

Looking back at this time, morale among our men was surprisingly good. Our battalion were all volunteers, and frankly, we wanted a bit of action. We thought the war could still be rescued. Of course, most of the time in action, you only have enough time to think of your own situation, not to be shot yourself. We were defending our Fatherland, and we thought we still had a good chance. You never spoke about it, whether someone was in the party or had been in the Hitler Youth. We had a bit of doubt about the conduct of the war, but we were confident. There were no deserters.

I was awarded the *Ritterkreuz* (Knight's Cross) in April for knocking out 44 tanks with my own gun in the space of eight weeks, and I was mentioned by name in the *Wehrmacht* Command Report."

VICTORY IN ITALY

Awaiting The End

Leaving Rome behind them, the Allies pushed north, meeting stiff resistance. After the terrible winter of 1944 amid ice and snow, the Eighth Army continued the offensive and took Lake Comacchio and opened the way for victory. The British and Americans worked with Italian partisans to overcome the formidable German defences

Günther Drössinger (20) was a corporal with the Paratrooper Storm battalion, 1st Company, who fought against the Allies at the River Po and in northern Italy until the capitulation.

"On about 16 April we were dug in near the Adige river when the English Air Force mounted their first night assault. We used to call them shift workers, because they would always attack by day and clock off before sunset. I had gone with one or two comrades from my company to fetch food supplies and what turned out to be the last postal delivery to the Italian front. When we got back to the battalion combat post, the barns where the soldiers were holed up were in flames. We had moved into the neighbouring farmhouse.

About midnight or one o'clock in the morning I went outside for a pee and left my machine pistol inside the house. The area was lit by the flames from the barns. I was standing in the shadows and on the street outside. I could see a group of Englishmen standing at the front door of the farmhouse. What could I do? If I had had my machine pistol with me, it would have been, 'Hands up or I'll shoot you', but I'd left my gun inside. They couldn't see me in the shadows, so you could say that we were both lucky. What really shocked me was how close the English soldiers were bunched together. We always had about 10 or 15 metres between each man. You could have picked these English off easily with a machine pistol. I've seen films of Cassino where the Americans were clumped together like bunches of grapes. Anyway, I managed to get away, but I had to jump over the hedge at the back and from there I had to make my way alone for about two km and came upon one of our rearguard units – 14th Company. I warned them about what was ahead.

On 19 or 20 April we were in San Benedetto by the Po and we had to get over the river. There were two of us. The other was a man from the battalion staff. He was not from my unit, and by the time of the capitulation we were left with about five or six men, but at this stage I could find no-one from my unit. They were all scattered or wounded or dead. You could hardly talk of organisation at this point, or a chain of command. This was more or less every man for himself. Still, morale was unbroken.

We were in the hills near Caldonazzo lake when we heard of the capitulation. It was about midday on 2 May. We felt like 14-year-old boys again. We were delighted. Of course we were delighted. And yet it does seems strange. We had gone through this grinding battle in the north of Italy, what had turned out in the end to be a mere battle for survival, and we had ended up defeated, yet now we were just so pleased that the war was over for us.

War is a filthy business for everyone, and yet when you have been in it for so long you become a creature of instinct. You can smell danger. When a shell is coming over, you can tell by its sound, by the whistle it makes, whether it is coming for you or not. And these old soldiers' instincts (and I was only 20 at the time, but still in war terms a veteran) are passed onto the young lads coming to the front for the first time, or to those who have had no experience.

We believed in it. The way I see it is this: the Americans. What were they fighting for? For the interests of big business. For the big capitalists. Not to defend their own country, their own people. Theirs was an anonymous fight. We were fighting for our homeland. It was an honour to wear the German uniform.

After the capitulation, we guarded the farmhouses side by side with the Americans against the partisans. You could hardly say that they had taken us prisoner at this stage; we hadn't even given up our weapons. It was two weeks before we had to give up half of our weapons, and it was not until the beginning of June that we had to give up all our guns. The partisans were a common enemy. You didn't know at this stage what side they were on. There were groups who were against us, groups who were against the Allies, and then groups who fought against both. Then there were Communists groups, Christian groups etc. The Americans were no longer shooting at us."

21-year-old Nardina Donnatini lived in the market town of Marradi in the Apennines. For weeks, German troops had been passing through the town, heading south to the front during June 1944.

"It was a time of sadness in my family, for, just two months earlier, my sister, who was 17, had died of meningitis. We didn't know where the Allies were, but everybody had heard that Rome had been liberated earlier in the month. We all knew it wouldn't be long before Marradi too would be liberated. There was a small German garrison, which came to our town when Mussolini fell from power. Their Kommandant was really very kind – he had lent his car to take my sister to the hospital in Florence. But many of our young men had been taken away to Germany to work – others had fled into the hills to hide or join the partisans.

We were always frightened of the SS because they would come into the town to look for our menfolk and take them away. Some we never saw again. The SS wore the best uniforms and were handsome – but very cruel, and we always ran and hid when SS patrols came.

The Americans bombed Marradi one market day. I was on my way down to the town from our house, when I heard the sound of the planes. I immediately knew, something told me, the Americans were coming to bomb the bridges. I turned and ran back to the house to my mother and father. 'They're coming to bomb! Run away, quick!' I warned. We ran up the hillside towards a cottage away from the town. My mother couldn't run fast enough and hid under a small shed which was built on stilts. My aunt and cousin hid in a tree. I watched the planes fly up the valley. They had big, white stars on the wings, the sky seemed to be full of planes. Some German guns, which guarded the bridges, opened fire.

The bombs started to fall, and I heard the scream as they fell. I threw myself flat on the ground and the bombs burst. I could feel the air beat over me and debris all over my head. When the bombers had finished, there wasn't much left of Marradi. The buildings in the square were flattened and there were fires everywhere. A terrible sound came from the town below – screams and moans of the injured and trapped, men's voices and animals in pain. Those sounds have stayed with me to this day. Many people were killed and injured – my aunt and cousin were among the dead. The railway bridge and the road bridge were untouched. The bombers had missed their targets, but had killed so many people – and destroyed our town.

We knew the Americans would come back and bomb Marradi again until the bridges were destroyed, so we decided to leave the town. We didn't come back to Marradi until Easter. By then the Allies had arrived and there were Indian soldiers living in our house – and the bridges were still standing."

Private William Ernest Wright of the Royal Irish Fusiliers had been in action in North Africa, Sicily, Cassino and through Italy – and by the time he and his company reached the Po, he felt that they had all become dehumanised by exposure to battle. The weather had deteriorated as they entered the mountains.

"After Rome, we were ducking from one side of Italy to the other. We were a crack force because, by then, we had been in the business for four years – we had to be good.

Just north of Rome, we took a castle which overlooked a lake. The whole of the wine cellar was completely intact. Why it hadn't been shipped to Germany, I'll never know. We found the most beautiful wines and brandies, and for four days were as drunk as lords!

We were told that we would be going into battle, so we laid off the booze. The next morning, we were all on parade – all except the stretcher-bearer, and we needed him for the other end of the stretcher. We searched and searched the castle, then someone suggested we look in the wine cellar which had, by then, been locked for two days. Just as he said this, there was a banging from inside the cellar door. When he was let out, the man marched out very straight – then fell flat on his face. He had been in there for a week. That man stayed with us right until the end, and saved many lives.

We were pretty well bogged down at the Po because of the weather. The Germans knew that it was only a matter of months before the war would be over, and we knew that it was nearing the end too – but then again, you can still get killed during the last minutes of the war.

What stood out most in my mind were the patrols. We would go out and shout things at them which we had learned in German – 'Put down your arms', and, 'Come on, don't be silly. Surrender.' Their answer used to be a bloody great burst of machine-gun fire. It was a bit stupid, shouting at them, but we were young. Sometimes we had a pint of vino in us too, which made us more daring. A lot of Germans did surrender – usually shell-shocked.

There was a wine tank near us, in the Po Valley. It was about 15 feet high, and it stood out in the yard of a deserted farmhouse. By this time we were virtually alcoholics – every time we went out, a sniper would have a go at the barrel and we would go and get the wine under cover of darkness. It was rough, but good. One night, the blinking wine stopped – just like that. By this time, I had a stripe – I was a lance corporal, so I could give orders. I said to this bloke 'Nip up and find out what's happened'. He came back and said, 'You're not going to like this. There's an old woman's body in there."

Troops enjoy the delights of Italy as they take a gondola through the canals of Venice

BATTLE OF BERLIN

Brothers in Arms

The Allies agreed to leave the ultimate prize, Berlin, to the Soviets as the Red Army pushed back the Germans through Eastern Europe. In April 1945 the battle entered the streets of Hitler's capital. Despite fierce German resistance, the Russians carried the day. The Führer committed suicide in his bunker. On 7 May, the Reich surrendered – the war in Europe was over

SS Untersturmfuhrer Heinz Landau had fought furiously through the Battle of Berlin, but as the Soviet tanks closed in, he was trapped in a cellar. Felled by a blow to the head, he finally came to, a POW of the Russians. His feelings were of being upside-down and moving along – and of not knowing where he was.

"My memory started flooding back. I got knocked out and, but for my helmet, I would be dead. I opened my eyes and, to my horror, took in what I already suspected, but would not admit to myself. Two Ivans were dragging me along, each hanging on to one of my feet, my shoulders and head bouncing all over the cobblestones.

When they noticed I had come round, I was turned the right way up, tottering to my feet. I had obviously been beaten and kicked while unconscious. I was covered in blood from head to toe and felt as though every bone, every muscle, in my body was damaged. Several teeth were broken – one, at least, missing. Someone turned up with a bucket of cold water, which was unceremoniously emptied over my head. I was now standing, and frightened to death, but would not let them know it. I was completely surrounded by 50 or 60 of them.

Why had they not killed me? What had they got in store for me?

One of them approached me, as cautiously as though I were still armed, put a hand out and flicked open one of my pockets, at the same time jumping back. This made me smile. These chaps were afraid of me, even under these circumstances. He came back shamefacedly and went through my pockets.

I figured out what was puzzling these chaps. It was my uniform. One of my captors must have ripped my sliver-grey epaulettes off, and without these, my uniform was simply that of a private in the tank corps. Furthermore, my flashes did not display any SS insignia.

The crowd was getting hostile again and the first punches and kicks were beginning to find their mark. A grim-looking, heavily armed party was making its way towards me, led by a poisonously green-peaked-capped NKVD officer. I was beginning to feel quite sick again. I was kicked, pushed and shoved into whatever direction I was supposed to take, and so my nightmare walk through Berlin started. Fortunately, they were never quite sure what exactly I was supposed to be.

Every Russian man or woman who felt so inclined was welcome to have a go at this German who no longer had the ability to defend himself. Thus I was slapped, kicked, rolled about on the ground, used as a football, then spat on, and even urinated on. The highlight of this introduction to 'civilisation' in 'barbarian Germany' was getting straddled by a Russian woman in uniform, minus underwear, who then proceeded to empty her bladder all over me to the delighted howls of the mob.

Eventually 'Nutcracker NKVD' got bored with the show and I was once more dragged away for another walkabout. The next couple of miles were a bit better, as I had to be literally dragged along and no-one could get near enough to do any further damage. It was about this time that I first noticed German women being dragged into the streets, knocked into the gutter and raped, sometimes to death.

A black-leather-clad Red Air Force pilot came up to me. His head was heavily bandaged and he made a beeline for me, put his left arm out, pushing his fist into my chest. Then he pulled his service pistol from its holster and pushed the barrel against my forehead.

'Kneel down and beg for your life, German dog!' I looked him in the eye and did nothing at all. His knee came up unexpectedly and caught me in the groin. Down I went on my knees. 'That's better, Nazi swine.' I got to my feet and looked him in the eye. He lifted his pistol high and hit me on the side of my neck. I fell to the ground but immediately scrambled to my feet. There followed a furious exchange of gems of the Russian language quite beyond my powers of description. NKVD convinced the man that he was responsible for me. I gathered I was to be taken to Divisional HQ for interrogation.

After further battering, I reach Div HQ late in the afternoon. I was led into the yard where there were a few other POWs, but I kept away from them. I sat for a couple of hours in the company of my guards, to whom time did not seem to matter. Another NKVD officer asked what had happened to my papers. I told him they were lost when I was captured. Night fell and we still sat in the yard. I lay down and slept the sleep of exhaustion."

Lieutenant-General Telegin was a member of the war council of the 1st Belorussian Front which, under Marshal Zhukov, shared the Berlin operation with the 1st Ukrainian Front under Marshal Koniev.

"Captain Archangelsk's tank company was halted by gun and rocket fire near a massive obstacle at a crossroads near the *Reichstag*. The leading tank, trying to ram the obstacle, was set on fire and fell out of action in the centre of a square.

The tank commander and the turret gunner, badly wounded, just managed to pull themselves out on to the paving stones through the lower hatch , and then sheltered behind the armour of the tank from enemy machine-gun fire. In the burning tank remained only the driver-mechanic, the Young Communist, Anatoli Ivanov – but after a few moments, the commander's hatch cover appeared, accompanied by his loud boyish voice, 'Forward, for motherland and victory!'

The burning tank, gathering speed, hurled itself at the obstruction – but another missile penetrated the tank's armour. The ammunition exploded and the tank was destroyed. Anatoli Ivanov likewise perished. The gap that Ivanov had succeeded in making was too small to allow tanks through.

Only a few minutes after the destruction of the tank, a fair-haired soldier jumped out from the window of a nearby house with a box of explosives on his back. He hurried to the place where Anatoli had met his end. Who was this hero? Most probably a soldier from the neighbouring assault group. The tank men covered this daring fellow with their cannon and machine guns. Wounded by an enemy bullet, he laboriously pulled himself along on his hands, crawling forward and dragging his box behind him. The tanks gave all the gun and machine fire they could, and the hero crawled to the gap made by Anatoli Ivanov. He placed his explosives, lit the fuse, then collapsed. There was an explosion that threw the obstacle completely aside. The road to the *Reichstag* was clear – but the unknown hero had perished."

Jean Porter was 22 when she was sent from her home town of Antwerp in Belgium to work in a restaurant in Berlin in 1943. She stayed there until the end of the war, and witnessed the final days when the Russians stormed into Berlin.

"I was sent to Germany in 1943. I got a letter, saying I had to go and work there. You had to report to a certain place; you were given money and coupons to buy some extra clothes. They asked you whether you wanted to work in a factory or privately, like in a restaurant or something, and I said I'd work in a restaurant, because I thought, you know, I don't want to go hungry. If you didn't go, they would find you and put you in prison.

So, they sent us on this train to Berlin. We didn't know where we were going at first. I worked in a cafe in the Anhalterstrasse near the Anhalter Bahnhof. Workers from the railway used to come in, lorry drivers, that sort of thing – there were a lot of people working you know, they weren't all in the war. They would all come in for a plate of stew, because you didn't need to use your coupons for it, as there was no meat in it. We stayed in a private house just round the corner. The boss rented this room. Me and this other girl from Belgium, Marie, stayed there. They were very good to us at the restaurant and in the house.

Life was very much the same from day to day. It was only at the end that the real action started for us. We knew there was something in the air. Nobody knew what was happening, but there were rumours going around that Russia was invading. The following day we went home to get some stuff. There were German soldiers on the corner of the streets with guns, lying dead. And when we got home, we just took what we could carry and went again to the shelter. And we could see on the bridge over the canal they'd piled up furniture ever so high, as a sort of barricade. I don't know how they could have built it so high. The next day we had to be evacuated, because the

Russians were almost on the doorstep, so to speak. We walked all the way alongside the rails in the underground from one station to the other through the tunnels; we had to be very quiet, everybody was saying 'shsssh'... In the meantime they had tried to stop the Russians coming in. We were up to our knees in water, and if you fell over the rails, that was your lot. You couldn't get up. You were so weak by then. In the underground there's like a ledge, and people were all trying to get up on there, but the people who couldn't get up there were walking in the water. It was very hard to get up on the ledge, because it was every man for himself. We had to walk in the water, and there was one couple with a new-born baby, and it must have been dead, because I saw them laying it down in the water. They had no food, and we had no food – we had no food for five days. We lived on a little bit of butter and sugar. The next day the Russians came into the underground and told us, 'All out, all out, the war is over.' So we all came out, and there was this girl there, and she said to me, 'I'm going to my boss, do you want to come with me?' So I said, 'All right, I'll come.' Well, we went home, and, of course, there was nothing standing. There were bodies everywhere, half-burned bodies and horses as well. It was terrible. Anyway, we went to this girl's boss's house, and we stayed there the night. The Russians were knocking on the doors, and they said, 'Any Frauleins here?' And the boss said, 'Oh no, no Frauleins here, upstairs.' And so he sent them upstairs. The next day he told us we'd better go.

We walked all the way from Berlin to Potsdam, and that was 40 km. There were thousands of us, and when we got to Potsdam, there were loads of people there staying in a farm. The Russians there were burning down all the houses. I think they were mostly pretty uneducated people, they were just doing it for the hell of it. We had to sleep in the hayloft, and the lady there gave us food. I just followed this Dutch chap. He seemed to know where he was going, and we thought, well, if we get to Potsdam, we must be on our way home. There were loads of Dutch people there at the farm, and the next day the lady from the farm gave us a horse and cart and we set off. There were streams of people along the roads, moving out like us. Well, after a while, the horse would get tired, and so, what we did, we just let it go and took another one from the fields. The horses didn't mind, of course. At that time, nobody bothered, you see, everything was still a shambles."

VICTORY IN BURMA

Jungle & Plain

Having driven the Japanese back from India, General Slim pursued them into north Burma, where in March 1945 he captured the strategic towns of Mandalay and Meiktila. With campaigns in coastal Arakan and in the central jungles, British and Indian troops raced down the pensinula, liberating the capital Rangoon in May to end three years' hard fighting

Lieutenant-Colonel James Lunt had fought through the first campaigns in Burma – during which time he had the opportunity, on numerous occasions, to meet 'Uncle Bill' Slim – the man whose masterly grasp of the later Burma campaign made him a major contributor to the victory.

"After the retreat from Burma in late 1942, I was posted as an instructor to the Indian Military Academy – the Indian Sandhurst. My son had just recently been born at this time, and I was sitting next to a lady at dinner whom I had never met before. I was talking, naturally, about my first-born, and beaming all over. I said I didn't know how on earth I was going to educate him. She said, 'You ought to do what my husband has done – he writes articles and short stories and so on – he educated his son by his pen.' As I was leaving, I asked who the lady was and it turned out that she was Aileen Slim – Bill Slim's wife.

I met Bill Slim first when we were really in a desperate situation. He was a most impressive man. There were two absolutely different British General types involved in the Burma campaign – one was Alexander – a terrific personality, a Guardsman and incredibly brave. He was always immaculately turned out with Sam Browne belt and nicely pressed shorts – he gave one confidence, but somehow he was remote. Slim was quite different. He was extraordinarily *simpatico*. I was a very young officer, just 23, and Slim would sit down beside you with a mug of tea and just chat. The thing I loved about him was that he was so down-to-earth. He'd say, 'You know, Jimmy, we haven't got a snowball's hope in hell of beating these buggers – but the point we must make to everyone is that we mustn't give up. Because once we give up, they will just corral us like cattle. We've got to fight... and maybe, who knows, we may suddenly find their weak spot or something of that nature, and that will give us the opportunity, because we've still got quite a lot of fight left in us.' That was what endeared me to Slim. He was a very ordinary man – hadn't been to Eton or Harrow. He'd served in the Indian Army – a poor man's army compared with the British Army. But he was called 'Uncle Bill' and it sums him up, really."

Hidetaro Kotani was a 2nd Lieutenant in the Japanese Fifteenth Army Supply as the battle began for Meiktila. Since no Japanese would be prepared to accept defeat, this was going to be a fight to the death.

The enemy tanks blazed away at us with guns and machine guns. We started to hurl grenades, jumping up on the tanks and trying to open the turrets and throw grenades inside, but many of us were cut down by gunfire.The enemy's small-arms fire began to increase in intensity, and in the end, I didn't dare raise my head above the level of the drainage ditch. The infantry began to close in. I could not make out where the firing was coming from, or how near the enemy infantry were, but the bullets were striking low, and with deadly accuracy.

The soldier lying next to me in the ditch was hit by a ricochet and wounded in the head. I ordered PFC Kato to give him first aid. Kato was an older man then the rest, who'd been called up when the older men were conscripted, and he was a cut above the rest in intelligence. He had a wife and child, and a great sense of responsibility. Kato hurled himself through the dense hail of bullets, so thick, in fact, that if you put out your hand, it would be shot to pieces. He was dead before he'd run more than a few yards. He was running towards the enemy, so they may have thought that he was putting in an attack. The bandage which was to be wrapped around the soldier's head fluttered from Kato's neck – and the soldier

Fourteenth Army soldiers advance through a banana grove, bayonets at the ready

himself was already dead.

Being alive in such an extreme situation was more painful than death. The stronger your feeling, 'I want to live', the more exhausted your spiritual strength became. I could see enemy aircraft diving down on positions on the opposite bank, but I could not make out at all the enemy situation close by. All I could think was, 'If the enemy appears in front of me, I fire.' After a short while, I began to wonder if I was still alive. I had no awareness of the passing of time, but at sunset the attack began to die down. It had been a long day.

When I came out of the ditch and looked around for survivors, peering into the holes in the ground, the surrounding scenery had changed completely from the night before. The place was like a vast rubbish dump – sheets of corrugated iron, bricks and stones, great chunks of broken concrete were all scattered far and wide. You could only walk with difficulty. The enemy troops were digging ditches about two or three hundred yards ahead of us – and waiting. Their tank attacks and artillery fire had reduced every one of our companies to a strength of no more than half a dozen men. The only officers still alive were Lieutenant Nakayama and myself. We were mixed up with troops from other units, with not the faintest idea of where they'd come from.

Those men who had fought to the very limit of their strength and had managed to stay alive had no hope of survival now that the road to retreat was cut. In order to put a bit of gloss on certain death, we spread the new blankets along the ditch – we could die in comfort.

From the north side of the group of houses, tracer shells began to come in, making a beautiful outline of smoke as they criss-crossed. The smoke made everything look as if we were in a mist, high up on the moors. Then, from time to time, star shells would burst overhead, lighting up the surrounding brickwork, and tugging me back to reality. I had the impression it was already light, and took out my note-book-cum-diary from my map-case – but it was dark as I wrote, using big characters on a white page. I was sure I would be dead by tomorrow, without fail, and I wanted to convey to human beings close to me just what that felt like. I've forgotten now what I wrote, but at the end, I remember writing my name and my address in Japan in Roman script. It seemed to me a cause for regret that I should be face-to-face with death here, and that no-one should know about it.

I went round the various units, distributing rice to each of them. The psychology of the battlefield is odd. The soldiers were delighted. 'Rice coming up' – in such an extreme situation, the arrival of rice could nonetheless have such an effect on them. There seemed to be more activity in them, as if the units had come back to life. I wanted to find out more about the general situation, and went to take a look behind the No. 2 Transport HQ. I was amazed to find 50 or 60 Japanese soldiers still there. They looked as if they had lost all will to fight. They had some equipment, but no rifles. Casualties from 107 Line of Command Hospital were just a bunch of human beings without any energy, left in the face of approaching death. Men shambling along, dropping their mess-tins, men crouching by the roadside, soldiers without caps, soldiers without boots – all alike, with bent backs and drooping heads, uniforms blackened, faces blackened. Nobody seemed to be in command.

From time to time a shell burst, but no-one seemed to take shelter – only here and there, occasional black, crouching human shapes. No human beings were going to survive this, I was sure. When all the skill and will to fight of a human being comes face to face with an enormous machine, whatever the differences between them, the result is the same. Tomorrow, in this confined space, the day would group them together – groups of corpses."

Gunner Charlie May was a Driver Mechanic with the 134th Field Regiment, serving in Burma since early 1942. After extensive jungle training, he was able to say that it all paid off – the Japanese were finally driven out of Burma.

"Once we crossed the Irrawaddy, we were really beating them. We threw them back, left, right and centre. The artillery boys had a terrible time. They were going down like flies. My own company lost about 14 blokes, which wasn't too bad, but then we weren't on the front line. We lived like rats in the jungle – our clothes were on until we stank. You hadn't got time to be depressed – you had your mates alongside you. A man would die for his mates.

At night we had a perimeter – like a border. The only people on this side would be us and the infantry. Each person, company and regiment would be responsible for the perimeter, so eventually you had a long chain. If anybody moved outside, it was not one of us. We used to take the bells from the pagodas and temples and tie them on to the bale we used as telephone lines, then stretch it around the outside.

When we heard the bells we would all throw grenades like fury. We knew precisely where the bells were. We used hand grenades because they couldn't tell where they were coming from. In the morning, we would find a dead Jap - sometimes we got a cow, which would finish up as steak.

We went through the jungle and then out into the open, onto the plains. Anything that moved was sorted out by our planes and the US Air Force. The Japanese dug into the sides of mountains, making strongholds like fortresses. They would fire on any convoys that went past. They used flashless powder, so when they fired, you never saw anything. When we fired our guns, it would leave a terrific flash. When the air force bombed the places where they thought they were, the Japs had gone right back into their tunnels. They would bring their guns out and fire on any convoys that went past.

As soon as the planes came, it would shut the Japs up, and we would nip past them, out of their line of fire. We would go like the clappers. We had them beaten – though I sometimes wonder how."

IWO JIMA AND OKINAWA

Last-ditch Bushido

In the US campaign through the Pacific, the islands of Iwo Jima and Okinawa were the last pieces in the chain that would allow an assault on Japan. In February 1945, Marines landed on the volcanic beaches of Iwo Jima, dominated by Mount Suribachi; two months later, they invaded Okinawa. On land and at sea, victory only came at a high price in the face of fierce resistance from Japanese troops determined to save their homeland

Admiral Sir Michael Denny was captain of the British carrier HMS Victorious, which was part of the British Pacific Fleet. He recalls the kamikaze attacks, which seemed to come at the most vulnerable moments.

"Our anti-aircraft fire was pretty effective, and the *Victorious* was an immensely handy ship to handle, with a big rudder. I could spin her around quite rapidly and so I ruined both my *kamikaze* attacks. They aimed originally for between the lifts – with American ships they could open up the flight deck and go right through into the hangar space below – but eventually they found that this didn't work on the British carriers' armoured decks.

Two *kamikazes* successfully striking an American carrier could put her out of action with regard to operating aircraft, but this did not work with the British carriers. This was possibly the reason why, later on, they seemed to go for the bridges of British ships, with a view to killing our command personnel. But this was a silly thing to do – they could do far more harm to us by going for the hull of the ship. Damage to the actual lifts, while less spectacular, was a far more effective way of putting a carrier out of action.

Our first *kamikaze* started out from almost astern of us, and my turn put him on my beam. He tried to pull up and start again, but he was not quick enough. I crossed ahead of him pretty close, and his wheels touched the flight deck at right angles. The undercarriage sheared right off and his plane broke up, sliding 80 feet across the flight deck on to the 4.5 inch guns. From the first moment I started to swing the ship, he had been trying to adjust and steer up the flight deck – which would have given him the length of the ship in which to drop his stick and hit – but he missed.

It is interesting to recall that each pilot would react differently – there appeared to be no set formula for an attack, other than the aiming point and the run-in. One could never tell whether one was up against a first-class pilot or not, until the moment one swung the ship and watched the pilot's reactions. If one's timing was good, and the pilot was forced to rethink his attack, the majority of them would veer in at a lower angle, which at once reduced their effectiveness if they did hit. If one could lead an enemy pilot to make a large alteration in his course, or if he failed to make an alteration at all, one felt secure that he would not score a hit. The fatal thing to do was for a carrier to steer a straight course, for in that case he would always get you.

In the cases where more than one aircraft approached, in all cases they would make separate attacks. One could watch them pick their targets, through a good pair of glasses, and as soon as the leading aircraft went into his dive, his wing-men would open up on either side of him, hoping to hit you, no matter how you turned."

Captain Koichi Ito, Commanding Officer of the 1st Battalion, 32nd Infantry regiment, witnessed the fight-to-the-death by many Japanese soldiers throughout the Pacific campaigns. Proudly he could say that his own battalion never surrendered at Okinawa.

"Early on 4 June, I took a roll-call. My battalion had been in the fighting since April, and our strength had dropped from a total of 700 to 120 men. That day, we arrived at the village of Zaawa from the Shure Line. From 11 June onward we fought off the enemy's overall offensive.

According to the US war history, the US forces sustained 1,500 casualties, killed or wounded, and lost 21 tanks in the fighting for Kuniyoshi, and the fierce Japanese counter-attacks made them rely on aircraft and tanks. The Army's right and centre collapsed, and soon the extreme left collapsed also. Our battalion continued to resist stubbornly, but was cut off from battalion headquarters, so that the state of units under command was totally unknown.

One night at the beginning of July, I went on a tour of inspection with Kashiki, my adjutant, at the eastern end of Kiniyoshi Village on the south side of the plateau. We met two men who said they had escaped from Mabuni. It was through them we learned that the GOC, Lieutenant-General Ushijima, had committed suicide on 23 June. I felt a huge shudder pass right through my body.

Now the Army's organised resistance was at an end, we moved over to guerrilla warfare, to be fought by each unit in the place where it had survived. In the case of my battalion, the headquarters was at Kuniyoshi, and we made up units of 20 men each from about 100 men who were still alive. In all, we could only muster ten rifles between us, but we did what we could to interfere with the enemy's mopping-up operations – but nine-tenths of the men were wounded or fell sick. I myself was suffering from a recurrence of amoebic dysentery, and for a long time I could not walk. If we put together all our arms and ammunition, we could seek a chance to die in one last attack on a nearly airfield, but although we put together a suicide unit, our physical condition was simply not up to it.

So to the night of 14 August. From time to time a cloud would pass over the moon, which was nearly at its full. As usual, enemy AA began to fire tracer then, as we watched, it seemed to spread over the whole island of Okinawa. I don't know how many thousands – tens of thousands – of star shells they fired. A red light criss-crossed with shafts of light from the searchlights, a stupendous barrage which went on until dawn. I heard that night my first and last noise of bombing by special attack planes. Everywhere the word for VICTORY was spelled our in V-shaped lights.

About 22 August, I heard someone call out, 'Battalion Commander!' A Japanese Army corporal stood there, guiding a US Army officer. He said he had spent 17 years in Japan and spoke fluent Japanese – he told me Japan had surrendered.

No *kamikaze* planes had flown since 14 August – I knew that – and enemy leaflets had been dropped on us on the 18th, telling us that Japan had surrendered. I put these things together in my head – the premonition I had had became reality. I waited for sunset that evening and went to see the regimental commander. We were to resist, whatever happened, I knew that – but I forced myself to recount the day's events to him. He seemed to be unconvinced, but

As smoke rises from Mt. Suribachi, US Marines face a 15 feet wall of volcanic ash

in the end, ordered me to act as a peace envoy.

Two days later, I met the American, Morse, again, and asked for certain proof that Japan had surrendered. 'I'll bet you listened to the recording of the Emperor's Rescript ending the war,' he said, 'and the news from Japan. Captain Ito, please accept what has happened.'

'No, that's not proof enough,' I answered. 'Please have me meet our Chief-of-Staff at Army GHQ, who has already been taken into camp.' Lieutenant Morse kept his temper, but refused. 'Well, the parley's broken down. Let's take up our rifles again,' I said. The adjutant and the rest of the men were holding their breath. It was the work of a second. The enemy officer granted my demand.

Straight away, I climbed into the jeep with Lieutenant Morse, and we turned towards Kadena, 30 km away to the north, where the US Army GHQ was. I had to get him to stop the jeep from time to time, for calls of nature, because of my dysentery – apart from that, the jeep sped on, through the shattered trees by the roadside. The mountains looked naked, as if they had been stripped bare, with a white, grainy texture like a coral reef.

Let me go back to the fate of the 10,000 officers and men who survived, and who were weaponless. They ended up in all sorts of ways – some were eventually killed in the fighting, some continued to resist, some escaped, and some surrendered. Some 3,000 men surrendered before the news of our defeat and became POWs –

thousands more ended up in US camps. So, even though organised combat by the army on Okinawa came to an end, it may be said there was no *gyokusai*, no fighting until annihilation. It was impossible to crush the Japanese soldier, however brave he was, even if he was weaponless.

Soon we reached US Army Intelligence HQ, and I listened hard to the recording of the Emperor's broadcast, which was very difficult to make out. I listened again and again. I asked for it to be repeated three times. 'Bear the unbearable...for the peace of the whole world...' the phrases stayed in my heart for ever.

Then north again, in the jeep. I met a colonel in a straw-thatched village house. He showed me the *New York Times* and explained the situation, from the Soviet invasion of Manchuria to the end of the war. 'I have no proof, but I do believe Japan has surrendered. Please make your own decision, so that your men do not become casualties wantonly and pointlessly.' Tears welled in his eyes as he said this.

Each unit, reduced to ten or 12 men, assembled, in ranks, in Kuniyoshi village. The soldiers' uniforms were faded and torn, and they could not conceal the pallor of fatigue. The US troops drove forward their vehicles to take up our casualties, and the severely wounded were taken to hospital. Next, a hundred local people from the area were removed to a camp for civilians.

On the night of 28 August, we carried out the ceremony of burning the regimental flag, which had been the symbol of our tradition and honour ever since 1899. The officers gave a final salute to the flag as it went up in flames. Next came the day of our disarming. The US Army demanded that the regimental commander read the surrender rescript. The road through Kuniyoshi village ran from east to west, and by that roadside, we laid down 30 rifles. Next, the 300 officers and men formed up in ranks.

Colonel Hongo Kakuro stood facing Major Train, who was in command of a ten-truck unit, led by one jeep. Both commanding officers walked towards each other and shook hands. 'We give ourselves up to the US Army, by the command of His Majesty the Emperor,' said Colonel Hongo, choosing his words with great care. I had asked that we could say it this way, because to use the word 'surrender' was shameful.

And that is how Japan's 32nd Infantry Regiment never, right to the end, employed the word *kofuku* – surrender."

BOMBING JAPAN

Rain of Terror

As US forces advanced on Japan, so the Air Force launched strategic bombing of enemy cities. But bad weather and long distances hampered their efforts until, late in 1944, the arrival of the B-29 bomber allowed them to make successful low-altitude raids aimed at burning the wooden and paper buildings below. In total, the bombing claimed more victims than the atom bombs that eventually ended the war

Masatake Obata, a resident of Tokyo, was a retired soldier with a manufacturing business making component parts for aircraft. On 9 March eight people were living in the Obata household. This was the night that American General Curtis LeMay decided that his bombers would 'burn up' Tokyo.

"In the house were my wife, four children, two sisters and myself. My sisters actually lived up by Ueno Park but they had stayed for dinner and were gossiping with my wife. At about eight o'clock that night of 9 March, Radio Tokyo broadcast a preliminary warning about an air raid. They decided to stay overnight.

The air raid began at about midnight. When I saw that it was serious I changed into my air raid warden's uniform and prepared to go on duty. I told my wife and children to get dressed and go out of the house. I took them all to Fuji Park and then went to a meeting of my neighbourhood association. There we decided all the families should go to Sumida Park, one of the big open spaces, where they would be comparatively safe.

After that I put on my helmet and began my patrol, moving from door to door, checking to see that no one in our neighbourhood had made the mistake of trying to wait out the air raid at home. I found

A B-29 Superfortress continues its bomb run over Osaka, June 1945, despite damage

some people, mostly young women with children and old women, and told them they had to go to Sumida Park.

Then I started back for Sumida Park myself to meet my family. The bombing had started, and many houses were burning from the incendiary bombs the B-29s were dropping. The smoke was very heavy and it was hard to breathe. I also noticed that a strong wind had sprung up and the fire was being carried by the wind from house to house. Everyone was wearing his air raid hood, but I saw some people whose hoods were burning, and if they took off their hoods their hair began to burn.

Suddenly a whole cluster of six pound bombs dropped not ten feet away from me. Before I could do anything, the cluster exploded and one bomb blew up directly in my face. I was wearing one of the conical Japanese army helmets, but it did not help because the bomb came up from underneath. The impact knocked me down. The steel helmet fell off and that is the last I knew. I became unconscious.

Maybe I was unconscious for an hour. I don't know. When I woke up I found that my shoes had burned off, and my toes had melted. My hands and arms were so badly burned that they were black. I had burns all over my body. I could not use my hands. I rolled on the ground, trying to put out the fires in my clothing. I got up somehow and walked towards a trench alongside the road. The bombers were still coming over, and the firestorm had begun. A fierce wind was blowing flames everywhere. I walked into the trench. I felt as if I was walking on tennis balls – my feet had swelled to three times their normal size. I went to an air-raid shelter and found several other people there, all badly burned.

When day came and the last American plane had gone, I knew I had to find help so I headed for Sensoji Hospital behind the Akasaka Shrine. When I got there, a doctor looked me over. A nurse took off my burned clothes and treated my burns with salve and bandaged them. When they were finished I was a mummy. I heard a nurse ask the doctor which ward she should send me to. The doctor said, 'No ward, take him down to the mortuary. He is as good as dead.'

So they took me to the morgue and I lay there for five days without food and water, until my sister finally found me and saved me. My wife, children and other sister had all been killed when the firestorm raged through Sumida Park. Thousands and thousands of people died that night, almost all women, children and old people. There are no records, but perhaps 200,000 people died that night in the firestorm over Tokyo. The bodies clogged the banks of the Sumida River like charred logs."

Mr Isemitsu Kozakai miraculously survived the air raid on Tokyo on 9/10 March 1945. The tragedy is so firmly etched on his memory that, having been a keen artist, he was only able to illustrate his impressions of the raid and its after effects years after that terrible event.

"I used to run a shoe-shop business and had a wife and three daughters. Since Tokyo was really a dangerous place to be in, I had my family evacuated. They went to my elder brother's place in the country, in Niigata. That was in December 1944. Only my second daughter was evacuated, with her school, to Yamagata.

My brother agreed to our going to him, but I came to the conclusion I was imposing on him too much – it was a burden for him. So I decided to come back to Tokyo with only my 15-year-old daughter, Mieko. It took five days to get back. The morning we were leaving, she turned to my wife and said, 'Let me see your face, just once more,' and gazed at her for some time. I wonder if she had a premonition that she was going to die.

Apart from my job, I was also the local section chief of the National Health Movement on behalf of the town council. This involved taking evacuation drills, or calling people out for their preventative injections. When the air-raid warning sounded, it was my job to be first to go out.

That morning, 10 March, the air-raid warning sounded as usual. However it seemed to go on for an awfully long time. I was surprised at this and thought it must be something serious. Incendiary bombs started falling straight away. Flames began to spread as we watched. There were enormous sheets of flame everywhere. When I went to look at the air-raid shelter, the fire seemed to have gone right through it – there was nothing but flames and smoke. I tried to go in first, with Mieko and a neighbour, but we could not get inside, and outside the fires were spreading. It became difficult to breathe in my air-raid hood, and fires were blazing in various places, but there was nothing we could do – so we came away.

An old lady appeared ahead of us. 'What dreadful things! It's better to be dead. Please, kill me!' Her voice trembled and she clung to me. I wondered where we could go, and looked here, there and everywhere, before I caught sight of some school buildings ablaze. It was Oshima No. 2 People's School, and I suddenly remembered – there was a pool in that school garden, and I crawled under the flames and plunged into the pool. There were already people in it before me, competing for their share of water. The flames began to lick at my air-raid hood. I didn't feel I was burning, but rather I had the impression the flames were on the move – and fast.

At the time, my whole attention was concentrated on the fires. 'If only dawn would come soon – if only it could be soon....' That's what I kept thinking, because apart from that, there was no hope at all. Finally dawn came and I went back to look at the air-raid shelter. The earth on top of it had fallen in, and it had collapsed. Next, I went towards the house. I wondered if perhaps Mieko had managed to escape, and I walked across the smouldering ground, calling out her name.

I retraced my steps to the air-raid shelter. Five or six of my neighbours had gathered there, and we dug up the ground with shovels. As we did so, the backs of two or three bodies came into sight in the dug-up earth. There didn't seem any point in going on. We tried to dig a little more, but our eyes had been damaged. What with the smoke and dust, we could hardly see. We decided it was pointless to go on, and agreed to meet again in three days' time.

I went back to my wife's parents' house in Gumma Prefecture. I had some medical treatment for my eyes, then came back to Tokyo. My younger brother and my daughter were lying on corrugated zinc sheeting. My daughter had on my wife's *mompe* [women's baggy work trousers]. There were burns all over her body. I collected firewood from all over and heaped great piles of it on top of the bodies. I set fire to it, but they wouldn't burn. However long the wood burned, it seemed as if they were half-roasting. It was only later I realised that the firewood should not have been piled on top of the corpses, they should have been put on top of the firewood.

So, for two whole days, we kept on burning. I looked for two unglazed jars, washed out the insides throughout, put the bones in them and went to Gumma Prefecture. Later, still carrying the bones, I went to Niigata, where the rest of the family were. When I got there, my wife clung to the bones, weeping almost without a sound. She would not be separated from them – I could not make her let go. When I said 'What is burned does not return,' she was furious with me.

My feelings – well, such things as 'how sad, how pitiful' – there was absolutely none of that. That was true when we burned the corpses too. It was so terribly practical, business-like, you see. There was nothing sad about it, however odd that may seem. Perhaps I did not really think about it at all.

My elder brother said, 'We must have a double funeral ceremony – for them both together.' We had a joint ceremony, a month after. The priest came and read a *sutra*. When he'd done that, I thought for the first time, 'How unbearably sad.' I remembered many things about them, and I could not stop myself from crying, crying and crying, on and on. I could not bear to lift my face up. I was so ashamed, you see. Tears poured down my face, on to my trousers. They were ringing wet. I think I had come back to myself.

The day after the raid the newspapers announced, 'The Prime Minister has proclaimed a resolution in the Diet. We will not allow the enemy to break his way into our divine country. We have accumulated reserves of strength for thousands of years. If the enemy lands, he will be annihilated.'

I came back to Tokyo. In the mornings, I used to sell fermented soy beans, and in the lunch hour I used to shine shoes. A man who had run a shoe shop introduced me to a basement store in Aeaji-cho. I now have a shoe shop repair business there. I am still keen on painting – but now I paint horses flying though the skies – pictures of horses flying away, into the distance. That's what I think of now."

THE ATOM BOMB

Under the Cloud

Since virtually the start of the war, scientists of the American Manhattan Project had been working to harness the power of the atom in a weapon. On 6 August 1945, rather than launch a costly amphibious invasion of the Japanese islands, the Americans dropped the bomb on Hiroshima. Three days later, another fell on Nagasaki. Faced with such awesome destruction, the Japanese surrendered the following month

Colonel Paul Tibbets was the man charged with piloting the Enola Gay *to drop the bomb on Hiroshima. After intensive work with the Manhattan Project, the time had come for the real mission.*

"I named the crews that were going to make these flights in each aeroplane and I said afterwards that there would be a further briefing at a certain time that evening to allow us to go in a little bit more detail into what these other crews would do – or more specifically what we wanted each one of them to do; things we wanted them to look for and be prepared for.

Again, this intensified the atmosphere, so that when we got around to the point that we had all of the briefings over with and we had had a midnight supper (which was commonplace – whenever they were going out on an early morning run, they'd have a midnight supper), I found that it wasn't just the flight crews and the operations people that were there, but everybody was there – the whole organisation. Nobody was sleeping that night. They didn't know *why* they weren't, but they weren't sleeping.

So, when we finally got down to the aircraft and loaded on board (now they all knew that we had loaded the weapon, because you can't hide the fact that an aeroplane has been loaded – they didn't see what was loaded, but everybody knew that that afternoon a bomb had been loaded in the aeroplane) and got to the time of take-off, the word had spread throughout the island.

I had plenty of faith in my aeroplane. I knew my engines were good. I wasn't even anticipating any great problem that evening. We started our take-off on time, which was about 2.45, I think, and the aeroplane went on down the runway. It was loaded quite heavily, but it responded exactly like I had anticipated it would. I had flown this aeroplane the same way before and there was no problem.

At the time the bomb was armed, we must have been somewhere close to five hours away from the target. Our next point was a rendezvous 600 miles away from Tinian. We had this rendezvous with Chuck Sweeney and George M... because they were going to fly aircraft that would escort me. These aircraft would contain scientific-type instruments that would be dropped from those aeroplanes at the same time my bomb dropped from my aeroplane.

We made the rendezvous quite successfully, then we had about an hour and a half or a little over that to go along in a lazy formation on a beautiful night out on the Pacific, with moon and cloud that looked like powderpuffs. It was quite peaceful, believe me, and nothing much went on – there was a bit of talk in the aeroplane, but that's always normal on a mission. But then you get a quiet period and while we were going along there, I guess everybody had been dreaming or something, because it was quiet. But we had to start thinking about climbing up to the altitude, pressurising and getting ready to get on this bomb-run before we got to the coastline of Japan, and if my memory serves me correctly, it was something like 6.40 in the morning when we prepared a climb to altitude in order that we would be in our bombing altitude before reaching the coastline of Japan.

We arrived over the 'initial point' and started in on the bomb-run, which had about 11 minutes to go – rather long for a bomb-run, but on the other hand, we felt that we needed this extra time in straight and level flight to stabilise the airspeed of the aeroplane, to get everything right down to the last detail.

After about three minutes on the bomb-run, I made the last-minute corrections. Now, when I did this, I was also required to advise the crew that they must put on these dark glasses – we had been given dark glasses to shield our eyes from the glare that the blast was expected to produce.

The problem after the release of the bomb is not to proceed

forward, but to turn away, so I immediately went into this steep turn, as did Sweeney and M... behind me, and we tried then to place distance between ourselves and the point of impact. In this particular case, that bomb took 53 seconds from the time it left the aeroplane until it exploded. That's how long it took to fall from the bombing altitude. This gave us adequate time, of course, to make the turn. Now we had just made the turn and rolled out in level flight, when it seemed like somebody had grabbed hold of my aeroplane and given it a real hard shaking, because this was the shock-wave that had come up.

This was something I was glad to feel – it gave me a moment of relief, after all, having worked on that bomb for well over a year. You know, that 53 seconds when I'm turning the aeroplane, I'm wondering, 'Is it, or is it not going to work?' and of course the shock-wave hitting us was an indication that it had worked.

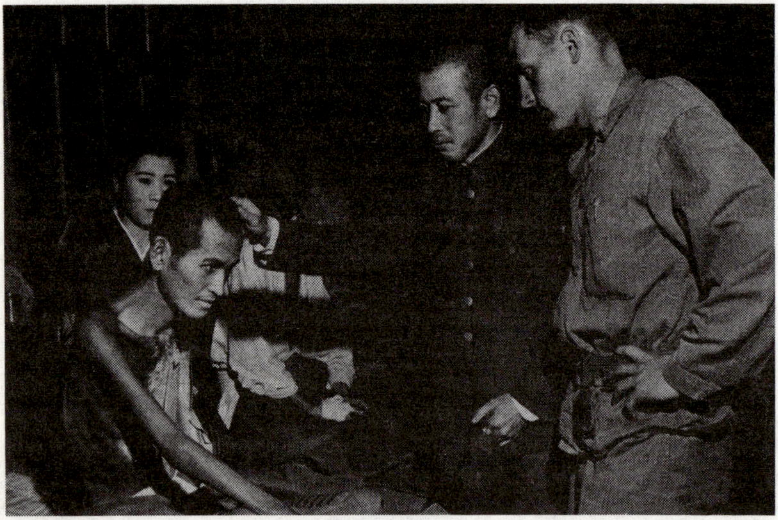

Flash-burn victims are studied in the US post-mortem

Now, after we had been hit by a second shock wave, not quite so strong as the first one, I decided we'd turn around and go back and take a look, because each of us in the three aircraft had hand-held cameras. We were looking through the front of the aircraft to take pictures as rapidly as we could of what was transpiring in front of us.

The day was clear when we dropped that bomb – it was a clear, sunshiny day. Visibility was unrestricted, so as we came back round again, facing the direction of Hiroshima, we saw this cloud coming up. The cloud by this time, in two minutes, was up at our altitude (we were at 33,000 feet at this time) and was continuing to go right on up in a boiling fashion. The surface was nothing but a black, boiling – the only thing I could say is a barrel of tar. That's the best description I can give. Where before there had been a city – distinctive houses, buildings and everything, that you could see from our altitude – now you couldn't see anything except the black, boiling debris below. It was terrible to look at really – a rather horrifying sight because you knew there were people underneath and you could speculate (but didn't want to see) what the result was.

I didn't want to delay too long in this air – I don't think that I could have stayed in the Hiroshima area more than about six minutes. It took me about two minutes to make the first turn to come back and take a look at it, then about four more minutes of slow flight, just kind of looking around so we could take these pictures. Pretty soon it became a rather routine flight home.

I've often been asked how I felt, and I think I have what you might call a rather straightforward stock answer to the question. I had been assigned a military mission to perform. I was most anxious to do the best that I could possibly do in the accomplishment of that mission. I'd been trained for that. As far as my personal feelings are concerned, I never let my personal feelings enter into it. I learned this back in the days when I was flying out of England and bombing targets in Europe. I knew there were people down below, getting hurt by this, and I felt that if I let my emotions get carried away and I got to worrying about who was going to get hurt by this, that I wouldn't be effective at all – so I had to school myself not to think about it.

Now, from this point of view, I was not affected emotionally. I haven't been up to this day, because it was something that had to be done. I was convinced that it had to be done, and I was convinced it was the right thing to do at that particular time. I've also been asked, would I do it again? My answer is, if you turn the clock backwards and get the same conditions existing today that you had in 1945, I'd probably do the same thing again with basically the same attitude. You can't turn the clock backwards – you can't erase it. It has been done. Let's hope we've learned a lesson from it and that we don't have to do it in the future."

Seiichi Nagai was just ten years old when the bomb exploded over his home town of Nagasaki. He remembers his father, a professor at the town's Medical University, who had previously been studying the use of radium, and X-rays and already had leukaemia – and the funeral of his mother killed in the bombing.

"Our house was about 50 metres from the epicentre – but at that time I was at my granny's at Kiba in Miyamacho, about 7 km away. My mother was killed in the blast. I don't know when I first found out, really. I just knew she was no longer alive. When granny went to meet her the day afterwards, she must have gone to our house in Urakami. Granny came back, but she didn't tell us straight away.

Father came back with the relief squad people on 12 August. He had a triangular bandage tied around his leg and one on his head. I felt bad about that, but he was alive and he had come back – that was enough. At the time the loss of my mother was the same for the whole family, but the sheer joy that father was still alive was stronger than my grief.

I remember my mother's funeral. All four of us walked, bunched close up together, thinking simply that the four of us must keep together whatever happened – that was what we promised mummy. The gravestone had been blown down and the stone cross was bent. We unwrapped the white cloth, and stared a long time at her, at that shape which had changed for ever. Our mummy carried about in a bucket – however many times Kayano and I cried out for her, she would never come back again, would she? Our mother had been burned and reduced to fragments, the rays of sun shone into the bucket and were reflected by those white bones.

A hole was dug on top of where my sisters Ikuko and Sasano were buried, and mummy's bones were placed in it. With a rustle and a clatter, our mother's bones were poured into that hole where her children were sleeping. We drew in our breaths, as if in greeting. The tears poured down my cheeks. Bending his face down towards his stick, daddy was crying too. We each poured a little earth on top of mummy's bones. A big pine tree inclined over the grave, and it was enveloped, as if by a perfume, with the fragrance of pine resin. On a new white cross were written the words: 'Marina Nagai Midori. Died in the Bombing, 9 August 1945. Aged 38 years.'"

CHINA

Merciless Invasion

In 1937, the Japanese had invaded Manchuria, in neighbouring China, launching a decade of bitter fighting that reduced China to a state of ruin. In August 1945, honouring a promise to the Western Allies, Stalin declared war on Japan and launched an attack on Manchuria, utterly defeating its defenders. In the aftermath, even the Japanese troops found it difficult to accept the brutality with which they had enforced their brief rule

Yuichi Hirata joined the Japanese Army in 1942, aged 22, having trained as a teacher. He recalls the appalling atrocities committed by the Japanese against the Chinese people and now, as a member of the Society for Planting Trees in China, he feels deeply the need for reconciliation.

"At that time, everything was clear-cut, wasn't it? I never doubted that it was a perfectly natural thing to go to the wars and die. Then I held fast to the maxim that I was living for the everlasting law of justice and right – but now I think this was not the case.

February 1942 was a lively time – but I was one of a group of young soldiers who were bound for North China. Shansi Province, it was. But when I got there, I saw that the garrison boundaries of the Japanese Army were moving. They went from 'area' to 'line' and then the 'lines' became 'points' – the lines were being cut. Then great numbers of troops went south and I recall they took their arms with them.

A situation was beginning to take shape where various points were just barely held on to because China was such a broad front. Shansi Province was under the domination of the Communist forces. They crossed the Yellow River and had begun to infiltrate their political activity into Shansi Province.

Nanking Station, Shanghai, lies in ruins after Japanese air raids in 1937

You want to think the people in the villages are friendly, but if you turn your back on them, you're done for. Three days before we made a move, they had the intelligence, 'the Japanese Army is coming'. They knew perfectly well. So if we look into that particular village, we'll not find a single chicken – not a single rush-mat. The Chinese people had led a life of suffering for a very long time. If we assume that the friends of these people, the peasants, are the Communist Army, then, whoever they are, we turn them into allies of the Communists. All the more so, since we're a foreign army – another people coming into their land and committing atrocities.

Some of these people were taken prisoner. When I was a cadet, I took part in an operation going down south from a place called Pingyao, just near Taiyuan. In the mountains, as we went into a village, we spotted people hiding under the shadow of a rock or under a tree. They were ordinary prisoners, but they were guerrillas. Sometimes we used the prisoners as guides to the roads, but before they were used as guides – we were trying to put up a show of what we'd captured – we wanted to collect rifles and ammunition. We assumed that without a doubt, they'd escaped after hiding their weapons. So we forced them to confess where that hiding place was.

We did awful things – you wanted me to speak out as an

eyewitness, so on behalf of humanity, I will. It was fire torture, water torture – things like that, to get the young soldiers slowly accustomed to such things. At first, we made a show of cutting off prisoners' heads then, when we went into operations, we used fire torture. We made them strip naked and hung a petrol tin down their backs and set fire to it. It's brutal and cruel, isn't it – even when you're merely thinking about it?

For the water torture, we turned a ladder into a sort of platform, made them lie on their backs, and fastened them to it. We put a piece of cloth into their mouths and poured water on them from above. If you do this they can't breathe, and they drink the water. The stomach swells up. This is torture. I don't know whether the Japanese Army invented these things, but they didn't confess. They were really tough, whether they were villagers who really knew nothing, or Communist Army soldiers. Many men died, I think, under such questioning. They were not prisoners of war, with treaty rights – just ordinary people, villagers.

It would have been very bad if prisoners had been allowed to escape, because they would have passed on to the enemy intelligence about the Japanese Army. I was an Intelligence Officer or, to put it simply, I was in charge of prisoners. So, as prisoners increased in numbers – and they were not to escape at any price – the company commander said we must kill them. I myself told my subordinates to kill them. A senior NCO, a real old sweat who'd been a long time in the battle zone, was used to dealing with prisoners. But in the end, I think he had some humanity. He said, 'Mr Hirata, I've already had enough of killing.' So I told them, when the Japanese Army finally goes, to go back home. I told them to make themselves scarce and told the Company Commander I'd killed them. It was a black mark, but I couldn't do anything else. That is some consolation for me.

The Chinese, until they were actually face-to-face with death, would plead, 'Master, master!' Even if they didn't understand a word, they could guess from the atmosphere – from our behaviour – that it was a question of 'to kill, or not to kill'. They made gestures as if to beg for their lives. But when it proved to be useless, they were splendid. They really showed courage. Is it because the Chinese have been great throughout their history?

There is a piece I contributed to a magazine back in 1960. It goes as follows: 'In November 1943, I took part in an operation in development territory, attached to 226 Infantry Regiment, 37 Division. I was 23 at the time. I passed out from the A-Class Staff

Cadet Unit at Paoting and had finished my local area training as a cadet. I believed absolutely in our cause. It was naive innocence on my part – all the more so because I was faced with a spiritual dilemma when I found out in the course of operations that these atrocities were ordered....'

One soldier, to start with, bayoneted an old woman. When that happened, one of the mothers who was holding her baby ran towards the valley – or rather hobbled there, because her feet had been bound. To bayonet her was not fast enough, and a shot rang out. It struck her in the back. I have no recollection at all of that mother's voice, but her expression, of an anguish that I have never seen before or since, had never left my mind. She had rounded her back as if to protect the child, and they both tumbled down a drop of 17 or 18 feet, into the valley. Two or three soldiers jumped down after her, and looked down at the mother, who was dead by this time. They looked up. 'Sir, the baby's still alive. What shall we do?' The platoon commander looked down and spoke one word. 'Kill!' I don't know whether the soldier shot or bayoneted the child.

That child's father may still be alive today. If he is alive, I beg his forgiveness for my crime. Of course, not words alone, but our everyday conduct, must be our foundation stone for peace. That is the last thing I can do in expiation. I clasp my hands in prayer.

I myself was taken prisoner of war by the Soviets, and I kept with me a black brush box and beads. I suppose I hung on to them as a form of peace of mind – against the thought of dying. Perhaps because, in the end, I did not die for the Emperor.

I was badly wounded in the lower abdomen – a thrust right through. I waited for death, and turned towards the East, praying to Buddha and reciting prayers with my rosary in my hand. I was in an excellent frame of mind. I thought, 'If I die, the troubles of the present will disappear.' In such a beautiful mood at that time, I thought I could die."

Mr Hatada, a colleague of Yuichi Hirata and founder of the Society for Planting Trees in China, was also in the Japanese forces which invaded China. It is out of remorse for the atrocities committed there that he still runs the society and works continually to atone in whatever way possible.

"I was a soldier from 1944 onwards, but I felt resentful and indignant at having to take part in such a foolish war as far as Japan and China were concerned. In 1982 I was 56 – what people think of as retirement age – and long before that I'd thought that I'd like to apologise to China in some way, within my own personal limits.

So with that in mind, I started the movement for planting trees in China. The Japanese Army had burned its way through so many of China's towns and villages, that even if they said they were sorry for five years, or ten years or 20 years, it will never be enough. We need to think in terms of centuries, and as far as China is concerned (and it's not only China, is it?), we must apologise into our children's age – into our grandchildren's age.

As far as planting trees is concerned, it's something that can be done whether you're educated or not. All sorts of people can do it, without discrimination. There had been some fairly severe criticisms by young people – did we realise that what we had done had humiliated the Chinese? And so on. It will be difficult to achieve even a normalisation of Japanese-Chinese relations, since we could not prevent such a violent war, and it's natural they should be even angrier with our generation than they are."

Three Chinese captured by the Japanese kneel, about to be beheaded

FAR EAST AFTERMATH

Back to the Jungle

The defeat of Japan left many problems for the victorious Allies. The vanquished had to be demilitarized, but their absence left a power vacuum in the Far East as the countries they had ruled fought for independence from their pre-war colonial masters. In Indonesia, French troops went back to the jungle to win back their imperial possession. But as the US would discover later in Korea and Vietnam, defeat was the inevitable outcome

Lieutenant-Colonel Hugh Astor was serving with a section of the SOE (Special Operations Executive) attached to Mountbatten's military mission to Indochina in 1945/46. Here he provides a unique insight into Allied post-war planning in south-east Asia, and into the causes of the region's persistent turmoil.

"I was with an organisation called Force 136, which operated behind enemy lines, so we had people behind the lines in Burma and Thailand during the war – but Indochina was a different situation as it was not part of our (British) theatre of operations and this was a big problem for us. Initially, Roosevelt was violently opposed to colonialism, especially French colonialism, and he had told us on one occasion that he would approve of anything that would help defeat the Japanese, provided it didn't help restore the French to power in Indochina. He felt very deeply about it. Indochina formed part of the Chinese theatre of operations under Chiang Kai-shek, with whom the Americans had two military advisors – Wedemeyer and Stilwell – who naturally shared the anti-colonial views. And at one point it looked as though the colonial French Army, before they were disarmed in 1945, would stage a coup against the Japanese. We were trying to make contact to give them advice, supplies and encouragement when Wedemeyer got news of this and said it was a misuse of Lease-Lend equipment – aircraft and so on – and if we didn't cease the operation it would be withdrawn. For one ally to say that to another is not very helpful, but it does indicate how strong the feelings were among the Allies.

I was on Mountbatten's staff at the time and the main thrust we were planning was Operation Zipper, which was against Malaya. The plan was to invade Malaya but the Japanese HQ was in Saigon and our lines of communication went through Indochina to Malaya. So Mountbatten was anxious to secure control over Indochina. He had raised this on a number of occasions, but it wasn't until the Potsdam meeting that we were given operational control over Indochina south of the 16th Parallel. North of that would remain in the Chinese theatre. This was the thinking behind the planning in 1945. But then the bomb was dropped and it all changed.

Indochina had been rather like Vichy France; it had retained a degree of autonomy and a titular head of state and they had not been very helpful to the Alllies – but when the French saw that it would only be a matter of time before the Japanese were overcome, they started to identify themselves increasingly with our war effort and wanted to be part of the victory campaign. Until this time they had been sitting very much on the fence, although they were to say that they had been planning a coup against the Japanese and it was only because security was so bad that it failed. The Japanese had pre-empted them by confining all the troops to barracks and disarming them.

At first we re-equipped them, which wasn't wholly satisfactory as they became rather carried away and took some very vindictive action. It was very unpleasant. We first went in at the end of September 1945. I went in with the British Mission. We were sent because our government had assumed that the old colonial powers would take control of their colonies when the fighting was over, but as there were no French troops we had to do it for them and the Americans were anxious to keep them out as long as possible. It was always understood by our planners that we would only be there working with the Japanese who had unconditionally surrendered to us until the French came. But we were under constant criticism that we were fighting a colonial war to restore the country to the French. I didn't see it like this. Our job was not to restore anything to anybody – it was to release the prisoners who had been held by the Japanese for a very long time.

Japanese POWs on Guam listen to the Emperor's announcement of final surrender

When the Emperor made his declaration of surrender it was on the basis of being absolute. This was taken literally by the Japanese and in Indochina, as well as Burma and Thailand, the Japanese came under the authority of the Allies. When I arrived in Indochina the reception committee were Japanese. I drove around with a Japanese driver and I have no doubt that they fought on our behalf when ordered to. In the villages I saw the dread on the faces of the people if the communists were to take over but neither did they want the French back. They wanted an independent government.

The Americans had a small OSS (Office of Strategic Services) mission there and we enjoyed very good relations with them, although they were busy arming the communists because they saw this as a way of impeding the return of the French. The US were strongly involved with the Chinese in the north and the Viet Minh received a certain amount of support from the US. The OSS had earlier parachuted into the north to train the communists to fight against the Japanese which, to a small extent, they did, but the main purpose was to stop the French returning. But the French eventually arrived and assumed control in the north after landing at Hanoi and were pretty much in control for a time."

Battery Sergeant Major Douglas Greensmith was with 232 Battery, 114 Field Regiment, RA (Sussex) (TA), part of the 20th Indian Division. The battery arrived in Indochina after leaving Burma at the end of the war and were astonished to find Japanese troops now under their command.

"One hundred troops were flown immediately to Saigon to try to hold the place. We were told to hold the communists, who got the blame for everything. Although the war was over I didn't mind going in, but I would say that more than 50 per cent of the regiment were of the mind that this wasn't our war. We had fought ours and if the country belonged to the French let them go and have a go because they haven't been doing much for the last five years.

However, we set sail for Saigon and coming up the Mekong the landscape was beautiful. We were in a converted hospital ship and we sailed past lush vegetation and huge trees – we had seen nothing like it in Burma. The river was very wide and bendy – just like the Thames. When the noise from the ship's engines dropped we were just rounding a bend and into view on the left bank of the river came Saigon, a city only about 20 years old. The first thing we noticed was the tarmac roads which we hadn't seen since we left India, except in Rangoon. It fascinated us and this was new too – Japanese soldiers walking around the docks!

The Gurkhas with us were astonished because they had only seen ragged, filthy troops, riddled with malnutrition and disease and left behind by their own soldiers. These Japs were very clean and smart. There were cars with officers in the back and chauffeurs – big French and American cars. It was astonishing. Then when we started to unload, we walked past the Japs and they all bowed. We couldn't get over this, some Gurkhas just kept walking up and down laughing while the Japanese were continually bowing. This was great fun.

The Japs had run the country but once the bomb had gone off, the Emperor told them to surrender and cooperate. I couldn't believe this. The Japs would never, never surrender but they did – 95 per cent of them. The other five per cent went off to fight with the communists out there. It was a hell of a mix up. The Japs had gone out to free the natives from the white man's yoke, then they had collaborated with the French; now they had turned around and joined us to fight the natives again. Fighting us were the people known as the Viet Minh and later still, the Viet Cong.

Sometimes we came across rebels, mixed groups of the Viet Minh and Japanese. One group got very close to Saigon. They held a position about four miles from the airfield and about the same distance from the city. The rebels had taken over a bungalow which had been occupied by a French plantation manager. He and his family, including children, had had their throats cut. Then the rebels had dug themselves in, under the house which was built on stilts, raised up a couple of feet from the ground. They were holding up a whole French battalion, about four or five hundred men. The French were badly trained, no discipline – awful colonial troops.

Only seven people were dug in – two Japs with machine guns and five riflemen. They were holding up the complete French advance. They called us up with our guns. We positioned the guns about 400 yards away and engaged the house over open sights. It brought the house down – it was just rubble. By this time the French had decided that they would go in, so a whistle was blown and everyone was shouting and bawling and firing. We stood looking at them in amazement. We'd been used to the Gurkhas who went in like snakes through the grass; you never heard anything. What an army this lot were, bugles going and everyone shouting. In the melée the rebels had escaped through the back of the house into the jungle. They had left behind an old man who had survived our shelling. He was about 60 and obviously a bearer. The rebels would go into a village at night and take the bearers. If they refused to go, they cut their throat. They would keep them for about four days for interrogation.

The old man was terrified. The French had brought him back to headquarters. His hands were tied behind his back and the French were kicking and beating him, I'd never seen anything like it. It was terrible. They were interrogating him – that's what they called it. We could see that he didn't know anything. Our battery commander, who spoke French, ran over and started to tell them what he thought of this. He was pushed aside and told to fight his war and let them fight theirs. He came back and told me we were getting out. 'I will not stay and witness a cold-blooded murder,' he said to me. Later he said, 'For two pins I would have turned the guns on them.'

If he had done so, he would have been fully backed up by the troops. That was French Indochina and we were glad to leave later that year and return home. It was the beginning of a mess the French were never going to get out of and, although I hated the Japanese, at least they were professional soldiers, however odd it felt to have them with you."

POST-WAR EUROPE

Out in the Cold

With their homes and factories devastated by air raids and ground fighting, little remained of German citizens' livelihoods. For many, the challenge of rebuilding ruined lives represented not the end of the fighting but the beginning of a new struggle. For others returning home from the front, life seemed boring and the social upheavals caused by the war had left a world virtually unrecognisable from that they had left

James Palmer, after a very active war in France, the desert, Burma and Italy, had, strictly speaking, finished his active service with the Royal Tank Regiment, but he spent a final year in a Reinforcement Unit in post-war Germany and witnessed the country in its disillusionment.

"When I went into Europe and Germany as the war was drawing to a close, I began thinking what it was all about. As I travelled with the Reinforcement Unit through Belgium, France and into Germany, over the bridges at the Rhine, I felt as if I was going into hostile territory. The Belgian and French people seemed pleased to be released from the German yoke, but at the same time, I felt that they would have been happy to stay under German control rather than suffer the saturation bombing and destruction of their land and homes by the Allied Forces.

The German people were completely confused at their defeat, and could not understand how it had happened. They had been on cloud nine when Hitler had *Blitzkreiged* through Europe – and they did believe that they were the 'master race', as Hitler had said. They could not understand why they had failed in Russia and why the Allied air forces had been able to flatten their cities. After Dunkirk they believed that they were masters of Europe, and Hitler was their god. The front-line German soldier was good at his job, and I often admired his courage and stamina. Their desert campaigns, and especially their defence of Cassino in Italy, were proof of their military thoroughness. Rommel, in my opinion, was a brilliant general, but I do not think he agreed with Hitler on many aspects of German policies. I believe he was involved, with other military generals, in the plot to blow up Hitler.

On my travels into Germany in the wake of the Allied offensive, I witnessed the appalling havoc our air forces had caused to the cities of Germany. The German people were resentful of our mass bombing, but it had been perfectly in order for the German air force to flatten Coventry, Manchester, Liverpool and a great part of London.

I was amazed at the number of German people who said that they did not want Hitler or anything to do with Nazism. Of course, this was only after we had done to them what they had done to the rest of Europe for four years. I don't think that the 'non-fraternisation' laws issued by the military control of the Allies were very helpful. It only made the Germans more bitter in their defeat.

My short stay at the Belsen camp sickened me more than anything I had experienced in my active campaigns, yet the German dignitaries of Celle said they did not know what had been going on. When they were brought into the camp to see the atrocities with their own eyes, they said that the whole situation was our fault because the Allied bombing had cut off all supplies to the camp. With that sort of reasoning, I could see no logic.

During my stay in Germany we moved around until we reached our final destination at Fallingbostel, and I found myself in a strange situation. The armistice had been signed on Lüneberg Heath and Allied military control had been established. The prison camps had been opened and thousands of Polish and Russian prisoners and displaced persons were in camps, awaiting repatriation.

Near Fallingbostel were two such DP camps, one for Poles and one for Russians. The Poles and Russians hated each other's guts, and there were continuous armed conflicts between the two camps. It was a regular thing for us to go into the camps to search for arms and ammunition, which we confiscated.

To add to the confusion, the Poles and the Russians each formed their own vengeance squads to go out and destroy the local German farms and communities. The situation was so bad that the British troops had to go out on security patrols to guard the isolated farms from the wrath of the Poles and Russian DPs and POWs. Machine-gun posts had to be set up each night in the local farms and villages.

In the German towns and villages, the black market was the main business of the Germans. Five marks for one cigarette and ten marks for a block of chocolate was the going rate. You could get anything, and I mean anything, for a block of chocolate, a packet of cigarettes or a bar of soap. The black market in Naples had been bad enough, but in Germany it was horrendous.

We in the army were paid in military marks, but there were millions of German marks floating around. The NAAFIs would only accept military marks and there was even a black market on currency. You could change your German marks for military marks at any street corner. You got one military mark for five German marks.

In an attempt to curb this, the army decreed that when you were given leave, your pay book must be endorsed with the amount of money you had been paid since your past leave. This was all you could change into British money when you came back home. Even this was liable to fiddles if you were well in with the Pay Clerk.

All in all, Germany after the armistice was a mess, and I was not particularly happy with my stay. There was too much bitterness and recrimination, and so much deceit about the situation."

George Clare was a Royal Artillery Bombardier attached as an interpreter to the control Commission for Germany (British Element). He was a second-generation Viennese Jew who had travelled to Britain after the Anschluss. He eventually arrived back in Berlin with the Allies and formed these impressions.

"I'd been in Berlin before the war and I spoke the language, so I was able to make some comparison when I returned in January 1946. I was first the deputy and then the British representative on a committee that was responsible for seeing that nobody who was a Nazi got back into culture or media life and so was in a position to watch as Germany and Germans emerged from their defeat. When I arrived, my first encounters with post-war Germans were with a heavily defeated people – a people that had lost whatever inner strength they had had – people who were starving and who only wanted to survive. They were quite prepared to lie, provided it would help them to survive.

My feelings towards them were made up neither of hate nor pity, because you cannot hate a whole nation or a city. They pitied themselves so much that no outside pity was actually required – they had brought their state upon themselves.

There wasn't a German left after the war who had ever been a Nazi although I once came across a Waffen-SS soldier who was honest and proud enough to admit it. He was a young man who had been conscripted into the SS late in the war and who only wanted to get back to a normal life. It was a rare moment of honesty. Most men would tell you about how they had been passionately in love with a young Jewish girl in the thirties but had had to break off the romance because of the situation. A rough count indicated to me that many times the complete Jewish population must have been in Berlin before the war and all in love with a nice German boy!

There were a few dyed-in-the-wool Nazis left, but these were people that had not committed a crime; they believed in the politics. They would appear before a denazification panel and if they were of no importance they were classified as 'fellow travellers' and given a low-value ration card which only lasted for a short time. It was the German authorities themselves who distributed the rations and the

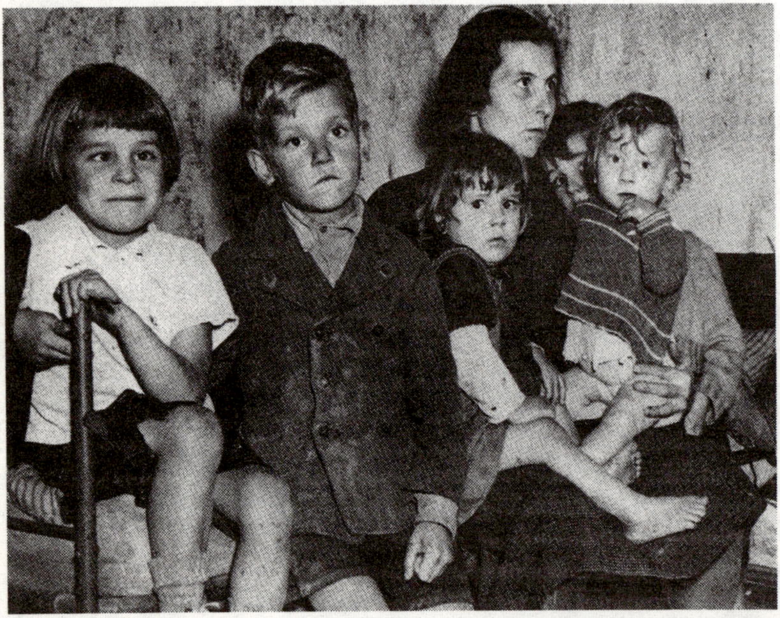

Many Berlin families now face years of poverty and a struggle for the basics of survival

quantity varied. For instance, coal miners in the Ruhr got more than some old biddy in Berlin. Everyone used the black market and most girls knew how to use their bodies to obtain favours from the Western powers. Those who worked for the occupying powers were generally better off.

Berlin at this time was governed by the four powers – the British, Americans, French and the Soviets, and for a time we all got on well, although the Soviets came to Berlin with the most dismal reputation of any nation except, perhaps, the Germans themselves. They had raped and pillaged on the way in and carried on when the war was over.

But slowly they tried to make up for this by convincing the world that they were basically a highly cultured nation. They immediately demonstrated this by getting the cinemas and theatres working again. The Western powers were at first a bit slow on this because they were looking after organising the ordinary services, from electricity to street-sweeping, but eventually they cottoned on that people who had nothing to eat would forget their hunger pains if they had some good entertainment. And so more and more theatres were opened in the Western sectors.

The early days of the cultural committee did not reflect the tension of the Cold War to come. The Soviet cultural officers were the most highly educated people in all the Control Commissions. They were all university professors who spoke perfect German and who knew the German culture inside out, while we just put in whoever seemed suitable. At first the Soviets selected highly efficient, educated people, who were then part of the so-called 'Leningrad mafia' from Leningrad University, many of whom had actually studied at German universities in their youth – but they were replaced by the Moscow mafia, which was a much stricter regime following the Stalin line. But life in Berlin was changing, people could and would disappear. Second-line anti-communist critics and journalists were kidnapped, never to be seen again.

But in the end, in my view, the Western allies, particularly the Americans and the British, laid the foundations for the best Germany we have ever had."

INDEX

Picture Credits

Hulton Picture Library: 14, 32, 254, 257. Imperial War Museum: 21, 26, 35, 37, 41, 54, 72, 77, 81, 82, 89, 97, 101, 102, 104, 109, 115, 116, 120, 122, 141, 142, 147, 151, 164, 167, 172, 187, 190, 195, 202, 227, 235, 266. Topham Picture Library: 11. US National Archives: 52, 61, 64, 67, 84, 131, 134, 157, 160, 176, 180, 205, 207, 212, 215, 217, 220, 241, 244, 250, 260.

ORDER THESE BOOKS POST & PACKING FREE!

KINNOCK
Dr George Drower
Introduction by the Rt Hon Gerald Kaufman, MP. Special contribution Glenys Kinnock.
Based on interviews with the former Labour leader and his political friends and enemies, this is a remarkable insight into the character and personality of the man who might have been.
Biography/politics
Hardback: 408pp with photographs; £16.99

A MAN DEPRIVED
Fiszel Lisner and Guy Nathan
Extremely harrowing and moving, this is the story of the man who survived the Nazi death camps for longer than anyone – one week short of five years.
Biography/history
Paperback; 208pp; £6.99

THE ANGEL WITHIN
Helen Wade
Foreword by the Lord Rix, CBE DL.
Humorous and harrowing but ultimately wonderfully uplifting and inspirational, this is the story of the life of a mother of a child with Down's Syndrome.
Biography/sociology
Paperback: 252pp; £6.99

THE DEVIL'S DAUGHTER
Christine Hart
Foreword by Colin Wilson
The incredible story of the girl who came to believe she was the daughter of notorious Moors murderer Ian Brady.
Autobiography
Paperback; 282pp; £5.99

GEORDIE PASSION
Mark Hannen
The captivating chronicle of the author's lifetime devotion to Newcastle United Football Club. From his early years in the late 1960s to the present day, this is a testimony, written from the heart, to a game that incorporates all of life's emotions in a way no other can.
Sport
Hardback; 164pp with photographs; £9.99

BIG JACK
Stan Liversedge
The life and times of one of the most widely-respected international football managers who guided Ireland to the 94 World Cup finals and the sensational victory over Italy. A fascinating and thoroughly enjoyable read.
Sport/biography
Hardback; 172pp with photographs; £9.99

LIVING, LOVING, LEARNING
Clarke Jaggard
Published posthumously, after the author's tragic death in a car accident when he was barely 20, this is a beautiful collection of Clarke Jaggard's poems of love and life and dreams.
Poetry
Paperback; 24pp; £3.95

THE A-Z OF USES FOR AN UNEMPLOYED PERSON
Miles
A sparkling collection of cartoons by the famous ex-cartoonist of several newspapers and publications.
Humour
Paperback; 28pp; £1.95

These books can be ordered post and packing free. Just send cash, cheque or postal order to the value of the book(s) to:

The Publishing Corporation UK Ltd,
Colson House
Knight Street
South Woodham Ferrers,
Essex CM3 5ZL
Tel/fax: 01245 320462